Psychology's War on Religion

Psychology's

on Religion

Edited by
Nicholas Cummings, Ph.D.
William O'Donohue, Ph.D.
Janet Cummings, Psy.D.

ZEIG, TUCKER & THEISEN, INC.
Phoenix Arizona

Library of Congress Cataloging-in-Publication Data

Psychology's war on religion. / Nicholas Cummings. William O'Donohue. Janet Cummings. — 1st edition.

p. cm.

Includes bibliographic references.
ISBN 978-1-934442-26-5 (alk. paper)
1. Mental health—religion 2. American Psychological Association—policies.
3. Mental health services
I. Nicholas Cummings II. O'Donohue, William III. Cummings, Janet
IV. Title

RA790.6.C85 2008
362.2'0973—dc21 98-50582

Published by

Zeig, Tucker & Theisen, Inc.
3618 North 24th Street
Phoenix, AZ 85016

Manufactured in the United States of America

Acknowledgements

The editors would like to thank Professor Dan Koren,
Dr. Arthur Goldberg and Professor Arthur Houts
for valuable suggestions regarding chapter authors.
In addition, we'd like to thank Linda Goddard
for all her valuable assistance in preparing
this manuscript for publication.

Contents

An End to the Hostilities?

Overview

This book is divided into three sections. The first section contains introductory material. Chapter 1, by William O'Donohue, is a description of the height and breadth of Psychology's war on religion. It discusses the beliefs that have caused the division and results of this rift for therapists, patients and graduate students in the field. Chapter 2, by former American Psychological Association (APA) President Nicholas A. Cummings, Ph.D. and his daughter Janet L. Cummings, Psy.D. on the history of the relationship between psychology and religion. Cummings and Cummings point out that many prominent early psychologists such as G. Stanley Hall and William James had deep interests in religion and developed respectful "psychologies of religion." They argue that psychology's antipathy toward religion probably began with Freud who saw religious belief as pathological—an indication of infantile wishes, e.g. This, they argue, has blinded psychology to the importance of religion in many peoples' lives and particularly the positive value of religion.

The next section is labeled: The Key Battles. In this section, authors examine some of the specific ways psychology fights, and thus harms, the religious. In his chapter, Dr. Michael Lavin who holds both a doctorate in philosophy and psychology, examines the intolerance organized psychology holds for those who have a negative evaluation of homosexuality. First, Lavin provides a careful exegesis of the Roman Catholic Church's, various Protestant churches', and Jewish views, on homosexuality and shows that they are much more nuanced and reasonable than the caricatures that predominate among the antireligious. He then examines prominent psychologist Gerald Davison's well-known argument that it is unethical to provide treatment to a gay individual who wants to become heterosexual. Lavin argues that Davison's argument contains the false assumption that religious individuals can't make informed, reasonable, authentic choices, based on their religious beliefs, to desire such a change. He also points out that Davison's argument forces religious psychologists to act as if they are secular psychologists and thus is insensitive to a cultural norm and grouping. He argues against what he reasonably calls "bullying secularism".

In the next chapter, Professor Mark Yarhouse of Regent University continues to examine battles over sexuality. He sees the skirmishes over abstinence-focused sex education, abortion, homosexuality, adult-child sexual contacts, and even cohabitation. Religion among sex researchers and counselors is often viewed as a negative constraint to normal sexual functioning.This of course, has not been shown to be the case, by any sort of research. There are certainly case examples of the religious who are inappropriately "sex negative" and perhaps dysfunctional, but there are also cases of the secular who are this way. More common, of course, is the problem associated with the secular view of unhealthy sexuality—leading to unwanted pregnancies, what some call the killing of babies, deadly venereal diseases, the sexual exploitation of women in the sex industry, and the break up of marriages and families, etc. These are the concerns of the religious and need to be balanced against the concerns of the secular in any fair appraisal of both positions. Professor Yarhouse points out that psychologists *qua* psychologists cannot speak to the truth claims of various religions. He then chronicles various movements within the APA regarding homosexuality, all of which do not take into account the views of the religious. He suggests that the antireligious ideology of organized psychology can trump science. He then surveys what he sees as open scholarly questions that are closed for debate within organized psychology. He then argues that training climates in psychology can be intolerant and thus harmful to the religious. Finally, he provides some very useful remedies for the current hostilities, such as owning up to ideology (religious or secular); and to actively allowing a full range of religious, as well as secular, perspectives in policy.

In the next chapter clinical psychologist Isachar Eshet writes of the struggle between scientific psychotherapy and Judaism. Judaism is one of the oldest major religions and provides roots to Christianity and other religions. The world knows all too well of how anti-Semitic prejudice has caused, and continues to cause, tremendous pain and injury. Dr. Eshet describes a Jewish worldview (which, given the various branches of Judaism, is not univocal). The kinds of commandments given by the Torah are discussed and how these define morality and immorality, with correlative religious concepts of sin and guilt. He then contrasts the egocentric nature of psychotherapy's worldview with the other-directedness of the commandments from the Torah. Similar to the famous philosopher of religion and science Ian Barbour's typology of relationships between science and religion, Dr.Eshet then examines three kinds of relationships between psychotherapy and religion: 1) struggle for dominance; 2) mutual respect, allowing the best of both worlds; and 3) synthesis.

In the next chapter, William Donohue, President of the Catholic League for Religious and Civil Rights, gives examples of the antireligious and anti-Catholic biases found in academic and clinical psychology (even a Jewish professor whose intellectual specialty was Catholic mysticism being denied tenure!). He then goes on to describe Freud's special hatred for the Catholic Church, as well as intellectually problematic and anti-Catholic *psychohistories* of witch burning and misrepresentation of religious practices such as praying the rosary as repressed anal-erotic desires. He also tries to correct the record on the relationship between Galileo and the Catholic Church. (Contrary to popular opinion, the Catholic Church presented Galileo with medals. Its issue with him was not his hypothesis of a solar centric system, but his presentation of this as fact rather than as an hypothesis needing further data.) Finally, Donohue describes some of the good works conducted by the Catholic Church, such as providing 27% of the HIV/AIDS services worldwide. The Catholic Church is seen as intellectually bureaucratically bound, non-progressive, as dogmatic and inflexible, and as philosophically unsophisticated. We have always been struck that many secular organizations, including the APA, fit these descriptors much better than an accurate portrayal of the Catholic Church. The many good works of the Catholic Church in healthcare, education, and care for the dying, orphans, and the poor are often ignored by the secular in their negative appraisals. Finally, the philosophical sophistication of the Catholic Church from Aquinas to Augustine, Descartes and the more modern philosophers, such as Chardin, needs to be better recognized.

In the next chapter, two of the book's editors Drs. Nicholas and Janet Cummings describe the varieties of the Protestant religious experience, to paraphrase William James. They talk about the initial European, and then subsequent American, roots of many of these denominations. They also describe the wide variety of positions these denominations have regarding key issues such as gay ordination, and gay marriage. They describe the role that Protestants had in both the Abolition movement and the later 20th century's Civil Rights Movement. They describe what they see as a moderating trend on a variety of social issues in Protestant churches of the last few decades. They then describe how the Protestant worldview is deeply engrained in American culture, from its views about individual freedom, to the importance of scientific inquiry to the rise of capitalism. They conclude with an indictment of psychology's bias toward religion that has suppressed research into questions of faith, given its ubiquity in the American population.

In the next chapter clinical psychologist Dr. Dean Byrd describes psychology's assault on Mormonism. The 2008 Republican primary gave rise to the question about the nation's views and a shockingly open prejudice against Mormons and Mormonism. The first decade of the 21st century seems to be to Mormonism what the 1960's was to Roman Catholicism: a presidential hopeful had to reassure Americans that his religion was not a reason to vote against him. Dr. Byrd describes an instance in which a film describing the Mormon Church's methods of instruction as "brainwashing" (among other egregious mischaracterizations) was shown at an APA convention. Despite numerous protests, the leadership of the APA did little to correct this problem, although after much protest they did write what Byrd regards as an insufficient letter of apology. Byrd then describes the Mormon religion in a way that combats the false images about it. He also describes the Mormon's views on homosexuals and homosexuality, gender and other issues. Finally, he suggests specific ways in which the APA can show more understanding, tolerance and sensitivity toward the Mormons.

In the next chapter, Dr. Cummings argues that psychology is not fighting a war against Islam. He sees Islam, including fundamentalist Islam, receiving a "free pass" from organized psychology—despite problematic positions on the rights of women, tolerance toward other religions, freedom of expression and other human rights issues. He sees this as sensitivity and political correctness gone awry. Cummings then describes distinctions that are necessary in order to understand modern Moslems, including those between fundamentalists and moderates and Shiites and Sunnis. He then describes Islamic psychology.

In the next chapter Japanese psychologist Akihiko Masuda, who holds a faculty position at Georgia State, and William O'Donohue describe psychology's infatuation with Zen Buddhism. They see psychology's relationship with Zen as fashionable but unsophisticated. Although Buddhism is sometimes not regarded as a religion, it's relative acceptance among psychologists may be tantamount to the "black friend" among white individuals trying to show their (obviously thin) diversity credentials. The major problem is that psychologists generally take a superficial view of it—creating "cafeteria Buddhists." They provide a short introduction into what they see as authentic Zen. They describe Zen perspectives and critiques on psychotherapy—is it a vain pursuit to better fulfill one's desires? In addition, they critique the recent trend in cognitive behavior therapy to include mindfulness perspectives, allegedly taken from Zen. There are no quick fixes in Zen; however a reasonable goal is to live fully with the sweetness and sourness of life.

The final section, entitled "An End to Hostilities?" contains two chapters that provide suggestions for a more peaceful relationship.

In the first chapter of this section, Arthur Houts, emeritus professor from the University of Memphis, analyzes the conflict between psychology and organized religion and sees reformed theology as a path to restoring a more productive relationship. Houts describes the current models of the relationship between psychology and religion as "intellectually empty." Houts sees part of the contemporary conflict between psychology and religion in the context of the antipathy between Athens (rational abstract knowledge) and Jerusalem (personal immediate experience). Second, he describes scientism—briefly an inflating of the value and power of science—and discusses scientism's role in perpetuating the schism between psychology and religion. Finally, he describes Reformed Protestantism and shows how it can provide the intellectual bulwark in understanding the evolution/creationism debate. This is a very intellectually rich and important chapter that deserves a careful reading.

In the final chapter, Cummings and Cummings describe faith-based interventions and how these are on the rise. They describe the religious roots of positive psychology, which is clearly on the rise. They illustrate the role of religion in helping convicts and substance abusers, in progressive social movements, in minority cultures such as African Americans, and the role of religion in decreasing sex-related problems. They argue that faith-based counseling, while still needing to be evidence-based, provides some unique advantages by allowing religious individuals to have a therapist who understands and is in sympathy with a major part of their lives. They conclude by providing a few case illustrations.

Introduction

Chapter 1

The Culture Wars and Psychology's Alliance

William T. O'Donohue, Ph.D.

The premise of this volume is that there is a war against the religious, fought by organized psychology, with individual psychologists as its soldiers. The war metaphor, we believe, is apt. There is more than a simple lack of understanding and respect toward the religious; there is also hostility, aggression, and at times a desire to harm or destroy. This war has been going on for the past few decades and its battles can be seen in:

- numerous policy statements of the American Psychological Association (APA) that are not only inconsistent with the beliefs of many of the major religions but show no sensitivity toward these beliefs,
- the writing of leading psychotherapists such as Albert Ellis (1980 and 2001) defining the religious as irrational or mentally ill,

- a search to find the pathological causal pathways related to religiosity in social psychological research,
- deriding (and mischaracterizing) the Catholic Church as dogmatic, irrational and anti-science, as well as displaying an open prejudice against those of certain religions, particularly the Mormons and Evangelicals (Hempel, 1965).

These hostilities go beyond their embodiment in organized psychology. One also witnesses hostile prejudicial statements, stated with impunity, made about the religious by individual psychologists—"Evangelicals are dumb," "Catholics are dogmatic," "Mormons are strange, and Stepford-like," etc .

If similar statements were made regarding one of organized psychology's "protected classes" the utterer would receive the harshest punishments. It is more than a little ironic that those who accuse the religious of being intolerant, are often showing intolerance themselves. Often the war's victims can be the unempowered such as religious graduate students who feel that they must stay "in the closet" about their religious beliefs.

We also want to acknowledge that there are dissenters among the ranks of psychologists. Historically, as the Cummings point out in the next chapter, there has been much less hostility. Some of our founders have written classic books regarding religion, probably the most famous being William James' *The Varieties of Religious Experience: A Study in Human Nature* (1902/1985). However, both Freud and Skinner were much more negative about religion. Carl Rogers, on the other hand, was trained in a seminary and his central notion of unconditional positive regard might have been influenced by Christian notions of love.

Currently a significant number of psychologists themselves are religious and often don't hold these views (at least regarding their own religion). One also is concerned that part of the animus is not due entirely to the secular-religious battle but to the centuries old inter-religious hostilities. In addition, there is a Psychology of Religion Division in the APA whose membership has been increasing dramatically in recent years (to over 2,000 members). These might be seen as the anti-war dissenters that any war has. It also raises the possibility that those leading psychology in this war against the religious are neither representative of the general population nor of psychologists.

Organized psychology is certainly not alone in the war. It has fellow travelers. Much of the academy is secular and politically to the left (Maranto and Redfield, in press). It has been recognized that there is a culture war in wider society occurring between the secular left and the religious right; this culture war is the larger context for psychology's war on the religious. However, there are special circumstances that place psychology's war on religion as particularly worrisome:

- Organized psychology allegedly embraces the meta-ethic of diversity. However, it does not seem to value religious diversity in the same way it values ethnic or sexual diversity.
- Organized psychology regards prejudice toward groups as wrong and harmful. However, there is a regrettable atmosphere of tolerance for prejudicial acts against the religious.
- Organized psychology allegedly embraces the value of sensitivity. However, there seems to be no sensitivity toward the religious. In typical cultural sensitivity classes, sensitivity toward the religious is seldom if ever covered. The policy statements by the APA are not sensitive toward the positions of many religions.
- Psychology often fails to recognize that there are many issues relating to theology of which psychologists have no special expertise, e.g., epistemology, theology and metaphysics. This should entail some caution in making judgments in this area, *qua* psychologists.
- Psychologists attempt to make sure their values do not intrude into their science or psychotherapy if this is possible (O'Donohue, 1989). However, secular values, particularly secular leftist's values, seem to predominate the APA's worldview (Wright and Cummings, 2005).
- While attempting to respect the values of the people they serve, particularly minority groups with strong religious ties such as Hispanics and African-Americans, psychologists often fail to understand and show respect for the religious beliefs of these groups (Pew, 2007).

- Psychologists often endorse progressive social movements and the religious have often been at the vanguard of progressive social movements (e.g., the American Revolution, Emancipation and 1960's the Civil Rights Movement). However, they fail to see a balanced view of the history of religions, i.e., the positive progressive role of religion as well as its negative history.

Why This Book?

We do not wish to be misunderstood. Thus we want to clarify a few points:

- We are not compiling this book to attempt to convert psychologists to any religious view. We believe a secular viewpoint is perfectly reasonable, provided it is not hostile or prejudicial toward the religious.
- We are not editing this book to argue that a particular religion is true. We have included chapters from most of the major religious traditions. We ourselves have a variety of religious beliefs (including one of us who is secular).
- We are not arguing that psychology should become pastoral or religious. We think psychology should be scientific. However, if some psychologists want to combine religious viewpoints in their therapies, if the client gives informed consent and if the intervention is tested according to usual research standards (Paul, 2007), then we believe this is permissible.
- We are not arguing that there are not problems with some religions or problems with some religious individuals (e.g., hypocrisy, past historical mistakes, or immoral behavior on the part of some of the religious).
- We are editing the book because we think there is a tolerated contemporary prejudice against the religious, which harms both the religious and psychology, and we wish this to end.

We argue that the hypocrisy regarding psychology's professed meta-values, insensitivity toward the religious, policy statements that openly conflict with the viewpoints of many major religions (without suggesting how these should be dealt with) and hostile, demeaning statements about the religious should end. Many epochs have their unique prejudices. It seems that humans, including some psychologists, have a difficult time learning that all prejudice is wrong. Rather they learn more specific lessons: i.e., a prejudice against a certain groups is wrong (e.g., the Holocaust has probably contributed to less prejudice within psychology toward Judaism). We want to call attention to this open prejudice and call for it to be no longer tolerated (Lilienfield and O'Donohue, 2007).

What is the Evidence of the War?

The larger culture is battling over a number of issues. Essentially we believe that the war is over the definition of right and wrong—over ethics. However, the specific battles are over issues such as:

- Abortion
- Homosexuality/gay rights
- Status of women
- Ethical absolutism v. ethical relativity
- Gay marriage
- Definition of normative sexual behavior
- Creationism/intelligent design/evolution
- Definition of mental health/abnormality
- Bioethics (e.g., stem cell research)
- Death penalty

In addition there are legitimate and complex debates about the role of religion in:

- Politics
- Schools
- Law
- World affairs

Oganized psychology has made policy statements that are in open conflict with the beliefs and values of many organized religions. For example, the APA Directorate's policy statement regarding abortion, conflicts with the views of Roman Catholics, many fundamental Protestants, Islam, and Orthodox Judaism. There are at least two problems with the APA's positions. First, they are not well argued. For example, the research regarding the consequences of abortion for women has many gaps, and the APA's position ignores the key questions of the moral status of killing an embryo (O'Donohue and Dyslin, 1996). Second, it in no way attempts to deal with the ramifications of this policy on many of the religious. How is a practicing Catholic (whether a psychologist or a consumer of psychology) to handle this pro-abortion statement? Resign from their professional organization? Refuse to become a client of a psychologist who is a member of the APA? It raises what we think are avoidable questions, such as whether they should join and pay dues to an organization professing values against their religious beliefs. Organized psychology's endorsement of gay rights presents the same problems. It appears that organized psychology is either ignorant of, or accepting of, its insensitivity toward the religious on these and other issues. At a minimum, we believe that organized psychology should explicitly discuss this problem and seek ways to minimize the alienation of the religious.

What Are the Effects of the War?

We believe the partisan position of organized psychology and many psychologists demeans psychology. First, we believe as a prejudice it—as all prejudice—presents psychology in a bad light. Second, we believe it drives away many people who psychologists would like to serve. This includes both psychologists and consumers. Third, we believe this harms people. A Mormon graduate student or a Catholic client can have difficulties with their experience of psychology. Fourth, we believe it shows a lack of intellectual sophistication. It does so in two main ways. Primarily, it is an example of inconsistency and, at minimum, intellectual positions need to be consistent. Psychologists profess values of diversity and sensitivity but then violate these with the religious. Second, it is a rather unsophisticated position. It typically shows no appreciation of the epistemological issues related to faith and knowledge; it shows little understanding of the complex history of science and religion, and it shows no understanding of the possible limitations of science for determining values. For example, the philosopher of science, Carl Hempel (1965) has suggested that science cannot determine values—the core issue underlying the culture wars. If this is correct, what is the intellectual substance of psychology's condemnation of the values of the religious? Hempel illustrates the relevance of science for moral considerations by a thought experiment invoking Laplace's demon. The demon is a perfect scientific intelligence (knows all that science can possibly know) that knows all the laws of nature, everything that is going on in the universe at any given moment, and moreover can calculate with infinite speed and precision from the state of the universe at any particular moment, its state at any other past or future moment. Hempel argues:

> Let us assume, then, that faced with a moral decision, we are able to call upon the Laplacean demon as a consultant. What help might we get from him? Suppose that we have to choose one of several alternative courses of action open to us and that we want to know which of these we ought to follow. The demon would then be able to tell us, for any contemplated choice, what its consequences would be for the future course of the universe, down to the most minute detail, however remote in space and time. But, having done this for each of the alternative courses of action under consideration, the demon would have completed its task; he would have given us all the information that an ideal science might prove under the circumstances. And yet he would not have resolved our moral problem, for this requires a decision as to which of the several alternative sets of consequences mapped out by the demon as attainable to us is the best; which of them we ought to bring about. And the burden of the decision would still fall upon our shoulders; it is we who

> would have to commit ourselves to an unconditional (absolute) judgment of the value by singling out one of the sets of consequences as superior to the alternatives (Hempel, 1965, pp. 88-89).

According to Hempel, science cannot determine values; it can simply determine facts about the world. This leaves the important domain to extra-scientific traditions and procedures. Religion, both revealed and natural, has long been a direct source, as well as an indirect one, of information (through religious philosophers such as Descartes, Kant, Kierkegaard, etc.) about these value questions.

Another Representative Battle in the War: Abortion

Some misleading and antagonistic positions on abortion are even codified in the APA's Policy Manual. These are written to give the false impression that the results of psychological research support these positions. However, all exceed the scope of psychology's expertise and are consistent with one side in the culture wars. The APA has asserted, for example, that:

> Whereas, termination of unwanted pregnancies is clearly a mental health and child welfare issue, and a legitimate concern of APA; be it resolved, that termination of pregnancy be considered a civil right of the pregnant woman, to be handled as other medical and surgical procedures in consultation with her physician.

Of course the question is what evidence derived from psychological research was used to support this pronouncement? Psychologists *qua* psychologists are not experts on civil rights nor are they experts on the key issue of the status of a fetus/baby. Psychologists could conduct research on psychological outcomes of abortion for the woman or psychological effects of adoption or being a mother of an unwanted baby; however there is very little of this research and no definitive conclusions can be made. Again, at a minimum we argue that the APA needs to acknowledge the criticism this directs towards the views of some religious individuals and seek to resolve this problem.

Another Battle in the War: Sexuality

The culture wars also battle over what is acceptable sexuality (see chapters 4 and 6 in this volume). In general, secular thought has influenced the normative dimensions of the study of sex and of sex therapy. It has helped to define healthy and unhealthy sexual behavior, and to identify sexual minorities that have been victimized. The culture wars have also battled over the importance of sex. The secular tend to value it (some even define themselves by it). Bloom (1988) has stated:

> As it now stands, students have powerful images of what a perfect body is and pursue it incessantly. But deprived of literary guidance, they no longer have any image of a perfect soul, and hence do not long to have one. They do not even imagine that there is such a thing. (p. 67)

Miriam Grossman (2006) in *Unprotected: A Campus Psychiatrist Reveals How Political Correctness in Her Profession Endangers Every Student* recently described how the values associated with the secular movement influence what is practiced in a typical university health clinic. She suggests that clinics exaggerate the protection for sexually transmitted diseases (STDs) provided by condoms, fail to inform students about how casual sex may be implicated in their emotional problems, fail to inform female students how long-term career plans and biological time determinants of fertility interact, and finally fail to discuss the emotional scars that can be left post-abortion. She suggests that the psychological and physical health of students would be better served if clinics declared war on the "hook-up culture" rather than more politically popular culprits like second-hand smoke.

The first problem is that these proffered norms regarding sex associated with the secular left have rarely been argued for. Rather they have been presented by *fiat* as some sort of unarguable apodictic *objective value.* The sexual norms offered are regarded as "sex positive" and in opposition to more traditional views of sex, which are viewed as "sex negative." The new norms are generally hypersexual and relativistic. For example, there is no hypersexual disorder in the DSM-IV, only a hyposexual disorder. This is despite the health and social problems caused by certain kinds of behavior. In the Politically Correct (PC) account there are few prohibitions placed on any sexual behavior or interest. The interaction between this view and sensitivity toward those practicing traditional religions is unclear.

Further, there has been a reluctance to diagnose certain kinds of sexual behavior as deviant. (This is perhaps due to the difficulties finding clear criteria for diagnostic inclusion or exclusion during the debates on the diagnostic status of homosexuality). For example, to be diagnosed a pedophile by DSM-IV criteria, the individual would have to be distressed by his pedophilic urges or acted on them; if a person is sexually attracted to children, and is not distressed by this and has not acted on this, then this person cannot be diagnosed as a pedophile. (See O'Donohue & Geer 1992, Volume 1 & 2).

Finally, in the secular view, sexual minorities that need protection have increased (transgendered is a recent addition). There is a movement in the past few decades endorsed by individuals such as Alfred Kinsey (see Reisman, 2003) and Theo Sandfort (see his 1989; recently elected to the presidency of the International Academy of Sex Research) to combat what they view as a modern prejudice against what they call "intergenerational sex." They view the new liberation movement as one that is directed toward liberating those who wish to engage in adult-child sexual contacts. I resigned from the International Academy of Sex Research several years ago when Sandfort was elected President. This background might have served to explain why Congress in 2000, for the first time ever, condemned a scientific article published in *Psychological Bulletin* which reported a meta-analysis of nearly 50 studies of the effects of child sexual abuse. This study concluded that some minors reported their experiences as neutral or positive and, in some studies, negative psychological effects were not found.

Finally, the secular leftist view is that many nongays are "homophobic." The scales that purport to measure homophobia—

all which have unacceptable validity—do not take the construct literally, i.e., a fear of homosexuals (see O'Donohue & Casselles, 2005). An examination of these scales and their items reveals that they load more on the construct of "viewing homosexuality as morally wrong" (O'Donohue & Casselles, 2005). However, we have argued that it is wrong to pathologize, as these scales do, an open ethical question and the ethical views of Orthodox Jews, Catholics, Muslims and fundamentalist Christians, among others. Claims about the ethical status of homosexual behavior can be criticized; but not made "pathological" by *fiat* in psychologists sneaking this view into test construction. Although the APA seems to hold a meta-ethical stance of diversity and sensitivity it does not seem to care about diversity and sensitivity regarding the sexual views of those belonging to many of the traditional religions. The APA is currently considering that any psychologist who performs restorative therapy (helping someone who has engaged in homosexual behavior and who wishes to end this) is behaving unethically and could lose their license to practice.

Why Might Psychologists Have These Anti-religious Views?

Miller et al provided a recent survey of the religious views of psychologists and compare these to a national sample. Within the sampling restrictions of the survey, Miller's data suggest that psychologists differ in two important dimensions from the general public:

- Psychologists place significantly less importance on religion in their lives.
- Psychologists attend services less than nonpsychologists.

Here are some of the other characteristics of psychologists with respect to religion.

Negative Stereotypes

It is also the case that many psychologists have very negative images of the religious. They think of the religious as hypocrites, poorly educated, not very intelligent, sex-negative, judgmental and retrogressive individuals. Elmer Gantry, the Church Lady, pedophile priests, prominent Evangelical ministers caught with prostitutes or who have gold doghouses are the (sometimes true) negative images. However to round out this picture we should also consider individuals such as: Ghandi, Dr. Martin Luther King, Mother Teresa, David Ben-Gurion, the Dalai Lama, Abraham Lincoln, John F. Kennedy, and Nelson Mandela.

All are or were religious. Even some of the contemporary heroes of the left such as Hillary Clinton, Barack Obama, Edward Kennedy, as well as some in the recent past such as Franklin Roosevelt were also religious.

To give a balanced picture we must also consider some of the villains of the secular movement. These are responsible for approximately 100 million deaths in the 20th century: Hitler, Stalin, Mao Zedong, Pol Pot, and Castro.

Thus, although we conjecture that when psychologists think of ideology resulting in murder they think of the Salem Witch Trials, the Crusades, or the Spanish Inquisition, it is clear that the secular ideologies have resulted in far more harm than the religious.

The American Religious Tradition

In addition, the American political tradition has had a central role for religion. Thus, we also want to point out that it is strange for the APA to be so hostile to religion. The first Europeans to populate our country were pilgrims seeking the freedom to practice their religion. In the Declaration of Independence, God is mentioned four times (although there is no mention in the constitution, there is mention in many states' constitutions). Jefferson mentioned God as a lawmaker ("the Laws of Nature and of Nature's God"); as a creator ("endowed by their Creator with certain unalienable rights;" as a judge ("the Supreme Judge of the world for the rectitude of our intentions") and as a protector ("the protection of Divine Providence"). Washington, during his inauguration, placed his right hand on the Bible and after taking the oath added "so help me God" and bent over and kissed the bible. The framers of our republic thought that democracy, which gave power to the people, could only survive if the people were virtuous, and religion, they thought, was the major way that individuals became virtuous. For example, John Adams stated:

> We have no government armed with power capable of contending with human passions unbridled by morality and religion. Avarice, ambition, revenge or gallantry, would break the strongest cords of our Constitution as a whale goes through a net. Our Constitution was made for a moral and religious people. It is wholly inadequate to the government of any other.

We could state many other ways in which our nation's history and current practice is associated with religious beliefs and practices, but we think the point is made. Hostility toward religion is not an American tradition. Certainly, the constitution wanted a separation between church and state, but part of the culture war is fought over the meaning of this. The First Amendment's second phrase is often forgotten:

> "Congress shall make no law respecting an establishment of religion, or prohibiting the free exercise thereof;"

Thus while there are important questions regarding the establishment clause, there are also important questions about the government not "prohibiting the free exercise thereof." We believe that these are both important considerations for organized psychology. To wit, does organized psychology conflict with the American political tradition when it interferes with the free exercise of religion?

The Relationship Between Religion and Science

Barbour (2000) in his classic *When Science Meets Religion* suggests that there are four major views of the relationship between science and religion:

- **Conflict**. In this view, religion and science oppose each other. Thus both cannot be true. Either the religious are right about their claims about creation or scientists are right about their claims regarding evolution. There has to be a winner and a loser.

- **Independence.** In this view religion and science are separate magisteria. Because they make different kind of claims about the same matter or because they simply deal with different questions, they can co-exist. Science deals with facts and laws; religion with meaning and values. Conflicts arise only when individuals ignore these boundaries.
- **Dialogue**. In this view science and religion can mutually explore questions. Science may tell us the big bang is responsible for many aspects of the universe but religion can still investigate why there was something rather than nothing for the Big Bang to operate on. Science can address how the universe is orderly and intelligible; religion can explore why it is.
- **Integration**. This view suggests that the interaction between science and religion should be more systematic than a dialogue. In what Barbour calls a theology of nature or a natural theology, results from the dialogue can be integrated to provide more comprehensive answers. Teilhard de Chardin, (2004) for example, attempted to integrate evolution with the Catholic religion, accepting the scientific results of evolution, while interpreting this for a Catholic point of view (suggesting an order to evolution, which is controversial).

We suggest that psychologists think not only of the first model of the relationship between science and religion—that of conflict—but also recognize that there are other models. Scientism—the incorrect belief that science can provide all answers to all questions—lacks the ability to see the limitations of science. *Scientistic* views such as those held by logical positivists were often hostile toward all metaphysics. However, no philosophical view has been more discredited than logical positivism. Its influence, direct and indirect, on psychology is still felt however. (See Smith, 1986 for another view, at least regarding behaviorism).

But we ought not to look simply at theology with its problems and prospects; we also need to look at theology's major rivals, i.e., the secular life. Has it with all its professed logic, scientific and material progress brought about human happiness and utopian existence?

The Problem of Meaning

Religion gives many individuals meaning. It provides answers to questions of morality, transcendence, and the meaning of death. Certainly even secular psychologists should embrace some of the *meaning structures* provided by religion (e.g., the importance of love, forgiveness, family and charity). One also wonders to what extent more secular views on life (importance of material possessions, sexual conquests, and other selfish pursuits) are responsible for both individual psychopathology as well as more widespread social problems (e.g., pollution, feminization of poverty). Psychologists rarely study the meaning structures of different traditions and understand their relative strengths.

Wisdom

Religion can also supply wisdom. Wisdom is seen as different from knowledge—as a shrewder more useful type of knowledge. It can teach us to value others, particularly those who may be in need of help. It can teach us to have a reverence toward life; the value of forgiveness, the importance of self denial, the importance of charity, the importance of love toward others, even enemies, the importance of quiet meditation, and the importance of peace, etc. A significant part of the good life that psychotherapists help their clients to achieve might rely on wisdom as well as knowledge.

Psychotherapy's Selfism vs. Religion's Other-Directedness

As Donohue notes in his chapter on Catholicism in this volume, (The War on Catholicism, pp. 129) the scholar Paul Vitz has critiqued, "psychology's deep commitment to narcissism, egoism, self-worship, the individual, isolated self" (p. x-xi). Religion typically teaches the individual that it is vital—one of life's key missions—to overcome this selfishness. It directs people to be focused on others, sometimes those they have duties toward such as their children but especially the unfortunate—the poor, the sick, the discriminated against. Psychotherapy can be seen at times as too much of a narcissistic exercise: how can my life and my needs or my wants be dealt with? Religion can teach that some of this is just plain narcissistic—it can be a corrective to the self-focus of psychotherapy. It would be interesting to attempt to understand how effective the message of focusing on the needs of others can itself be curative for some of the unhappiness that motivates individuals to come to therapy.

A More Positive Vision of the Future Relationship Between Psychology and the Religious

We hope this book can promote the following changes:

- A change in practice by organized psychology, particularly the APA, so that it is more cognizant of and respectful of the intellectual positions of the religious.
- An increase in intolerance for prejudicial and discriminatory statements and practices by psychologists toward the religious.

Secondarily, we would also like to see:

- An elimination of the stereotypes of the religious and religions as uninformed, dogmatic, anti-science, immoral, and mentally disordered.
- An appreciation of the positive qualities and contributions of religion and the religious, including the positive contributions of religion to mental health.
- A realization of the intellectual complexity of both the present and historical issues between science and religion and more humility on the part of organized psychology and individual psychologists regarding these metaphysical, epistemological, philosophical and moral questions. At times we fear there is an anti-intellectualism in contemporary psychology that attempts to reduce these questions to cartoon form.

References

Adams, J. (1854). *The works of John Adams, second president of the United States.* (Vol. IX) C. F. Adams, Ed. Boston: Little, Brown and Co.)

Barbour, I.G. (2000). *When science meets religion: Enemies, strangers or partners?* New York: Harper Collins.

Bloom, A. (1988). *The closing of the American mind.* New York: Simon & Schuster.

Delaney, H. D., Miller, W. R., & Bisono, A. (in press). Religiosity and spirituality among psychologists: A survey of clinician members of APA. *Professional Psychology.*

Ellis, A. (1980). *The case against religiosity.* Unpublished manuscript.

Ellis, A., Nielsen, S., & Johnson, W. B. (Eds.) (2001). *Counseling and psychotherapy with religious persons: A rational emotive behavior therapy approach.* Mahwah, NJ: Lawrence Erlbaum Associates.

Grossman, M. (2006). *Unprotected: A campus psychiatrist reveals how political correctness in her profession endangers every student.* Penguin Group (USA) Inc.

Hempel, C. G. (1965). Science and human values. In C. Hempel (Ed.), *Aspects of scientific explanation.* New York: Free Press.

Lilienfeld, S. & O'Donohue, W. (Eds.) (2007). *Great ideas in clinical psychology.* New York: Bruner-Taylor.

Maranto, R. & Redfield, R. (in press). *Reforming the politically correct university.* Washington, DC: American Enterprise Institute Press.

O'Donohue, W. T. (1989). The (even) bolder model: The clinical psychologist as metaphysician-scientist-practitioner. *American Psychologist, 44(12),* 1460-1468. Spanish translation in *Clinica y Salud,* 1991.

O'Donohue, W. T., & Casselles, C. (1993). Homophobia: Conceptual, definitional, and value issues. *Journal of Psychopathology and Behavioral Assessment, 15(3),*177-195.

O'Donohue, W., & Dyslin, C. (1996). Abortion, boxing and Zionism: Politics and the American Psychological Association. *New Ideas in Psychology, 14 (1),* 1-10.

O'Donohue, W. T., & Geer, J. H. (Eds.) (1992). *The sexual abuse of children: Volume 1: Theory and research.* Hillsdale, NJ: Lawrence Erlbaum Associates.

O'Donohue, W. T., & Geer, J. H. (Eds.) (1992). *The sexual abuse of children: Volume 2: Clinical Issues.* Hillsdale, NJ: Lawrence Erlbaum Associates.

Pew Research Center (2007). *Trends in political values and core attitudes: 1987-2007.* Retrieved from http://pewresearch.org/pubs/434/trends-in-political-values-and-core-attitudes-1987-2007.

Reisman, J. (1998). *Kinsey: Crimes and consequences.* New York: Institute for Media Education.

Sandfort, T. (1992). The argument for adult-child sexual contact: a critical appraisal and new data. In W. T. O'Donohue & J. H. Geer (Eds.), *The sexual abuse of children: Theory and research.* Hillsdale, NJ; Lawrence Earlbaum Associates.

Smith, L.D. (1986). *Behaviorism and logical positivism.* Stanford, CA: Stanford University Press.

Teilhard de Chardin, P. (2004) *The divine milieu* (S. Cowell, Trans.). Brighton: Sussex Academic Press.

Wright, R. H. & Cummings, N.A. (2005). *Destructive trends in mental health: The well-intentioned path to harm.* New York: Routledge.

Chapter 2

Psychology and Religion: A Brief History of a Paradoxical Relationship

Nicholas A. Cummings, Ph.D., Sc.D.
and **Janet L. Cummings, Psy.D.**

At its very beginnings psychology regarded the study of religion to be of integral, if not of paramount importance to the field. As will be seen, if the founders of our discipline had been given their way, psychology would have also included the study of religion and education (G. Stanley Hall) or religion and philosophy (William James). In time psychology's determination to be accepted as a hard science comparable to physics resulted in its turning away from religious study, and there emerged a growing disdain of anything spiritual. But it was a mixed picture. Some prominent psychologists, such as O. Hobart Mowrer, who served as president of the American Psychological Association (APA) in

1954, was unabashedly religious, while others, such as B.F. Skinner, eschewed faith and saw the technological ideal of science as the way to social reform[1] (Smith, 1992). Freud regarded religiosity as a manifestation of pathology, a view held by most psychotherapists of the mid to late 20th century.

As mainstream psychology drifted farther away from religious studies and the APA even issued position statements seen in some circles to be in opposition to religion (as will be discussed below), religions paradoxically espoused psychology. Humanistic psychology was openly and profoundly spiritual, but in a way different from the more doctrinaire manner of evangelical denominations which promoted and proliferated pastoral and other psychological counselors for their members. In the 1960s and beyond many clerics openly stated that they would like to have become psychologists rather than priests and ministers. As president of the nation's first professional school, the California School of Professional Psychology, I "re-treaded" many a cleric on one of our four campuses. In fact, in the 1970s, I received a formal letter of complaint from the Roman Catholic archbishop in San Francisco that I was depleting the ranks of the priesthood.

More recently Buddhism, renamed "mindfulness," has become a standard approach to treatment in cognitive behavioral therapy [2], while other psychologists openly adhere to Zen principles[3]. These same psychologists may have little or no interest in the more mainstream Christianity or Judaism. Nonetheless, there is now a heightened interest in all aspects of religion as evidenced by the number of publications on the subject. In the sixty years between 1900 and 1959 there were a total of only 3,803 articles in the psychological literature that addressed religion or spirituality, while in the six years between 2000 and 2006 alone there were 8,193 such articles (Bartoli, 2007). After decades in which such publications were relatively sparse, there was a sharp increase in the 1980s, and this has continued to the present.

All of this describes the paradoxical relationship between psychology and religion, where emotions frequently clash and there is often a lack of common ground. Some have attempted to resolve the contentiousness by separating religion and spirituality. The former is seen as essentially sectarian, while the latter is regarded as more secular. This distinction itself is questionable inasmuch as there is considerable overlap between religious faith or conviction and spiritual feeling or enlightenment. Nonetheless, while the heightened interest in spirituality continues, there is a growing distrust of psychology and mainstream psychotherapy by evangelical denominations and other religious groups, resulting in a burgeoning of faith-based treatment centers as described in a later chapter, by Cummings and Cummings, of this volume.

The Religious Beginnings of Psychology

Both G. Stanley Hall and William James have been called "the father of American psychology," and it depends upon one's point of view who deserves the appellation. Some historians would choose the former because he founded the APA, convened its first meeting in 1892, and became its first president. Others would choose William James because he founded the first chair in psychology, even though he gave it to Hugo Munsterberg while he, a physician who never practiced medicine, retained his chair in philosophy. He served as the APA's third president and is the only such president to later be re-elected. Both men profoundly molded the emerging discipline in America, and their roles as *the* founders are indisputable. Whichever of these two pioneering psychologists you choose to designate the "father," it is clear both were deeply spiritual and regarded the study of religion as integral to the new discipline. Such were psychology's roots.

When G. Stanley Hall invited seven individuals to his home in 1892 to form the American Psychological Association, the main item on the agenda was to define who was a psychologist, and whom to invite to membership. The first year saw 31 original members who joined upon invitation, an exceedingly diverse group that varied from those who were biology-oriented on one end of the small spectrum, and those identified with religion and philosophy on the opposite end. As the APA grew from this small group, the pressure heightened from within that it become more scientific by emulating biology and physics and by discarding its interest in religion. Society, however, would have none of this, as Americans in the latter 19th century were intensely interested in psychic phenomena and expected that the new discipline of psychology would become its prime investigator.

It was difficult to ignore this societal clamor for investigation of spiritualism and other psychic phenomena because the fledgling profession relied upon public support and funding. Among many religiously disposed psychologists such as Hall, psychic phenomena, and especially spiritualism, were regarded as heretical. He was joined by Joseph Jastrow, a student of James, in conducting research to establish that table tapping and other phenomena at séances were a fraud. But it was difficult inasmuch as the most influential psychologist of the time, William James, fueled the public's clamor for research that would validate psychic phenomena. When James established the official psychological laboratory at Harvard in 1890, he stocked it not only with the usual scientific apparatus such as chronoscopes, kymographs, tuning forks, and physiological models, but also with a hypnotizer and Ouija board[4]. Later Hall, who was president of Clark University, was highly embarrassed when the first major bequest in 1906 to the university was specifically restricted to research in spiritualism (Sokal, 1992). By 1913 both Harvard and Stanford Universities had received large bequests for psychic research, the substitute name for spiritualism proposed by Hall in embarrassment and desperation a few years earlier (Coon, 1992).

Hall's religiosity was quite apparent throughout his career, and it pervaded his intense pedagogical interests. An ambitious man who was an ordained Congregational minister, he was surprised to have been outdone by his spiritualist opponent William James when he published his wide-ranging *Varieties of Religious Experience,* which seemingly overnight became a classic[5]. He responded by founding the Clark School of Religious Psychology, where he installed many of the courses he had promoted when he was previously teaching religious psychology at Johns Hopkins University. He insisted on what he termed the "real definition of psychology" (Hall, 1911, pp 351-352):

> As natural, it reestablishes unity with nature; as ethical, a reunion of conduct with conscience; as theoretical, it is a re-atonement of the mind with truth; as feeling, it is the ecstatic

> closing in of the highest love with its supreme object, or fresh impulse along a forsaken but recovered path. The common element is atonement with implication of previous estrangement....Religion is the reinstallation of the individual or race into its true place in the world, recovery to health and wholeness.

The 19th century was one fraught with tremendous change, resulting in intellectual and emotional insecurity and one seeking to fill the moral gap created by the Industrial Revolution, Darwinism, and the weakening of religion. This was the age of distress resulting from an evolving naturalistic materialism, and by efforts to ameliorate this distress. It is understandable, as social historians have pointed out, that thoughtful people—among them philosophers and scientists—would seek answers in the occult and would eagerly look to science to provide evidence and define the parameters. Thus three seemingly unrelated movements captured the public's attention, with the adherents of one very likely being adherents of one or both of the others:

- Mesmerism, the belief that an imponderable fluid permeated the universe and could be manipulated to cure diseases.
- Phrenology, the belief that bumps on the head correspond to well developed portions of the brain that correspond to highly developed faculties.
- Spiritualism, the belief that there is a plane of existence apart from material existence that can be revealed through certain occult experiences and practices.

Psychology was caught up in all three, with the first contributing to our understanding of hypnosis, the second to the mapping of the areas of brain functioning, and the third the study of abnormal mental states. The perennial question of whether society influences the direction of science, or whether science influences social change is illustrated in the history of early psychology. The answer undoubtedly is that there is an interaction between the two, with the constant evolving of each as it is influenced or directed by the other. Now, as then, societal pressure and funding determine what science investigates, and, in turn, these results instigate changes in society.

The Beginnings of Experimental Psychology

The beginnings of psychology as an experimental science began at the same time that most of the early discipline was engrossed in the study of spiritualism and other occult phenomena. Historians (Leahy, 1992) would date this beginning to the publication, in 1860, of the book, *Elements of Psychophysics,* by Gustav Theodore Fechner who was not a psychologist, but a retired German physicist. He conducted the first research in experimental psychology that produced mathematical laws in an era in which it was widely assumed that the mind was not subject to experimentation, and was certainly not subject to mathematical scrutiny. Coincidentally in the same era Hermann von Helmholtz timed and measured nervous transmission. These experiments sparked an intense interest in sensation, perception and the temporal extension of thought, all now proven to be measurable[7] (Boring, 1950).

With Edward Titchener as its nominal leader, experimental psychology rapidly gained ground. But as psychology evolved into a quantifiable, laboratory-based science, this "New Psychology" as it was eventually termed, had to live side-by-side with those who directed their attention to whether people could communicate by direct thought transference or whether gifted people could foretell the future. At the beginning of this schism in psychology, both the public's and psychology's interest in psychic research dominated in the popular and literary magazines. But as this New Psychology increasingly came to the attention of the public, there occurred a noticeable shift as the public turned to this new cadre of mental experts to answer their questions about the mysterious powers of the mind and spirit (Sokal, 1992).

The Impact of Psychoanalysis

Psychoanalysis and behaviorism were becoming important aspects of psychology at about the same time (1915 and beyond), the first with the public at large and the second within psychology. In the early part of the 20th century no one suspected that it would become another "one hundred years' war" (Hornstein, 1992), inasmuch as the early discourse between the two was mutually critical but cordial. The *Journal of Abnormal Psychology* regularly reviewed books by Freud, Jung and A.A. Brill, and it published articles by psychoanalytically oriented writers.

However, it was not long before this relationship deteriorated into one of conflict. By the 1920s psychoanalysis had so captured the imagination of the American public that it threatened to eclipse experimental psychology. The initial response of psychology was to retreat into positivism, thus further limiting its relevance and scope (Hornstein, 1992). As the conflict heated up, attacks on psychoanalysis by experimental psychologists increased, and by 1932 Joseph Jastrow himself published a very critical book, *The House that Freud Built* (1932). But psychoanalysis continued to garner wide public interest, and in the 1950s entered its Golden Age as it was heralded in popular psychology books, magazine articles, motion pictures and novels. Most independently practicing psychologists at the time were psychodynamic in their therapeutic orientation, and clinical psychology's decidedly psychoanalytic doctoral programs had been established in such major institutions as New York and Adelphi Universities. Perhaps out of necessity a new strategy emerged within psychology, that of subjecting psychoanalytic concepts to experimental scrutiny[8]. This reestablished experimental psychology as the arbiter of the mental health world, and interestingly, at the same time the adoption of many psychoanalytic techniques markedly broadened clinical psychology.

By the 1950s the field of psychology, striving to be unequivocally scientific, had largely abandoned religion as an important psychological study, and had even become antagonistic to it. O. Hobart Mowrer, who served in 1954, was the last APA president to openly declare his religious affiliation. At the same time psychoanalysis had popularized the idea that religion was a manifestation of psychopathology, a position openly taken by Freud[9]. Experimental psychology's disdain for the lack of scientific scrutiny in psychoanalysis was curiously suspended as it widely disseminated the Freudian assumption that belief in a deity, heaven and hell, and religious morality were based on infantile fixations and wishes.

This paradoxical relationship to psychoanalysis extended even to B.F. Skinner, an avowed atheist but also a hard scientist. In personal conversations with me, he readily confessed that he was fascinated with Freudian theory, that he had extensively read Freud's work, and marveled at its internal consistency, even while it completely lacked experimental validity. In our discussions he was amused by my calling him a "closet Freudian." Within the general public, the Freudian ideal of a permissive childhood free from the so-called "ego stifling" strictures of discipline and inhibition gained wide acceptance, and it prevails to this day in a large sector of society. It permeated much of experimental child psychology as it strove for decades to establish the efficacy of Freudian permissiveness in parenting. It is only recently that psychology has begun to question this thrust, as shown in its concern for the apparent ill-effects of the early sexualizing of girls[10]. By this time psychoanalysis had declined and was no longer the psychotherapeutic force it once was, having been replaced by the cognitive revolution, and more recently by the biomedical revolution[11]. The belief that repression creates emotional maladjustment lingers in society even while Freudian psychology has all but disappeared.

Nonetheless, psychology's antagonism toward religion continues, as shown in a series of proclamations by the APA. Psychology's disdain of religion is essentially toward the Roman Catholic Church and evangelical Christian denominations. The mid-twentieth century in America was characterized by anti-Semitism, but psychology's record in this regard is exemplary, perhaps because Jews are overly represented in its ranks and its leadership, leaving Christianity as the vulnerable recipient.

Paradoxes Abound

It has been well over one hundred years since 1902 when William James wrote *Varieties of Religious Experience,* but it was reprinted in 1985 and this classic continues to be read in departments of psychology and philosophy in the United States. Psychology has lost its religious roots, but James continues to be highly regarded by these two disciplines to which he has contributed so much.

Even within psychoanalysis there was a difference of opinion as to whether religion was a manifestation of pathology. The second most popular psychoanalyst after Freud was his student Carl Jung, with whom Freud very bitterly broke early in their careers. In contrast to his teacher, Jung, who called his system "analytic psychology" to differentiate it from Freudianism (Jung was a Ph.D., not an M.D. like Freud), was fascinated with religion. His archetypes were heavily dependent on the religious symbolism of Christianity, Hinduism and Buddhism.

Jung's system also lacked psychoanalysis' less-than-flattering view of women, such as Freud's belief that "moral masochism" was an inherent characteristic of femininity. It seems no accident, therefore, that during the ascendancy of psychoanalysis most Jungian analysts were women, while most Freudian analysts were men. The late Professor Donald McKinnon, an ardent student of Jung's who was on the faculty at Swathmore College, relayed the following to me during a conversation in the mid-1960s. Jung was asked by a professor in the audience whether he was a Christian. Jung unabashedly replied, "Yes. I can't help it because it is in my every pore." Paradoxically, before he died, Freud mended some fences with Jung and thanked him for saving psychoanalysis from becoming a "Jewish movement."

In the recent Association for Psychological Science (APS) poll, Carl Rogers and Albert Ellis were voted the most famous American clinical psychologists. Rogers recalls that he felt called to enter the ministry, and he spent two years in a seminary. This influence would seem to be reflected in his concept of "unconditional positive regard" which closely resembles Christianity's notion of unconditional love. On the other hand Albert Ellis, who proudly referred to himself as an atheist, often stated in his lectures that the Bible has helped more people than all of the psychotherapists combined.

Alcoholics Anonymous (AA), founded in the early 1930s, and

its offshoot Narcotics Anonymous (NA), maintain that sobriety is achieved by surrendering to a Higher Power. Twelve-step programs have proliferated and have become the foundation for most of the substance abuse treatment centers in the United States. Following the basic tenet of AA, these programs teach that an alcoholic is never cured but is always "recovering," and abstinence is the only way to prevent slipping back into alcoholism. Cognitive substance abuse methodologies, as championed by psychology, eliminate the concept of a Higher Power, further reject the necessity of life-long abstinence and assert that alcoholics can be restructured to become social drinkers. With the current advances in the understanding of brain function it is apparent that cognitive psychology missed the aspect of actual physiological changes in alcoholism, and AA, as founded seven decades ago, is closer to current scientific knowledge. Curiously, recovering alcoholics who were also avowed atheists accepted the concept of surrendering to a Higher Power as a necessity for their continued recovery.

Since the early 1980s there is an explosion in the number faith-based counseling centers, along with the proliferation of Christian-oriented psychotherapists. The Christian Association for Psychological Studies (CAPS) is rapidly becoming a strong voice in the psychotherapy profession as patients distrustful of mainstream practitioners flock to the office of its members. All of this is occurring while referrals for psychotherapy are generally declining as patients are turning more to the new psychotropic medications. This recent phenomenon is discussed in a later chapter of this volume.

There is considerable discussion within psychological circles that the Holocaust contributed to the decline of religion as more and more people questioned how a compassionate God could allow this to happen. Lacking evidence to support this notion, it would seem that this is more discussion than fact, and the people making the assertion are the same ones who would use every tragedy to question the existence of God. One is reminded of the statement of Clarence Darrow who was defending Scopes in the 1920s court fight about teaching the theory of evolution, dubbed the "monkey trial." As replayed in the Broadway play, *Inherit the*

Wind, Darrow declared that the Bible tells us that God made man in his own image, and man, being a gentleman, returned the compliment.

The Attack on Faith-Based Doctoral Training Programs

The Clark School of Religious Psychology, founded in 1911, may have been a first, but within three decades there were psychology departments in most Catholic universities such as Fordham and Loyola. Following the Vail Conference in the 1970s, a number of evangelical Christian clinical training programs in psychology sprung up, such as Fuller and Rosemead. At this same time the clinical psychology program at Yeshiva University was established. No one seemed to regard these programs as constituting a problem, but when the more evangelical faith-based programs were established, there suddenly erupted a strong movement to disenfranchise from APA approval the faith-based clinical doctoral programs. In 1979 a strong, well-orchestrated effort was launched to do just that (Routh, 1994).

That was the year that, as president, I was presiding over the APA Council of Representatives where a series of resolutions were introduced, one at the beginning of each session of the Council. In essence they sought to ban the application for approval of any educational institution that required a creedal oath for admission to its program. The contention was that limiting admission to those who would sign the creedal oath somehow results in a markedly inferior educational and training program to the extent it does not merit approval. On the other side of the issue is, of course, the constitutional right of freedom of religion. The institutions targeted were private, not public, and they had the right to not only exist, but to exercise their religion. If a required creedal oath or any other religious aspect of a program did, indeed, render the program educationally and professionally deficient, then the institution should be denied approval on the basis it does not meet defined standards of excellence. In the absence of such determination, to ban a program from participation in the approvals process would come back to haunt us both legally and morally. The graduates of the banned institutions would be ineligible for psychology licensure in most states, and those so effected might have legal recourse on grounds of the violation of their religious freedom.

It was apparent, after an informal vote count, that such resolutions had the strength to pass and become APA policy. Psychology could ill-afford being labeled by the press, the courts and the public as a religiously intolerant organization, a fight that could weave itself in and out of the courts for years. So I ruled such legally questionable resolutions out of order, and indicated the chair would not entertain them unless they were based solely on the educational and training requirements and standards as enunciated by the APA approvals process. If the targeted doctoral programs were not meeting specified accreditations standards, for whatever reason, then APA approval should be denied. If they met these standards, religious affiliation and belief were irrelevant. The proponents were never able to frame their resolutions in such an acceptable manner, and one by one, they were ruled out of order. This allowed cooler heads in the profession to prevail, and now there are rules in the approvals process that guarantee the religious rights of the applying institutions. The proponents for disenfranchising faith-based clinical psychology doctoral programs indicate that, should the opportunity arise, they would mount such an effort again.

This degree of concern is unprecedented in the healthcare field, which has a history of religious involvement in training and practice. Nurse nuns have been a hallmark for generations, as only one manifestation of the various religions' extensive eleemosynary participation in health. In the early part of the 20th century the Seventh Day Adventist denomination founded the College of Medical Evangelists whose avowed purpose was to train physicians and other healthcare professionals for service in their foreign mission fields. Later renamed the Loma Linda School of Medicine, it remains one of California's major medical schools, turning out not only excellent physicians, but also nurses, clinical psychologists and other healthcare personnel. It has never been scrutinized by the American Medical Association on other than its merits in scientific medical education and training.

The Battle Over Intelligent Design

In 1982 the APA Council of Representatives adopted a resolution that stated creationism does not conform to the criteria of science. In 2007, and building on the previous resolution, the APA Council adopted as APA policy a resolution opposing the teaching of intelligent design as scientific theory[12]. In so doing it joined several other organizations taking similar positions, notably the American Association for the Advancement of Science (AAAS), the Federation of American Societies for Experimental Biology (FASEB) and the National Association of Biology Teachers (NABT). These organizations, far from being the major scientific bodies in America, nonetheless have a stake in making such a pronouncement. Why the APA, when confronted with so many psychological problems clamoring for attention and often left neglected, chose to get involved in something that is essentially tangential to its primary mission, is a question.

Perhaps psychology still feels inferior to the so-called hard sciences and is over-reaching in its determination to establish its credentials. Or this may be another in a long line of gratuitous proclamations on subjects for which there is little scientific evidence, but are responsive to the latest hot-button item in political correctness. Consider these subjects, all translated into past proclamations and all lacking scientific evidence: boxing, Zionism, abortion, gay marriage, and the naming of athletic mascots. Now comes the ban on teaching intelligent design.

In 1973 the APA adopted the Leona Tyler Principle, which states that when we or the APA speak as psychologists, we speak from scientific evidence or sound clinical determination. Every psychologist, as a citizen, has a right to speak out through a myriad of political and activist organizations. But when representing the discipline of psychology, evidence is required. Gratuitously rendering proclamations lacking such evidence will cause the APA to lose credibility as a scientific body, and become just another political organization seeking to be heard in a vast arena of contentious voices. Some say that has already occurred (Wright and Cummings, 2005). Beginning in the mid-1980s the Leona Tyler Principle, which has never been repealed, has been largely ignored. As a result, the public has lost much of its confidence that the APA is reflecting scientific fact, and regards its proclamations as essentially political in nature.

Taking at face value the assertion that the proclamation is intended to further science, it would be interesting to ascertain what a noted scientist might say about intelligent design. The three giants of the 20th century were Sigmund Freud, Charles Darwin and Albert Einstein. We have already seen that Freud considered religion a manifestation of psychopathology. Darwin in his *Origins of the Species and the Decent of Man* makes abundantly clear that the theory of evolution implies random selection. Although Einstein lived before he could have heard the recent term "intelligent design," he had strong opinions about such matters and he frequently voiced them. In the words of his biographer, "He was the odd breed, a reverential rebel, and he was guided by faith, which he wore lightly and with a twinkle in his eye, in a God who would not play dice by allowing things to happen by chance" (Isaacson, 2007, p. 4). An earlier biographer and longtime friend Phillip Frank underscored this when he wrote of Einstein's aversion to the practice of any traditional religion, even to attending religious services. Yet he had a profound reverence for the harmony and beauty of what he called the mind of God as it was expressed in the creation of its universe and laws (Frank, 1947).

Einstein drew from Spinoza a faith in determinism: a sense that the laws of nature, once we could fathom them, decreed immutable causes and effects, and God did not play dice by allowing any events to be random or undetermined. Even when quantum mechanics seemed to show this was wrong, Einstein steadfastly believed it was right (Isaacson, 2007, p. 84). Rather than assert that quantum mechanics was wrong, Einstein would say it is incomplete, as there must be a fuller explanation of how the universe operates. Such an explanation would incorporate both relativity theory and quantum mechanics.

Would the APA proclamation that would ban the teaching of intelligent design stifle Einstein's teaching and his lectures? Would it have discouraged the years of interchange between Einstein and Niels Bohr about the meaning of the quantum that social philosopher C.P. Snow proclaimed, "No more profound intellectual debate has ever been conducted" (Isaacson, 2007, pp. 325-326)? Such proclamations, if taken seriously, have the effect of ending debate. The proclamation flatly states intelligent design is not testable, is not supported by empirical evidence, and is not subject to disconfirmation. Thus intelligent design lacks a basis in science. Obviously Einstein would have found this conclusion untenable, and more recently it would be challenged by Stephen Wolfram, a scientist whose academic credentials are dazzling.

Wolfram attended Oxford on a scholarship and, by age fourteen, he had written a book on particle physics. At age 17 he published a scientific paper in the journal *Nuclear Physics,* and shortly thereafter went to work in the High Energy Physics Groups at the Argonne National Laboratory. While there, and at the age of eighteen, he wrote a scientific paper on heavy quark production that soon became a classic in the field. At nineteen he received an invitation from the legendary scientist Murray Gell-Mann to attend the California Institute of Technology (Cal Tech) where he earned his Ph.D. in just one year. The following year he joined the Cal Tech faculty, and at age 21 was awarded a MacArthur "Genius" Fellowship. Now in his forties, his latest book, *A New Kind of Science,* published in 2002, puts forth his innovative conceptualizations of cellular automata, all based on years of empirical research. This book was one of the most highly anticipated in physics, and its prepublication orders exceeded any in the entire history of the field. Yet because his conclusions do not coincide with today's conventional wisdom, there is hardly a mention in the media, and certainly the crafters of the APA resolution on intelligent design had never heard of him. His highly remarkable conceptualizations challenge much of the fundamentals of mathematics, as well as the basic notion of natural selection in biology[13] (Mangelsdorf, 2000). Demonstrating that there are over-arching principles that govern and even limit the forms that cells can acquire would also challenge the hasty conclusion that intelligent design is not subject to empirical scrutiny and experimentation. In the least, it is fertile ground for scientific debate, a debate the APA proclamation would seem to close.

Psychology's Appropriate Role in the Study of Religion: Some Considerations

Perhaps one of the most direct responses by Einstein was to Rabbi Herbert Goldstein who sent him a telegram with the question, "Do you believe in God? He prepaid for a response of fifty words from Einstein, who used only half of the allotted number: "I believe in Spinoza's God, who reveals himself in the lawful harmony of all that exists, but not a God who concerns himself with the fate and the doings of mankind."[14] He resolved his difference between science's predetermination and his belief in the importance of free will by looking at the latter as something useful, if not necessary for a civilized society, prompting people to take responsibility for their own actions. In Einstein's words, "I am compelled to act as if free will existed because if I wish to live in a civilized society I must act responsibly" (Isaacson, 2007, p. 392).

Excluding anti-religious ideologues, this is not unlike how most scientists balance their personal and scientific lives. As one prominent psychologist stated, "Trained in science and brought up to live in a moral world, there is always the paradox of how to keep these two views from crashing into each other. When evaluating psychology research, I wear my science hat; when dealing with the sticky life moral issues, I turn to my upbringing, church teachings, and faith in a God-based moral order."

Surveys repeatedly reveal that 90% of Americans believe in God. How psychology can reconnect with this population that we are committed to serve but too often have alienated is the subject of another chapter (see Chapter 7 in this volume). Of interest here is the question, what is the origin of morality? For decades psychology has been promoting the idea, now under serious question, that morality is socially determined. Society (or the culture), to protect itself, has created moral rules and religion to keep people from tearing each other apart, to establish social order, and to institute a system of fair play. These theories pointed to the environment as a determiner of moral sense. We are now hearing from the behavioral geneticists that a sense of right and wrong may be built into the individual at birth, a position taken by philosophers and theologians for centuries. Animals that live in groups have curbed their selfishness. Could the behaviors evolved by social animals to make societies work be the foundation from which human morality evolved (Wade, 2007)? The relatively new science of behavioral genetics suggests that the answer may be yes.

One example of a refreshing new empirical view of the origins of morality is the extensive work of psychologist Jonathan Haidt at the University of Virginia (Haidt, 2007). In probing the emotion of disgust, he tested people's reactions to behaviors such as those of a hungry family that cooked and ate its pet dog after it had become road kill. His research led him to explore what he termed *moral dumbfounding,* when people feel strongly that something is wrong but can not explain why. His pursuit of moral dumbfounding led him to the view that morality is driven by two separate mental systems, one ancient and one modern, even though one's mind is scarcely aware of the difference. He labeled the ancient system *moral intuition,* inasmuch as it is based on emotion-laden moral behaviors that evolved before the development of language. The modern system, which he terms *moral judgment,* came after language when people were able to articulate why something was right or wrong. To get his point across, he borrows from his experiences while doing research in India and its culture. He describes the first system as the elephant and the second its rider. Social theories of the development of morality have concentrated on the rider and have missed the elephant (Haidt, 2007; and elaborated by Wade, 2007).

Haidt believes religion has played an important role in human evolution by strengthening and extending the cohesion provided by the moral systems. "If we didn't have religious minds we would not have stepped through the transition to groupishness. We'd still be small bands roving around. Religious behavior may be the result of natural selection, shaped at a time when human groups were competing with each other. Those who found ways to bind themselves together were more successful (2007, p. 2)."

Summary and Conclusion

To establish itself as an empirical science, psychology early entered into a contentious era of conflict between its religious/philosophical roots and the emerging experimental psychology, and this conflict still lingers, often needlessly. In the 19th century the public's intense interest in psychic research spurred investigation into these phenomena, but ultimately empiricism won out, and psychology was enriched by these early, now long forgotten investigations. Similarly the public's interest in psychoanalysis fostered its dominance long beyond its usefulness, but this prolonged interaction between psychology and psychoanalysis ultimately enriched clinical psychology once we began separating the wheat from the chaff. What still lingers in many circles is the unfortunate belief that religion is a manifestation of pathology, along with the conviction that there is no place for religion in scientific discourse.

In the present era, the conflict between science and religion is not a simplistic dichotomy of science versus religion as is implied in debate-stifling proclamations such as those concerning intelligent design. The unequivocally pivotal role of religion in the evolution of humans, societies and even civilizations may be a fruitful empirical question as shown in the intriguing early findings by the relatively new science of behavioral genetics. Important questions for psychology, as discussed in other chapters in this volume, pertain to the perception that decline in religion is often accompanied by social disorganization.

End Notes

[1] For Skinner's early personal idealism of science, see B.F. Skinner (1948), *Walden Two.* New York: Macmillan.

[2] Although "mindfulness" has become standard in cognitive behavioral therapy, Marsha Linehan was one of its early and important proponents. See Linehan, M. (1993), *Cognitive behavioral treatment of borderline personality disorder.* New York: Guilford.

[3] Mike Sayama is both a psychologist and a Zen master. As a master psychotherapist he co-authored N. Cummings & M. Sayama (1995), *Focused psychotherapy: A casebook of brief, intermittent psychotherapy throughout her life cycle.* New York: Brunner Mazel. As a Zen master he wrote M. Sayama (1986), *Samadhi.* Albany, NY: State University of New York Press.

[4] *Account book* [of the Psychological Laboratory], *1890-c.1890.* Cambridge, MA: Harvard University Archives, Nathan Marsh Pusey Library.

[5] James, W. (1985). *Varieties of religious experience.* Cambridge, MA: Harvard University Press. (Original work published 1902.) See also D.E. Leary (1992), William James and the art of human understanding. *American Psychologist, 47(2),* 152-160.

[6] For a discussion of Hall's religiosity and the founding of the Clark School of Religious Psychology, see Hendrika Vande Kemp (1992), G. Stanley Hall and the Clark School of Religious Psychology. *American Psychologist, 47(2),* 290-298.

[7] For the actual experiments of Helmholtz and of Fechner, see also Wayne Dennis (1948), *Readings in the history of psychology.* New York: Appleton-Century-Crofts.

[8] An example of the intense experimental psychology scrutiny of psychoanalysis is H.J. Eysenck & G.D. Wilson (1973), *The experimental study of Freudian theories.* London: Methuen.

[9] Freud's belief that neuroses are the product of repression of thoughts and feelings largely imposed by civilization and relig-

ion permeates all of his writings. Regarded as his three masterpieces are *The Interpretation of Dreams* (1900, New York: Avon), *Three Essays on the Theory of Sexuality* (1905, New York: Avon), and *Civilization and Its Discontents* (1930, New York: Norton). The third, written late in his life, sets out to indict civilization and religious morality, and has had the most profound and lasting effect on society.

[10] In 2007 the APA took a stand following publication of extensive research reporting the deleterious effects of the early sexualizing of girls. See Rhea K. Farberman, (2007), APA Council adopts reports on military mental health, sexualization of girls. *Monitor on Psychology, 38(4),* 32-3 3. The research upon which this proclamation is based can be found on www.apa.org/releases/design.html

[11] In the mid-1980s managed care, objecting to the prolonged nature of psychoanalysis, stopped reimbursing for such therapy and substituted brief therapies. In 1986 none other than Hans Eysenck prophetically published his book, *The decline and fall of the Freudian empire,* Harmondsworth, England: Penguin. See also F.J. Sulloway (1991), *Reassessing Freud's case histories: The social construction of psychoanalysis. Isis, 82,* 245-275.

[12] American Psychological Association. (2007, March 1). [Press Release] APA adopts policy statement opposing the teaching of intelligent design as scientific theory. Retrieved from www.apa.org/releaszes/design.html. See also Rhea K. Farberman (2007), APA Council adopts reports on military mental health, sexualization of girls. *Monitor on Psychology, 38(4),* 32.

[13] For information concerning Wolfram's highly successful software that he developed in his empirical studies of cellular automata, see N.A. Cummings (2002), Medical cost offset as a roadmap to behavioral entrepreneurship: Lessons from the Hawaii Project. In N.A. Cummings, W.T. O'Donohue & K.E. Ferguson (2002), *The impact of medical cost offset on practice and research: Making it work for you.* Foundation for Behavioral Health: Healthcare Utilization and Cost Series, vol. 5, pp. 27-45. Reno, NV: Context Press.

[14] Einstein to Herbert S. Goldstein, Apr. 25, 1929, AEA 33-272; "Einstein believes in Spinoza's God," *New York Times,* Apr. 25, 1929; Holton, G. (2002, Fall). "Einstein's third paradise." *Daedalus.* 26-34. Note that Goldstein was the rabbi of the Institutional Synagogue in Harlem and the longtime president of the Union of Orthodox Jewish Congregations of America.

References

Bartoli, E. (2007). Religious and spiritual issues in psychotherapy practice: Training the trainer. *Psychotherapy: Theory, Research, Practice, Training, 44(1),* 34-85.

Boring, E. G. (1950). *A history of experimental psychology* (2nd ed.). New York: Appleton-Century-Crofts.

Coon, D. B. (1992). Testing the limits of sense and science: American experimental psychologists combat spiritualism. *American Psychologist, 47(2),* 143-151.

Frank, P. (1947). *Einstein, his life and times* (G. Rosen, Trans.). New York: Da Capo Press. (Reprinted 2002.)

Haidt, J. (2007). *The happiness hypothesis.* Richmond: University of Virginia Press.

Hall, G. S. (1911). *Adolescence, its psychology and its relations to physiology, anthropology, sociology, sex, crime, religion and education* (Vol. 2). New York: D. Appleton.

Hornstein, G. A. (1992). The return of the repressed: Psychology's problematic relations with psychoanalysis, 1909-1960. *American Psychologist, 47(2),* 254-263.

Isaacson, W. (2007). *Einstein, his life and universe.* New York: Simon and Schuster.

Jastrow, J. (1932). *The house that Freud built.* New York: Chilton.

Leahy, T. H. (1992). *A history of psychology* (3rd ed.). Englewood Cliffs, NJ: Prentice Hall.

Mangelsdorf, M.L. (2000, November 27). The Inc. 500. *Inc Magazine*, 57-69.

Routh, D. K. (1994). *Clinical psychology since 1917: Science, practice and organization.* New York: Plenum.

Smith, L. D. (1992). On prediction and control: B.F. Skinner and the technological ideal of science. *American Psychologist, 47*, 216-223.

Sokal, M. S. (1992). Origins and early years of the American Psychological Association, 1890-1906. *American Psychologist, 47 (2),* 111-122.

Wade, N. (2007, September 18). Is "do unto others" written into our genes? *New York Times.*

Wright, R.H., & Cummings, N.A. (Eds.). (2005). *Destructive trends in mental health: The well-intentioned path to harm.* New York: Routledge (Taylor and Francis Group)

Psychology's WAR on Religion

The Key Battles

Chapter 3

Intolerance in Psychology: The Problem of Religious Gays

Michael Lavin, Ph.D.

Why do psychologists, at least in the chief professional organization of psychologists in the United States, the American Psychological Association (APA), have hostility towards religion? And why is the hostility narrowly focused on traditional, conservative religions. If the venerable anthropologist from Mars came to study the ways of psychologists, I doubt he would discover universal disdain for religion among psychologists. If anything, religions that favor the ordination of women, gay marriage and adoption, greater equality in the distribution of wealth, leniency to people in the United States illegally, as well as opposition to the war in Iraq are beloved by professional psychology. For the most part, psychology is a profession of people enamored of lefty politics. The APA's pompous political posturing on matters like passing self-satisfied resolutions (O'Donohue & Dyslin, 1996) alleging it is always unethical for an APA member to assist in torture—presumably no matter how many lives might be saved by torture in extraordinary circumstances—are typical of what sane members already endure. After all, in the case of torture, it is already illegal for even non-APA members to assist in torturing people, but the APA wishes to make sure potentially wicked members are not without guidance if this matter comes up in their classroom or practice.

Battles over how people have sex are one more instance of a general pattern in APA behavior. Organized, APA psychology simply has a hard time letting conservative or traditional members sort out for themselves matters that excite the political left. On some topics, the left insists on right think. Sex is among them.

Psychologists and the clergy both have something to say about sex. Psychologists, as one might guess, have fewer reservations about varieties of sexual expression than do traditional clergy. So, while the APA has an official group for gay, lesbian, bisexual, and transgendered psychologists, the Catholic Church, to take but one example, has yet to establish a Holy Order for anybody but the chaste. If anything, the position of the Church and other traditional religions places it on a collision course with positions promulgated by the APA (1998).

Religious Teachings: The Facts

The Catechism of the Catholic Church (U.S. Catholic Church, 2003) makes these observations about homosexuality:

> **2357:** Homosexuality refers to relations between men or between women who experience an exclusive or predominant sexual attraction toward persons of the same sex. It has taken a great variety of forms through the centuries and in different cultures. Its psychological genesis remains largely unexplained. Basing itself on Sacred Scripture, which presents homosexual acts as acts of grave depravity, tradition has always declared

that "homosexual acts are intrinsically disordered." They are contrary to the natural law. They close the sexual act to the gift of life. They do not proceed from a genuine affective and sexual complementarity. Under no circumstances can they be approved.

2358: The number of men and women who have deep-seated homosexual tendencies is not negligible. This inclination, which is objectively disordered, constitutes for most of them a trial. They must be accepted with respect, compassion, and sensitivity. Every sign of unjust discrimination in their regard should be avoided. These persons are called to fulfill God's will in their lives and, if they are Christians, to unite to the sacrifice of the Lord's Cross the difficulties they may encounter from their condition.

2359: Homosexual persons are called to chastity. By the virtues of self-mastery that teach them inner freedom, at times by the support of disinterested friendship, by prayer and sacramental grace, they can and should gradually and resolutely approach Christian perfection.

Catholics who accept the Church's teaching believe that (a) homosexual acts are proscribed, (b) homosexuality is a trial for the homosexual person, and (c) unjust discrimination against homosexual persons is proscribed, (d) homosexuals are to be treated with respect, compassion and sensitivity, and (e) homosexuals are to live in chastity and may succeed in being chaste with effort that involves a variety of means. Further the Church's Catechism lacks any manifestly false empirical assumptions. To be sure, there are linguistic differences. What psychologists might call an "orientation" is characterized in the Catechism as a person's predominant or exclusive attraction to person (notice the plain English), in the gay person's case, of the same sex. The Church grants that homosexuality is not a statistically rare condition. Although the Catechism fails to spell out what just discrimination against homosexuals might be, the Church's practices imply that just discrimination would include, for example, a refusal of a priest to provide the sacrament of marriage to a homosexual couple. However, although the sacrament of marriage is unavailable to homosexual couples, the sacrament of ordination is available to gay persons. What's more, nothing in the Catechism requires homosexuals to cease being homosexuals. Instead, like all unmarried Catholics, they are told to be chaste. Sex is reserved for the married. Nothing in the Catechism forbids homosexuals from seeking to become heterosexuals, as improbable a project as available science shows that to be, or from accepting their orientation (see Jones & Yarhouse, 2007).

Protestant positions on homosexuality range from tolerant to intolerant. Of the large Protestant denominations, the Southern Baptist Convention has taken a hard line on homosexuality. The Convention and its Ethics and Religious Liberty Commission have endorsed the view that Biblical passages proscribing homosexuality are valid. The Commission website (erlc.com/article/homosexuality-your-questions-answered) is forthright and detailed in setting forth what it takes to be the truth about homosexuality (Fellows of Research Institute, 2005). The Commission did go beyond the scientific consensus when it blamed homosexuality on unhealthy relationships between their parents and homosexual children. In addition the Commission contends, in defiance of scientific consensus, that people can change their sexual orientation, but only because, according to the Commission, there is no such thing as a homosexual orientation, but rather there is simply homosexual behavior. The Commission also accepts the idea that homosexuality and heterosexuality are not dichotomous variables, but in fact homosexuality and heterosexuality represent a continuum of behavior from exclusive homosexuality and heterosexuality to varying degrees of bisexuality. Further, the Commission embraces the theological claim, though it claims it is scientific, despite long-standing scientific rejection of this view (American Academy of Pediatrics, 1983), that there is no such thing as what is ordinarily thought of as an orientation. Instead, homosexuality is a behavior.

> [A] homosexual person simply does not exist. Homosexuality

> should be considered as an adjective—a behavior—and not as a noun or label defining a person. Dr. Joseph Nicolosi, one of the foremost experts on the causes of homosexuality as a sexual disorder and founder of NARTH, National Association of Research and Therapy of Homosexuality, states, "There is no such thing as a homosexual person. We are all heterosexuals. Homosexuality is a description of a condition. It is not a description of the intrinsic nature of the person" (NARTH's Statement of Policy. Given his statement, then, men and women who consider themselves homosexual are really intrinsically heterosexual but they have a sexual identity problem and, as a result, might engage in homosexual behavior. (Fellows of the Research Institute, 2005)

Like the Catholic Church, the Commission recognizes chastity as an avenue for a homosexual person leading a moral life. Finally, the Commission endorses (apparently) a broader spectrum of permissible discrimination against homosexuals than does the Catholic Church. So a homosexual person, according to the Commission, ought to be discriminated against to protect the family and other important social institutions. However, a caveat is in order. The Commission denies it is favoring discrimination. Instead, it argues it is opposed to favoring homosexuality or what it views as a gay agenda to reform society in ways the Commission and Convention believe are at odds with biblical demands.

On the whole the Commission is less cautious than the Catechism. The contention that a homosexual can become a heterosexual is at best scientifically controversial, as is the posited etiology for the development of a preference for same-sex sex. However, it is worth keeping in mind that Spitzer, who championed removing homosexuality during the controversy over its inclusion in the American Psychiatric Association's diagnostic manual (Bayer, 1981), now believes, based on a study he conducted (Spitzer, 2003), that it is possible for some gay persons to become straighter, if they choose to enter treatment.

Even though it may break the hearts of some APA activists, Conservative and Orthodox Jews and even conservative Moslems have viewed having same-sex sex, or indeed any sex outside of marriage as morally proscribed. The traditions of Abraham die hard, even if it is unappealing for APA radicals to attack them with the gusto that they allow themselves to go after mere Christians. Anti-Semite and xenophobe loom as ugly epithets in the academic Temples of Feel-Good APA Activism while being anti-Christian, or at least anti-Evangelical has a cachet.

A Theoretical Clarification

Confusion can arise over what words mean. Again consider orientation. The idea that people have a sexual orientation, even if it has a purchase on features of human sexual consciousness through the ages, is modern. John Money (1986) is probably justly credited with introducing the idea. One feature of orientation in its modern usage is that one could have a particular orientation without ever having engaged in the sex acts characteristic of that orientation. A man can hold his orientation in his secret heart. Nobody else need know until he declares it.

Likewise, behavior is an unreliable guide to orientation. A man may have sex with other men and deny that his orientation is homosexual. Likewise a man might have fantasies of same-sex sex without ever having had same-sex sex or feeling that his orientation is not heterosexual. An additional wrinkle, and one that Money was much taken with, has to do with the question of anatomical sex. There are phenomena of nature, such as being a hermaphrodite, that confound tidy biological categorizations of sex based on egg size as the field biologist have it, or based on the look of genitals as most ordinary people judge it. Intersex phenomena, as exemplified in the contemporary social construct of a transgendered person, are an example.

What matters ethically and politically is that psychologists, at least in their chief professional organization, the APA, have joined the political battle for extending to heterosexuals to homosexuals, bisexual, and transgendered persons as well, and this joining of the battle has led the APA (Committee on Lesbian, Gay, and Bisexual Concerns Joint Task Force, 2000) to denounce the religious sensibilities of at least some of its members.

Davison's Absolutist Argument

Organized psychology's embrace of a left political agenda for gay, bisexual and transgendered persons is a context for comprehending the profession's hostility, or at least contemptuous indifference, to traditional religious beliefs, and surely to the right's political agenda. Prominent psychologists such as Gerald Davison (1991, 2005) have gone so far as to argue that it is wrong for any psychologist to assist a gay person in becoming heterosexual, contending that a request for "conversion" therapy from a gay person cannot, in the current social climate, be voluntary. His positions are well summed up in Waldheter (2006).

Davison advanced several arguments to support his belief that it is wrong for psychologists to attempt to convert a gay person into a heterosexual person. However, the preceding survey of the Catholic Catechism and a position of the Southern Baptists demonstrates that religious persons could wish to have assistance in changing their orientation or, more modestly, their sexual fantasies and behavior. In particular, a person who is gay might wish to change his orientation or behavior. A gay person might also wish to stop having fantasies of same-sex sex or may wish to stop engaging in same-sex sex. If a religious gay person makes such requests, how should a psychologist proceed?

Gerald Davison is unequivocal in maintaining that assisting a person to achieve these changes is unethical for a psychologist. The first premise of his argument is that psychologists have no duty to do whatever their clients ask them to do. Davison has no difficulty in establishing the first premise of his argument. Although clients seeking a psychologist's assistance normally are encouraged to set their goals, a psychologist need not acquiesce to his patients' goals like a mindless robot.

At least two broad grounds exist for a psychologist refusing to ally with a client's goal. There are technical reasons and moral reasons.

Technical reasons have many forms. A client may wish me to assist him with a problem outside my area of expertise. A psychologist might, for example, treat only adults. Sometimes, the psychologist knows the patient is asking for something impossible, as would be the case of a desperate person who consulted me to help cure their end-stage cancer. Or, less dramatically, a psychologist might decline to help the person because the goal is too expensive.

Moral reasons are omnipresent. A psychologist might decline to assist a person whose goal is reprehensible. No psychologist is going to agree to help a pedophile to enhance his enjoyment of sex with babies. Although a psychologist may not share all his client's values, he does not leave his own values at the consulting room door like an umbrella. He may refuse to do things while working as a psychologist that he believes to be wrong. A patient may need my "help" to get disability income, but my being in his employ does not entitle him to lying representations from me, no matter how much he or I want the money.

With that understood, Davison has his first premise. It is straightforward that a psychologist has no duty to assist a person in changing his sexual orientation, fantasies, or behavior. On the technical side, most psychologists would likely believe they lack the necessary expertise. On the moral side they may, as I do, view the patient's goal as misguided. So far, the relevant conclusion is that a psychologist may decline to assist a gay person in making himself "straighter." But Davison argues for a far stronger conclusion. He contends it is wrong for *any* psychologist, in circumstances where hostility toward gay people is rampant, to assist a gay patient in making himself straighter.

How does Davison reach the absolutist conclusion that a psychologist may never assist a gay patient in becoming straight? If I have understood Davison, he believes that numerous social pressures have demonized a morally neutral preference—sex with a person of one's own sex—in a way that makes it impossible for a person to make a voluntary request to change his preference for same-sex sex. Instead, patients making this request are in the grip of vicious social forces that have fostered hatred of their own sexual orientation or behavior.

All psychologists, according to Davison, have an obligation to refuse to ally with a patient's embrace social prejudices against his own sexual orientation and behavior. These prejudices make it impossible for a gay patient to make a fully voluntary request, or make it impossible for a psychologist to spot voluntary requests for aid in changing his sexual behavior, fantasies, or orientation. For Davison, an ethical psychologist's duty is to dissolve the patient's prejudice against his own orientation. Attempts of a psychologist to side with a patient in favor of being "straighter" are objectionable and morally indefensible assaults on the patient's sexual identity taking place without the patient's genuine consent.

In clinical language, the appropriate target of a psychologist's efforts when working with patients of this kind is their *homonegativity*. It is unfortunate that Davison skips explaining his criteria for deciding which social pressures make consent impossible, especially since the social pressures against being a pedophile or morbidly obese are perhaps even greater than the opprobrium attached to being gay. Does Davison, in these cases, believe he is treating patients with consent or is he merely siding with prevailing social winds that no longer have much use for men who keep catamites or are as fat as walruses? I take it as a given that he is not trying to make them tolerant of their predilections.

A Reply for the Religious

To accept this argument, psychologists must accept a premise at variance with the beliefs of many traditional religious people. In particular, devout Catholics, as well as many other persons with conservative religious beliefs such as Orthodox Jews and Muslims, deny the impossibility of patients making a fully voluntary request to align their sexuality with their religious beliefs. At a minimum, persons with these beliefs have fully comprehensible reasons for seeking assistance in helping them to stop engaging in same-sex sex. Likewise, psychologists sharing these beliefs also have reason to assist patients in doing so. People with these beliefs are free to disagree that a sincerely religious person cannot give informed consent to therapy targeting his sexual orientation, fantasies, or behavior. Davison's crucial premise, the impossibility of gay people giving informed consent to change their gayness, hinges on a rejection of religious beliefs held by many of the people seeking or providing this mode of treatment.

Undoubtedly many beliefs of the patients and psychologists trying to assist a person to be less gay are contrary to the official position of major mental health organizations on homosexuality—namely, that it is a normal developmental outcome for a minority of persons, rather like left-handedness. But the key premise in Davison's argument rests on the impossibility of an authentic choice, and it seems Davison has come close to asserting, on the sly, that no devout Catholic or Baptist can have authentic preferences regarding a homosexual preference. If one takes Davison seriously, religious psychologists should look to him or the APA, rather than their own Catechism or Convention's teachings, to determine how they may respond to gay patients making treatment requests.

My use of the term "treatment requests" is deliberate and is intended to highlight how common clinical distinctions made by psychologists can obscure key issues in arguments against what is commonly made out to be an effort to change a patient's orientation. A religious psychologist might, on scientific grounds, agree that orientation may be impossible to change, or even doubt that the construct of an orientation makes sense, but still believe it possible to get a person willing to make the effort to stop engaging in same-sex sex, to engage in heterosexual behavior, or to reduce the amount of homosexual fantasy or behavior in his life (Spitzer, 2003, Jones and Yarhouse, 2007, Yarhouse, this volume). Moreover, if a psychologist accepts that gay and straight orientation lies along a continuum, a person's point on that continuum may well have shifts overtime, even if nobody ever moves from one end of the continuum to the other.

The Status of Religious Beliefs

Might one wish to argue that religious beliefs should be subordinated to psychological science, even if they seem to be sincerely held? For starters, the question is suspect. Psychological science helps us to discover what the case is. It does not fall within the scope of psychological science to tell anybody what ought to be the case, even if the APA itself proclaims some expertise in this area.

Its ethics code may bind APA members, but even the code's enthusiasts do not claim it is one of the findings of psychological science.

Of course some religious beliefs can collide with facts, as when Christians asserted that the sun and other planets orbit the earth. As already pointed out, the Catechism at least seems insulated from empirical refutation. Southern Baptist claims regarding the etiology of homosexuality are on perilous ground. The refusal to recognize orientation puts them at risk of making it difficult to join debates on the topic. The Southern Baptist position that everybody is heterosexual, no matter their behavior, seems a theological thesis, though the rejection of orientation as a construct in favor of focusing on sexual behavior suggests a line of familiar behaviorist defenses, of the rejection of inner states.

Davison's argument fails, by begging questions, to explain why religious psychologists should respond as if they were secular psychologists. As Waldheter has explained, other psychologists (Throckmorton, 1998) have pointed out, against the Davison's line of argument, that the APA ethics code (2002) requires that religious diversity, a cherished commitment of the left, be respected.

The most straightforward reading of the respect requirement would be to allow religious psychologists the right to conscientiously refuse to adopt positions at odds with their faith. If so, the door to psychologists helping willing patients to change their orientation, same-sex sex fantasies, or homosexual behavior reopens. This level of tolerance has not appealed to all. One means of blocking it is to contend that respect for religious diversity does not mean anything as extravagantly straightforward as just proposed. Instead, Haldeman (2002) has argued for holding that religious beliefs are one belief among many. Waldheter (2006) glosses Haldeman as holding that "religion should not be accorded higher importance than sexual orientation, or vice versa" (p. 50). He goes on to quote Haldeman (2004) approvingly, as holding the ideal:

> Treatment philosophy is antidogmatic; rather than encourage either 'coming out,' repressing sexuality in the service of religious belief, or advocating for any particular outcome at all, a

treatment framework is offered that enables the client to make decisions for himself. (p. 712)

These views are models of bullying secularism. No account is even attempted to explain how the idea that religion is of no higher importance than sexual orientation squares with traditional beliefs. Nor is it explained how a devout Christian is to understand the secularist assertion that ideas contrary to the teachings of his own church are decisions "to make for himself." Let anybody with knowledge of Catholicism explain, for example, the sense in which what Haldeman is saying is so. The idea that a devout person seeking somebody to assist him to honor his faith commitments is seeking an "antidogmatic" is a shameless substitution of a secular goal for therapy for a religiously informed one.

A Conjecture About the Source of Psychology's Intolerance

What has gone wrong? Liberal secularism has failed to understand its own underpinnings. Perhaps psychology has become too sophisticated. As the profession has become more sophisticated, proportionally fewer devout people have studied it to the doctoral level. The profession has grown liberal and secular. While its tolerance for groups it perceives as oppressed has grown, the liberal animus towards more conservative elements of society, especially if they are powerful, has established itself. Politically, psychology has taken sides. (O'Donohue & Dyslin, 1996) So, when dealing with persons who are not liberal, who do not come from a tradition that espouses tolerance for all points of view, many psychologists have wished either to convert them or to treat them as if they might wish to be treated if—contrary to fact—they were old-fashioned liberals with an unshakeable commitment to personal choice and individual liberty. Haldeman's treatment recommendations, for example, make perfectly good sense, provided a patient is viewed as a pluralistic democracy that is trying to give all people or preferences their due. In a secular democracy, we do aspire to the type of balance Haldeman strives to achieve with his patient. Of course few actual patients are plausible microcosms of pluralistic democracies.

The Way Things Ought To Be

It is worth underlining the obvious import of my argument. No secular psychologists, if they believe as Davison or I believe, is being asked to practice in a manner inconsistent with their own ethical convictions. I am unapologetic in my belief, which I also believe are supported by the best available evidence, that preference for same-sex sex, as well as a gay orientation and fantasy life, is a developmentally normal outcome for a minority of children. However, if my patient is unwilling to consider the desirability of rethinking his religiously driven desire to behave as if he were a heterosexual, I think it clear that I am not the appropriate psychologist for him. And I am prepared to tell him so. It disrespects the patient to treat him with the goal of using my clinical skills to get him thinking as I think.

What, though, of a psychologist whose religion condemns same-sex sex? As attentive readers will notice, I believe the APA should limit itself to stating what the best psychological science has shown. It is to move well beyond the scope of science when the APA or groups of psychologists attempt to draw "oughts" from the facts about homosexuality.

Not all readers will know about the is/ought gap. Hume first insisted upon the gap. In an oft quoted passage from Hume's *Treatise* (1739/1974), Hume wrote:

> In every system of morality I have always remark'd, that the author proceeds for some time in the ordinary way of reasoning, and establishes the being of a God, or makes observations concerning human affairs; when of a sudden I am surpriz'd to find, that instead of the usual copulations of propositions, *is,* and *is not,* I meet with no proposition that is not connected with an *ought,* or an *ought not.* The change is imperceptible; but is, however, of the last consequence. For as this *ought,* or *ought not,* expresses some new relation or affirmation, 'tis necessary that it shou'd be observ'd and explain'd; and at the same time that a reason should be given, for what seems altogether inconceivable, how this new relation can be a deduc-

tion from others, which are entirely different from it (Book III, Part 1, Section 1). (Italics in the original)

Despite the old-fashioned English, the point is easy to grasp. Statements of fact do not tell us what ought to be, unless supplemented by value judgments. So, from the factual premises, the argument would be as follows: (a) Fritz and Mort enjoy having same-sex together. (b) Fritz and Mort are both able to give legal consent. (c) There is no injury to anybody else when they have same-sex sex. However, the moral conclusion—Fritz and Mort ought to be allowed to have same-sex sex—does not follow. To reach that conclusion, you would need a value premise (VP). For example, (VP 1) People ought be allowed to engage in consensual activities that do not harm others will do the trick. Likewise, it does not follow from the fact that sometimes brutes, like rats, sometimes endure pain when psychologists use them in experiments that psychologists ought not to use them in experiments. Nor does it follow from the fact that seals suffer when Inuit hunters, polar bears, or sharks kill them that Inuit, polar bears, and sharks ought to knock it off or ought to be stopped, perhaps by PETA cops, from killing seals. To get a conclusion that exciting, a value premise is clearly needed.

The distinction does not say that facts are irrelevant to moral thinking or to helping identify plausible moral principles. The fact that people dislike suffering might be a reason to embrace principles that limit it; however, Hume's passage points out that facts don't entail moral principles or conclusions.

As controversial as the is/ought gap may be, I am contending that genuine tolerance requires that APA psychologists do not seek to impose controversial ethical positions on its members. And I suggest that the present case is one in which the membership organization—with grand moral pretenses—has an opportunity to temper its paternalistic impulsivity. After all, patients decide from whom to seek assistance. They also decide from whom to continue to receive assistance. Although the particulars of cases matter, it is difficult to see the grounds for denying, given the actual position of the Catholic Church and the Southern Baptist Convention in the United States, that some religious persons have compelling, readily comprehensible spiritual reasons for seeking to bring their sexuality into better harmony with their religious convictions. The treating psychologist, if religious, may believe they are treating a "disorder," but it is also possible to reframe their project. They are engaged in assisting a person, perhaps against very long odds, in living closer to his own values. Nor should one be especially quick to condemn the religious psychologist as unscientific for persisting in a belief that homosexuality can be viewed as a disorder. Let it be recalled that homosexuality was eliminated as a psychiatric diagnosis because of political pressures. The politics of diagnosis is discussed by Bayer (1981), Lavin (1986), and O'Donohue & Casselles (2005). Although I share the regnant view in mental health that homosexuality is not a mental disorder, humility is in order. Disagreements about what is and is not a mental disorder are common, and there are theoreticians, Szasz (1961) for example, to name but one, who have challenged the coherence of the idea of mental illness. I would confess that I tend to view the DSM more as a listing of reimbursable constellations of symptoms than the as diagnostic equivalent of the periodic table of elements. Am I alone?

One risk of religion is that the religious project, like any serious enterprise, may fail. So, a religious homosexual may inflict avoidable damage to himself in pursuit of his spiritual quest to become less gay. Even though I view the quest as folly and am unwilling to assist in it, I cannot imagine by what right, by what spiritual hubris of my own, I could imagine myself entitled to block competent adults—a religious therapeutic dyad for example—from pursuing it. I urge other skeptical psychologists to join me in respecting the religious beliefs remote from our own beliefs, and show enough respect to our religious colleagues and patients to treat them as consenting adults. Perhaps it might even lead to a lessening of the grip of paternalistic thinking on organized mental health. If so, we all may one day learn to start treating even our patients as grown ups.

References

American Academy of Pediatrics. (1983). Policy statement: Homosexuality and adolescence. *Pediatrics, 92,* 631-634.
American Psychological Association. (1998). Appropriate therapeutic responses to sexual orientation in the proceedings of the American Psychological Association, Incorporated, for the legislative year 1997. *American Psychologist, 53,* 882-939.
American Psychological Association. (2002). Ethical principles of psychologists and code of conduct. *American Psychologist, 57,* 1060–1073.
Fellows of Research Institute. (2005, June 15). *Homosexuality: Your questions answered.* The Ethics and Religious Liberty Commission of the Southern Baptist Convention. Retrieved February, 03, 2008 from erlc.com/article/homosexuality-your-questions-answered.
Bayer, R. (1981). *Homosexuality and American psychiatry: The politics of diagnosis.* New York: Basic.
Committee on Lesbian, Gay, and Bisexual Concerns Joint Task Force. (2000). Guidelines for psychotherapy with lesbian, gay, and bisexual clients. *American Psychologist, 55,* 1440-1451.
Davison, G. (1991). Constructionism and morality in therapy for homosexuality. In J. Gonsiorek & J. Weinrich (Eds.). *Homosexuality: Research implications for public policy* (pp. 137-148). Newbury Park, CA: Sage.
Davison, G. (2005). Issues and nonissues in the gay-affirmative treatment of patients who are gay, lesbian, or bisexual. *Clinical Psychology: Science and Practice, 12,* 25-28.
Haldeman, D.C. (2002). Gay rights, patient rights: The implications of sexual orientation conversion therapy. *Professional Psychology: Research and Practice, 33,* 260-264.
Haldeman, D.C. (2004). When sexual and religious orientation collide: Considerations in working with conflicted same-sex attracted male clients. *The Counseling Psychologist, 32,* 691-715.
Hume, D. (1974). *Treatise of human nature.* P.H. Nidditch (Ed.). Oxford: Clarendon Press. (Original printed in 1739.)
Jones, S. L., & Yarhouse, M.A. (2007). *Ex-gays? A longitudinal study of religiously mediated change in sexual orientation.* Downers Grove, IL: Inter Varsity Press Academic.
Lavin, M. (1986). Review of homosexuality and American psychiatry: The politics of diagnosis. *Philosophy of the Social Sciences, 16*, 252-254.
Money, J. (1986). *Lovemaps: Clinical concepts of sexual/erotic health and pathology, paraphilia, and gender transposition in childhood, adolescence, and maturity.* New York: Irvington.
O'Donohue, W., & Dyslin, C. (1996). Abortion, boxing and Zionism: Politics and the American Psychological Association. *New Ideas in Psychology, 14(1)*, 1-10.

O'Donohue, W.T., & Caselles, C.E. (2005). Homophobia: Conceptual, definitional, and value issues. In R.H. Wright & N.A. Cummings (Eds.), *Destructive trends in mental health: the well-intentioned path to harm.* New York: Routledge.

Spitzer, R.L. (2003). Can some gay men and lesbians change their sexual orientation? 200 participants reporting a change from homosexual to heterosexual orientation. *Archives of Sexual Behavior, 32,* 403-417.

Szasz, T. (1961). *The myth of mental illness.* New York: Harper.

Throckmorton, W. (1998). Efforts to modify sexual orientation: A review of outcome literature and ethical issues. *Journal of Mental Health Counseling, 20,* 283-305.

U.S. Catholic Church. (2003). *Catechism of the Catholic Church: Second Edition.* New York: Doubleday Religion.

Waldheter, E. J. (2006, Spring). Ethical issues in the practice of sexual orientation conversion therapy. *The Register Report, 32,* 46-54.

Chapter 4

The Battle Regarding Sexuality

Mark A. Yarhouse, Psy.D.

Introduction

Is there really a war on religion in the area of sexuality? I tend to shy away from these kinds of metaphors, but I do think that some people in the general population, as well as some students and professionals in the mental health field, may feel like there is a war against some expressions of religion by some persons in the mental health establishment. Certainly if you are a member of the Metropolitan Community Church (MCC), a gay affirming church, you would be unlikely to describe a war against sexuality by the mental health establishment. Such individuals may feel marginalized within the broader culture, and such feelings may be intensified in certain regions of the country. But they would unlikely feel embattled within the mental health field. If anything, numerous policies and position papers have been adopted or published in support of a worldview endorsed by the MCC and other gay-affirmative religious organizations. But if you are a member of a traditional faith community—if you are a conservative Catholic, a conservative or Orthodox Jew, a conservative Muslim or an evangelical or otherwise conservative Protestant Christian, you might feel embattled in the area of sexuality.

- If you are involved in reproductive health education and believe that there may be value in promoting self-control and abstinence-focused education, you might feel embattled.

- If you provide services to women who have undergone abortions and are concerned about the potential after-effects on the emotional and psychological well-being of both women and men, you might feel embattled.

- If you work with conservative religious clients who are conflicted about their experiences of same-sex attraction and are looking for an alternative to exclusively gay affirmative therapy, you might feel embattled.

- If you believe that "child sexual abuse" is the proper designation for sex between an adult and a child (rather than referring to is as "adult-child sex"), you might feel embattled.

- If you are a conservative Catholic undergraduate psychology major who hears deriding comments about abstinence, celibacy, virginity pledges, as well as social agendas with positive portrayals of cohabitation and "safer sex" programming, you might feel embattled.

- If you are a devout Christian or Mormon in graduate training in psychology who hears derogatory comments about evangelical and fundamentalist religions, you might feel embattled.

- If you are a conservative Christian student who has applied to numerous programs for graduate study in psychology but have been denied acceptance or have received added scrutiny for your religious background, you might have a sense for why some people feel embattled.

What contributes to these experiences? How do some people end up feeling embattled in the area of sexuality? In the space that follows we will consider the following: (1) negative attitudinal set; (2) ignoring or overlooking religious perspectives; (3) instances when ideology trumps science; (4) topics closed to rational discussion; and (5) intolerant training climates in matters related to religion and sexuality.

Feeling Embattled in the Study of Sexuality

Negative Attitudinal Set[1]

Is religion an important variable in the study of human sexuality and sexual behavior? Does religion merely constrain sexual behavior and sexual freedom, leading to repression and negative emotions, such as anger and resentment, or is it a key variable in the meaning structures around sexuality for some persons?

There is an increasing awareness within the field of psychology of the importance of religion in promoting psychological well-being. This research is coming from several fronts, but has taken on a kind of prominence in the field of positive psychology. Research suggests, for example, that Judeo-Christian religious practices are linked to health-related physiological processes, such as immune function and neuroendocrine processes (Seeman, Dubin, & Seeman, 2003). Indeed, those who are religiously-involved are at lower risk of cardiovascular disease (Powell, Shahabi, & Thoresen, 2003) and mortality (McCullough, Hoyt, Larson, Koenig & Thoresen, 2000).

The scientific study of sexuality has been perhaps a little slower to recognize religion as an important primary variable in promoting well-being. Religion is often portrayed as a phenomenon that has shaped human understandings of sexuality, but in negative ways. This is evidenced in mainstream human sexuality textbooks in which mention of religion is limited to historical footnotes of ways in which religion has shaped various cultures' views of sexuality and sexual behavior, often in "restrictive" or "judgmental" ways. For example, Crooks and Baur (2002) discuss historical Judaic and Christian traditions and how sex became associated with sin following early attempts to set Christianity apart from various religious practices associated with a number of "exotic cults" (p. 9). Masters, Johnson, and Kolodny (1992) offer a similar historical overview, mentioning Christianity only in derogatory ways, underscoring negative attitudes, rigidity, and hypocrisy. There are kernels of truth in these historical analyses; organized religion is certainly not without fault. However, when religion is brought up in only a few instances, and when these are largely derogatory, there is a risk of implicit bias against religion in the scientific study of sexuality.

Many psychologists may be unaware of some interesting findings on some noted effects of religion on sexuality, effects that can be argued to be (but are not indisputably) positive. For the purposes of this chapter we will limit our discussion to examples from a Judeo-Christian religious perspective. Both Judaism and Christianity set limits on sexual behavior, particularly nonmarital sexual behavior. These limits appear to protect individuals from specific negative consequences, such as unwanted pregnancy and sexually transmitted diseases. Research suggests that religiously-affiliated persons report lower rates of participation in premarital and extramarital sex, delayed sexual debut, and fewer lifetime sex partners (e.g., Beck, Cole & Hammond, 1991; Cochran & Beeghley, 1991; Rosenbaum & Kandel, 1990; see Waite & Gallagher, 2000, for a review). In this sense, religion might be viewed as prescribing a more cautious sexual ethic. The effects of religion on sexuality might be viewed as positive, though there are some who might disagree.

In terms of practical application, religion is sometimes raised as an issue when it is viewed as a constraint to normal sexual functioning. This comes up in sex therapy at times, when, for example, religious beliefs are said to be in conflict with more open approaches to sex (Wincze & Carey, 2001, p. 155). Similarly, in their limited discussion of religion, Masters et al. (1992) say that someone raised with religious views of sin and shame "may be handicapped in later sexual enjoyment" (p. 550). These kinds of comments in the sex therapy literature—that strict religious upbringing is an etiological variable in sexual distress—are based more on stereotypes and clinical sampling than on research and adds to the unfairly negative view of the impact of religion on sexuality. In this way it can be compared to the assumptions in the 1960s that all homosexuals were manifestly disturbed. This is why Evelyn Hooker's famous studies in the 1960s were so compelling; she was able to challenge the assumptions widely held at that time—assumption about manifest pathology among homosexuals were based in part on clinical samples. Sex therapists do something similar when they "see" religion as a negative variable because of clinical sampling. Again, it is not that religious perspectives have *never* constrained sexual enjoyment; however, when this is one of the few ways religion is addressed in human sexuality, it hardly seems to be a full and rich engagement of the topic of religion.

Interestingly, the majority of the U.S. population continues to embrace some form of religion. The population is primarily Protestant (58%), Catholic (Roman and Orthodox combined represent 26%), and Jewish (2%). Other religious traditions (e.g., Hindu, Muslim, and Buddhist) account for approximately 3% of the population. Only six percent of the general population claims no religious preference (Gallup Poll, 2000). About 45% of the U.S. population would describe themselves as "born-again" or evangelical.

What about psychologists? In one study, 72% of psychologists reported belief in God, yet 51% of psychologists reported that religion was not very important to them (compared to only 11% of the general population) (Shafranske, 2000). Most Americans believe in the "healing power of personal prayer" (Wulff, 1997, p. 175). About two-thirds of Americans indicate that religion can answer all or most of today's problems (Gallup, 2001), and three-fourths of Americans agreed with the statement, "I try hard to live by my religious beliefs" (Bergin, 1991, p. 396). These data suggest to some that there is a fairly significant disconnect between professionals in the mental health community and the public they serve.

What about in the area of human sexuality? Religion often does interact positively with sexuality and sexual behavior. It provides a foundational understanding of human sexuality by tying sexuality and its expression to transcendent meaning. It can also have practical applications, ranging from protective factors (by encouraging sex in the context of marriage, which reduces risk of sexually transmitted disease) to pleasure and enjoyment with a committed partner. Greeley (1991), in his review of two major studies sponsored by the Gallup Poll and *Psychology Today*, noted that couples who pray together have the highest rates of sexual satisfaction. Laumann, Gagnon, Michael and Michaels (1994) found that religious affiliation was actually associated with higher rates of orgasm among women.

A final consideration related to negative attributional set is that criticisms of religious perspectives on sexual behavior as "rigid" are themselves value-laden. They presume that a more liberal view is right and do not see the need to argue for it. Again, religion can and often does interact positively with sexuality and sexual behavior and, in many cases, there may be important reasons to follow a more cautious sexual ethic often supported by religious views. Unfortunately, there exists a negative attitudinal set within the sexuality literature in regards to religion that lacks nuance or balance, and the negative reactions fail to reflect the real state of affairs in the empirical literature.

Ignoring or Overlooking Religious Perspectives

There are many examples of psychology ignoring or overlooking religious perspectives. In the space that follows, let me address three areas: sex education, same-sex marriage and parenting, and appropriate clinical responses to sexual orientation.

Sex education. In the area of sex education, how have religious perspectives been ignored or overlooked? Consider the APA's policy titled *Resolution in Favor of Empirically Supported Sex Education and HIV Prevention Programs for Adolescents*. On the surface this certainly seems like a noble project. A scientific organization ought to be examining the research and identifying programs with empirical support. It is interesting, however, that the draft resolution was titled *Draft Resolution in Opposition to Abstinence-Only and Abstinence Until Marriage Programs to Prevent HIV/AIDS Among Youth.* The phrase "in opposition to" seemed "adversarial" according to the final adopted resolution. That is a fair assumption, if the attempt to establish policy was motivated by opposition to one type of educational program. It could leave some readers wondering if the final resolution title is merely window dressing on a conclusion reached well in advance of the work of the committee.

For the purposes of the present discussion, the policy fails to do justice to the religious perspectives themselves—to the religious beliefs, values and theological underpinnings that lie beneath the very preference for abstinence. Psychology as a profession cannot speak to the truth claims of various religions, but it is surprising to see so little engagement of religion in matters of sex education because of the predominantly religious cultural context in which contemporary psychology operates. Put differently, critics seem so consumed with decrying abstinence-focused curricula that they overlook the very people they are intending to serve, as well as the respect that is to be afforded those who adhere to religion as a meaningful orienting system for understanding the world (Grossman, 2006).

An additional concern is that the policy seems to foreclose on the possibility of ever developing sex education programs that value abstinence. It is as if the "jury is in" and there is no more discussion.

Although abstinence programs are completely contrary to the social agenda advanced by some in the mental health field (see Grossman, 2006), Thomas (2000) summarizes the rationale for abstinence-based programs. These include, most importantly, that they provide "the only absolute protection against teen pregnancy and sexually transmitted diseases" (p. 6), but they also offer a more consistent message and may provide some protection from the potential harm from "premature sexual relationships" (p. 6). Finally, peer pressure may lead some teens to engage in sexual activities and programs designed to recognize these pressures and provide skill acquisition required to resist pressure can be valuable.

Related to abstinence-based programs are virginity pledges, which have become increasingly popular in recent years. There are some interesting findings from some of the studies conducted thus far. Does psychology really want to be perceived by the public as against abstinence? The key question that psychology can ask today is: *In what ways are abstinence-focused programs working?* and *How might they be improved?* The main finding being proclaimed by critics of these programs is that if young people break their pledge, they are at greater risk of not using protection (Bearman & Bruckner, 2001). But what is often not stated is that those who make virginity pledges are over 30% less likely to be sexually active, and that those who abstain from sex are better off on emotional and behavioral measures than those who are sexually active. Also, a concern has been raised for the emotional well-being of those who make and subsequently break their virginity pledge. However, Bearman and Bruckner reported that those who broke their virginity pledge were no worse off emotionally than those who were sexually active but did not make a pledge.

Of course, virginity pledges and abstinence-based programs cannot be offered in isolation, and this is an area in which psychology as a behavioral science could provide much needed assistance. According to Thomas, abstinence-based programs that show promise have "a firm grounding in contemporary theories of health behavior" and the "reinforcement of clear and appropriate values to make abstinence the subjective social norm among adolescent peer groups" (p. 14). It is also promising to include material that addresses media and social influences on sexual behavior. It appears to also be helpful "to include parents in the program to increase their sense of involvement and their level of communication with their adolescents" (p. 14).

In his conclusion Thomas (2000) noted that "the message that abstinence is the only absolute protection against these dangers is gaining acceptance and has shown some positive effect upon adolescents' attitudes and sexual behavior" (p. 16).

Because conventional religious beliefs often support an abstinence message, greater sensitivity and respect for religious beliefs and values might build upon what appears to be helpful and what appears to be promising. And who is better equipped than those trained in the behavioral sciences to assist people in managing their behavior and their environment in such a way as to meet abstinence goals? Perhaps the more pressing question is whether those who press a social agenda will be willing to tolerate the beliefs and principles that are foundations to some people's preference for abstinence.

Finally, there is an underlying assumption that abstinence-focused programs are grounded in ideology while standard sex education is grounded in science. The reality is that all views are grounded in moral and metaphysical views (O'Donohue, 1989), and the scientific data is complex and puzzling.

Same-sex marriage and parenting. Another example can be seen in two resolutions approved by the APA's Council of Representatives in 2004. The two resolutions were the *Resolution on Sexual Orientation and Marriage*, which supported broadening the meaning of marriage to include same-sex couples and the *Resolution on Sexual Orientation, Parents, and Children*, which took an affirmative stance on child custody and adoption/foster care for same-sex couples.

The empirical evidence cited to support these policies suffers from several methodological flaws, including relatively small sample sizes. But of equal concern is the issue of moving the preliminary findings of their being little evidence of harm in same-sex marriage and parenting to the moral judgment that such relationships or family arrangements are a good that society ought to endorse. The behavioral sciences are not able to address this issue and many professionals—gay, lesbian and bisexual (GLB) scholars among them—have expressed concern over the redefining of marriage in response to a social agenda.

For example, while Young and Nathanson (2003; http://www.marriageinstitute.ca/pages/keep.htm) support same-sex relationships and the benefits they believe same-sex couples ought to derive from being a "common-law" couple, they challenge the idea of transforming the meaning of marriage to include same-sex couples: "the essential function of marriage has always been to provide the necessary cultural framework for straight couples and their children." They believe that "heterosexuality must indeed be deliberately fostered and nurtured by a distinctive, supportive culture." Their argument is that "society needs a specifically heterosexual contribution more than any homosexual counterpart. Therefore, the need to provide cultural support for heterosexuality is greater than for homosexuality" (http://www. marriageinstitute.ca/pages/keep.htm).

Young and Nathanson (2003; http://www.marriageinstitute.ca/pages/keep.htm) compare redefining marriage to a "massive human experiment," much like the experiment conducted through changing divorce laws in an attempt to be compassionate to those who wanted easier access to divorce, which "set in motion social forces that would not be evident for 40 years."

As an important aside, the APA division concerned with religious issues (Division 36: Psychology of Religion) had requested representation on the Working Group on Same-Sex Families and Relationships that drafted the resolutions. They were not given representation on the Working Group. The APA committee on Ethnic Minority Affairs asked for Division 36 approval prior to a formal vote on the resolutions. As Hathaway (2004/2005) reports, there was an attempt to add a "friendly amendment" that would have addressed the fact that the APA was "speaking only to the psychological issues pertaining to same-sex families and marriage" and that "the APA supports the right of religious groups to create, endorse and support family arrangements that are consistent with their own religious beliefs, within constitutionally and legally defined limits" (p. 13). The friendly amendment was rejected by the Working Group, which stated that they "deliberately avoided the religious aspects of the issues ... because the APA is a secular organization" (p. 13). However, as Hathaway correctly observes, "There is nothing in [APA] organizational mission that precludes APA attending to religious issues as long as it does so from a psychological perspective" (p. 13).

Instead, the results are two resolutions that fail to take seriously the religious beliefs and principles surrounding marriage and family. Buried in background documents are two statements that state that both religious and gay persons might be stakeholders in these discussions, and the APA is limiting itself to "stating positions on civil marriage and on parental rights and to the psychological issues pertaining to these public policy issues" (p. 14). But this is not the public or professional perception of these resolutions, and they were written without regard for religion as a primary diversity variable.

Clinical response to sexual orientation. Following the removal of homosexuality as a mental disorder from the DSM in the 1970s, there has been considerable focus on developing affirmative approaches to persons who identify as gay, lesbian, or bisexual. Such efforts led to aspirational guidelines approved by the APA Council of Representatives in 1997. The guidelines focused on not condoning discriminatory practices, removing stigma, disseminating accurate information, respecting the values of others, respecting self-determination of clients, and so on.

The APA was asked by Parents and Friends of Lesbians and Gays (PFLAG) and the National Gay and Lesbian Task Force to review and update these guidelines. The formation of this Task Force is the most recent example of ignoring religious interests.[2] Again, the general charge was to "revise and update the Association's 1997 resolution on Appropriate Therapeutic Responses to Sexual Orientation," but specific bullet points included having the task force address "affirmative therapeutic interventions for children," adolescents, and adults who "present a desire to change either their sexual orientation or their behavioral expression of their sexual orientation." The Call also addressed "The presence of adolescent inpatient facilities that offer coercive treatment designed to change sexual orientation or the behavioral expression of sexual orientation," as well as the use of "stereotyped gender-normative behavior to mitigate behaviors that are perceived to be indicators that a child will develop a homosexual orientation in adolescence and adulthood."

There are many concerns with this Call for Nominations, but the focus of this chapter is really on how little is offered by way of understanding religious beliefs and values that might bring a person to seek professional services, whether they are centered on sexual attractions, orientation, or "the behavioral expression of sexual orientation." This later point is particularly disturbing because it expands the discussion beyond sexual orientation to "behavioral expression," which is a radical departure even among the most vocal critics of sexual reorientation therapy. There is great consensus among scholars—including gay scholars—that behavioral expression is precisely the moral concern under question and that people are capable of controlling their behavior to live in ways that reflect a particular moral vision (e.g., Stein, 1999).

Interestingly, although many qualified conservative psychologists were nominated to serve on the task force, each was rejected. The director of the APA's Lesbian, Gay, and Bisexual Concerns Office, Clinton Anderson, defended the decision: "We cannot take into account what are fundamentally negative religious perceptions of homosexuality—they don't fit into our world view" (Crarey, 2007; http://findarticles.com/p/articles/mi_qn4176/is_20070711/ai_n19358074). A sociocultural and/or religiously conservative perspective is not welcome because it does not fit into the APA's worldview? And the APA purports to respect religion as an aspect of diversity? It appears as though the only "perceptions of homosexuality" that will be tolerated are those that uniformly endorse same-sex behavior as a moral good. This exclusion is justified despite clients who, for personal and/or religious reasons, may seek the assistance of mental health professionals in managing behavior expression. Religion is welcome as long as it behaves itself or fits into the preexisting grid.

When Ideology Trumps Science

There are many ways in which ideology trumps science in the field of psychology. The reader is encouraged to read *Destructive Trends in Mental Health* (Wright & Cummings, 2005) with particular attention to the chapters dealing with political correctness, the culture of victimhood, and sociopolitical diversity. In the area of human sexuality, ideology trumps science in health information on sexual activity, cohabitation, and abortion, to name but three examples.

Health information on sexual activity. There is a kind of "anything-goes" mentality or climate in some segments of sexual studies in psychology that has affected college campuses and health centers today (Grossman, 2006). Miriam Grossman, psychiatrist at the UCLA health clinic and author of *Unprotected*, cites numerous ways in which social agendas trump science in ways that place students at risk, particularly by emphasizing risk reduction rather than actual prevention. It was Grossman who drew attention to the "ask Alice" health education website at Columbia University, which mentions the following:

- Providing the counsel to "give it a try" when asked by a married man about a threesome (so long as they all consent and use protection)
- Referrals to the student bondage and domination sadomasochism campus discussion organization
- Instructions on how to clean a "cat o' nine tails," particularly if it has drawn blood, with instructions for leather and plastic/rubber versions
- Recommendations on the use of "sounds" or inserting steel rods into the man's urethra
- Tips for the proper use of anal beads

In her area of expertise—reproductive health—Grossman states:

> This discipline has been permeated by an ideology promoting permissiveness and experimentation; in order to preserve that ideology, the bar has been lowered. Instead of aiming for disease prevention, as is done in the fight against heart disease or obesity, the goal is risk reduction—a.k.a. "safer sex"—followed, when it fails to be safe enough, by damage control. Instead of the grim facts, women are fed oversimplified and whitewashed information. And when "safer sex" fails, the consequences—both physical and emotional—are minimized. (p. 16).

It is extremely difficult to get a hearing on a number of subjects in sexuality. As Grossman indicates, there is a general attitude of "the more sex the better" that has permeated mental health circles. This is an interesting lingering effect from the days when Freudian notions of repressed sexuality permeated the mental health field. But the more recent expression of psychology as a behavioral science would seem to lend itself to partnering with a number of innovative applications that would lend themselves to behavioral management.

It is not paranoia to suppose that some of the resistance to clear messages that promote abstinence is that abstinence is a principle valued within conservative expressions of religion. If religion is rejected by most psychologists personally and professionally, then it is not a leap to suggest that formed judgments and a more cautious sexual ethic tied to religion may be rejected as well.

Cohabitation. Cohabitation is another example that comes up in sex education and human sexuality courses, as well as clinical settings when working with couples. It remains popular among professionals, and is often mentioned or recommended by experts, to ensure sexual and relational compatibility before marriage (e.g., King, 1999; Masters et al., 1992). Cohabitation may in some ways reflect a preference grounded in a broader social agenda coming out of the sexual revolution and a subsequent preference to challenge existing social structures.

However, the empirical evidence suggests that those who cohabit report lower rates of relational satisfaction, higher rates of abuse, increased risk of extra-relationship sex, and increased likelihood of adultery and divorce after marriage, experiences often associated with various negative emotions (Bracher, Santow, Morgan, & Trussel, 1993; Brown & Booth, 1996; Bumpass & Sweet, 1989; DeMaris & Rao, 1992; Stanton, 1997; Waite & Gallagher, 2000). These findings suggest that the religiously grounded hesitations about this life pattern are not without pragmatic merit.

It may be that religious involvement reduces the likelihood of cohabitation and indirectly leads to married persons' experience of the gains mentioned above, such as higher rates of relational satisfaction, lower rates of abuse, and so on. But what about the sex life of those who marry? After all, isn't it commonly understood that religion restricts sexual enjoyment in some way? This is the impression a reader might have from the June 2003 *Newsweek* cover story "No Sex, Please, We're Married," in which the writer actually cited empirical data that married couples report having sex an average of 68.5 times per year (or just over one time per week), but dismissed this as inflated because some psychologists report (from clinical samples!) seeing couples who have sex far less often. So the entire cover story is based upon impressions formed from providing clinical services despite data suggesting that the clinical presentation is a departure from the norm.

Post-abortion negative emotional sequelae. Women making a decision about abortion are caught in the middle of a political minefield. Talk about feeling embattled. From the mental health field they would have the impression that abortion is just another elective procedure with few if any risks. This and other myths were recently discussed and refuted by Miriam Grossman (2006), psychiatrist at UCLA who wrote *Unprotected*, a book documenting the misinformation that is regularly a part of reproductive health services on college and university campuses today.

The professionals who seem to acknowledge the existence of postabortion distress tend to be religious. For example, Hart, Hart-Webber and Taylor (1998) review some of the data, including a national poll in which over half (56%) of women reported guilt over the decision to have an abortion:

> Symptoms [of postabortion distress] can range from mild to full-blown post-traumatic stress disorder. There may be sleep problems, nightmares, repeated remembering of the abortion, avoidance of small children or pregnant mothers, a numbing or detachment from emotions associated with the abortion or with pregnancy and mothering, irritability, difficulty concentrating, decreased participation in activities previously enjoyed, eating problems, depression, and suicidal feelings. (p. 191)

Perhaps a conservative religious perspective leaves room for why it might be distressing to some women and men. This material is not typically addressed as even a possibility in most human sexuality textbooks. Rather, the focus tends to be on whether the public supports the right to have an abortion and the controversies over efforts to hinder abortions (e.g., Crooks & Baur, 2007; King, 1999).

In presentations on abortion in human sexuality, the tendency at times is to frame the two sides in ways that reflect the author's own biases. For example, Crooks and Baur (2007), in their discussion of the controversies around abortion, refer to pro-life groups as "antiabortion groups" (p. 350) in most of the material, while referring to the other side as "pro-choice advocates" (pp. 351). This might be viewed by some as a preference on the part of the authors to favor one side over the other by, on the one hand, using the less preferred language for those who view abortion as a moral concern, and drawing upon the preferred language when referring to those who favor legalized abortion.

Topics Closed to Rational Discussion

There are a number of topics that seem closed to discussion in professional circles today. They have taken on an "everybody knows" quality about them. The most obvious example today is whether sexual orientation can change.

Most mental health organization policy statements claim that there is no evidence to suggest that sexual orientation can change (Jones & Yarhouse, 2007). For example, the APA has on its official website a "Q & A" format that includes the question "Can therapy change sexual orientation?" The answer is "No." It goes on to say "...some homosexual or bisexual people may seek to change their sexual orientation through therapy, sometimes pressured by family members or religious groups to try and do so. The reality is that homosexuality ... is not changeable" (APA, 2005).

Another question on the fact sheet is "What about so-called 'conversion therapies'?" The answer is:

> Some therapists who undertake so-called conversion therapy report that they have been able to change their clients' sexual orientation from homosexual to heterosexual. Close scrutiny of these reports however show several factors that cast doubt on their claims. For example, many of the claims come from organizations with an ideological perspective which condemns homosexuality. Furthermore, their claims are poorly documented. For example, treatment outcome is not followed and reported over time as would be the standard to test the validity

of any mental health intervention (APA, 2005).

The initial response to the question of whether sexual orientation can change alludes to religious motivations but obviously in a negative and derogatory fashion, saying that "religious groups" may try to pressure people to seek change.

Other research clearly documents personal and religious motivations for seeking therapy regarding sexual attractions and orientation (e.g., Jones & Yarhouse, 2007; Spitzer, 2003), and the failure to recognize these motivations while only referencing groups that allegedly pressure people to pursue change falls far short of a rich engagement with religion.

The American Psychiatric Association has made similar claims on its website:

> [T]here is no published scientific evidence supporting the efficacy of "reparative therapy" as a treatment to change one's sexual orientation. The potential risks of "reparative therapy" are great, including depression, anxiety and self-destructive behavior. (Position Statement on Psychiatric Treatment and Sexual Orientation," American Psychiatric Association. Retrieved December 12, 2005, from www.psych.org/archives/news_room/press_releases/rep_therapy.cfm)

All of this to say that the "everybody knows" quality of the discussion has been fascinating to witness. It is based primarily upon anecdotal accounts rather than empirical study.

The most common form of bias is by those who cite the study by Shidlo and Schroeder (2002) as evidence of the harmfulness of such therapies, while also rejecting the study by Spitzer (2003) in which no evidence of harm was noted and self-reported change of sexual orientation was reported. The Spitzer study is usually rejected because it relied upon a convenience sample and recall memory. But so did the Shidlo and Schroeder study. Both studies were of about 200 persons. The study by Shidlo and Schroeder is helpful to those who want to make the case that efforts to change sexual orientation are intrinsically harmful. After all, some of the participants in the study reported harm. What is rarely acknowledged is that the study was originally titled "Homophobic Therapies: Documenting the Damage," because of the explicit focus on finding cases of harm. (What approach to therapy would fare well if an entire study was dedicated to finding those who did not benefit from the approach?) The title was only later changed to "Changing Sexual Orientation: Does Counseling Work?" because the researchers found that some people reported benefits to reorientation therapy, including, in a few instances, change of orientation (see Shidlo & Schroeder, 2002, pp. 251, 259).

Though the percentages of success ("self-perceived success") were modest (n = 26 or 13%) in the Shidlo and Schroeder (2002) study, we cannot draw conclusions from their study as to the likelihood of successful change (or unsuccessful change or harm) because the study is of a *convenience sample* originally sought out to "document the damage" and not representative of the population of persons who have a homosexual orientation and seek change. This is in no way meant to detract from the possibility that some people may report harm from their experience in reorientation therapy, and this is an empirical question that should be explored further, but anyone familiar with the research in this area would have to acknowledge that the limitations discussed in these two studies sound similar. To reject one study on methodological grounds means rejecting the other. Of course, the other option is to try to learn what we can from both studies while keeping in mind the methodological limitations of each.

Since that time a study (Jones & Yarhouse, 2007) has been published that addressed the limitations of both of these studies. The study was of religiously mediated change in sexual orientation (not reorientation therapy as such). It was prospective and longitudinal and used the best psychosexual measures available to date in the study of change of sexual orientation. Those who reject it will do so on *ideological* grounds simply because some topics are treated by a small but vocal minority as beyond rational discussion.

Whatever happened to the likes of Camille Paglia (1994), a lesbian activist who once wrote, "Is the gay identity so fragile that it cannot bear the thought that some people may not wish to be gay? Sexuality is highly fluid and reversals are theoretically possible" (p. 109). I would only add that there is *empirical* support that is both longitudinal and prospective (e.g., Jones & Yarhouse, 2007) for what Paglia deemed a "theoretical possibility."

Intolerant Training Climates

Most psychology programs will list religion among the expressions of diversity that are to be respected in terms of fostering a training climate conducive to diversity and multiculturalism. However, the pecking order of what constitutes a recognized diversity variable often treats conservative religious perspectives as suspect and ultimately subject to other expressions of diversity.[3]

For example, in the name of promoting openness to a wide variety of sexual behaviors, some students in clinical programs will talk about feeling quite conflicted when they believe such behavior to be sinful or immoral. Training climates will want to balance a respect for client interest in various sexual practices with respect for students' beliefs and values and how best to work with a range of presenting concerns.

A graduate student recently attended a workshop on sexual identity and shared her experiences in class at a secular training program as she participated in a discussion of the *Bruff v. North Mississippi Health Service* case. In this case Sandra Bruff, a licensed professional counselor with an Employment Assistance Program, asked her employer to accommodate her religious beliefs about not counseling a lesbian client on her same-sex relationship. The jury in that case awarded Bruff over $2 million dollars in damages, but she lost on appeal because the judge believed it would have been an undue hardship to accommodate Bruff's religious beliefs (Hermann & Herlihy, 2006). The case was complex and provided a tremendous opportunity to process the number of issues involved in respecting differences. But the student proceeded to share how the professor and other students ridiculed Bruff for this position, leaving the student feeling quite confused about how to think about her own religious beliefs and values, her responsibilities to clients and her employer, and so on. Does such an experience really recognize diversity and equip students to address the complexities of religious beliefs, principles, and values in a clinical setting?

Similarly, a professional shared with me that he was once asked during his internship about his personal beliefs and values about homosexuality. He attempted to sidestep the question, recognizing that his own values about sexual behavior *might not be tolerated* by his colleague. But it was asked again in light of his Mormon background. He shared that he affirmed the official teachings of his faith community, and these were that God's intention for sexual expression is in the context of heterosexual marriage, and that behaviors that fell outside of that revealed will are a moral concern. The reaction to his formed judgment (not prejudice, by definition) was very strong and negative, such that he felt his internship might be in jeopardy. He had neither initiated this discussion nor had any interest in disclosing his religiously formed judgments about sexual behavior.

We have also begun to see a move toward scale development to measure "competency" which appear to preclude students or clinicians who hold to traditional or conservative religious beliefs and values about human sexuality and sexual behavior. The examples that follow are in the field of counseling rather than psychology, but to the extent that they reflect a direction that may be picked up in psychology, they are worth mentioning.

In the development of The Sexual Orientation Counselor Competency Scale, Bidell (2005) distinguishes skills, attitudes, and knowledge, and suggests that attitudes are a critical piece to competence (although no empirical support is offered for this assumption) and utilizes items of questionable validity in so far as they fail to fully appreciate a conventionally religious world and life view. At least three items are problematic in this way:

- "The lifestyle of a LGB client is unnatural or immoral"
- "Personally, I think homosexuality is a mental disorder or a sin and can be treated through counseling or spiritual help."
- "When it comes to homosexuality, I agree with the statement: 'You should love the sinner but hate or condemn the sin'" (p. 273)

The first item confuses what is "unnatural" with what is "immoral." It does not allow for a counselor to affirm something as occurring in nature but take issue with whether specific behavioral expression is morally problematic. The second item conflates psychopathology and sin, as well as counseling and spiritual assistance. The clinician completing this scale cannot make religiously-informed moral decisions as distinct from statements regarding mental illness. The third sentence gets right at a familiar phrase in some conservative religious circles. Granted, this phrase may be rejected by gay, lesbian, and bisexual persons as untenable, but it is an orienting framework that has been meaningful to some conservative religious persons, particularly as they have sought out ways to hold in tension a high regard for the person while being faithful to theological ethics in the matter of human sexuality.

Bidell (2005) also introduces political views surrounding domestic partnership benefits with the following item:

> "I believe that LGB couples don't need special rights (domestic partner benefits, or the right to marry) because that would undermine normal and traditional family values" (p. 273).

The main point of this and other scales, of course, is whether competency is determined by attitudes and political beliefs. Does a counselor's view of domestic-partner benefits in some way qualify him or her to work competently with a gay or lesbian client suffering from dysthymia or panic attacks? Would it make sense to determine the extent to which counselors are competent to treat specific mental health concerns? Or if we see an emerging professional consensus that attitudes and political beliefs are critical determinants of competence, how will we ensure that proper, accepting, supportive attitudes and political beliefs exist (are taught, supported, nurtured) toward conservative religious clients?

In any case, in nearly every ethics textbook published to date (e.g., Corey, Corey & Callanan, 2007) the assumption is that counselors will encounter clients with whom they disagree on some aspect of personal belief or value. In some cases it is appropriate to make a referral. This long-standing assumption may soon be replaced with a social agenda that redefines competency in clinical practice.

Discussing the study by Ford and Hendrick (2003), Corey et al.

(2007) state that "this research supports previous conclusions that the practice of therapy is not value free, particularly where sexual values are concerned" (p. 78). Forty percent of respondents in the Ford and Hendrick survey indicated that they made a referral when they experienced value conflicts with a client in the area of sexual values. This is generally how real value differences are handled in clinical practice.

One can only conclude from these scales that competence is determined by both endorsing who a person is and what a person does apart from any moral evaluative framework held by the counselor. Do we know that specific attitudes toward legislation or the moral status of a particular behavior corresponds with actual competence in providing clinical services? Is a conventionally religious student incompetent by virtue of having formed judgments (rather than prejudice) regarding the moral status of any particular sexual behavior? And if this becomes the new standard for competency, how will training programs prepare psychologists and other mental health providers—who are disproportionately not as religious as the client population—to work competently with clients who adhere to a religiously informed worldview? The demographics also suggest that students will be much more likely to work with social and religious conservatives than with GLB clients in the years to come. Are training programs adequately preparing students to work with *both*?

Based on the view that religion is an important dimension of diversity, psychologists can ask themselves the question: what would it mean to be in a constructive relationship with religion, to take religion seriously as a primary variable in the meaning structures around sexuality?

Suggestions for Meaningful Engagement of Religion and Sexuality

Much of this chapter has revolved around the ways in which religion is misrepresented, ignored, caricatured, targeted, and so on—and how some people might feel embattled in discussions surrounding human sexuality and sexual behavior. But what of efforts to be in meaningful dialogue? What suggestions are there for meaningful engagement of religion in the scientific study of and clinical practices regarding sexuality? Here are suggestions for what psychology might do to move toward meaningful engagement of religion in the study of sexuality:

Own Up: Ideology is Ideology, Religious or Otherwise. It is important that mental health professions reflect on the ideological assumptions that underlie contemporary psychology and the valuative dimension of contemporary psychology. It has been argued that there is a valuative dimension inherent in psychology that influences not only problem conceptualization, but also policy development.

Sociopolitical ideology often functions in ways similar to that of religion insofar as it is a lens through which people "see" topics in psychology (Jones, 1994; O'Donohue, 1989; Redding, 2001). What are influential are the assumptions held by scientists. These assumptions may be grounded in sociopolitical ideologies or religious principles or any number of evaluative frameworks. But these assumptions shape what researchers then take to be true as well as what has to be argued for, as well as what must be asked and how best to provide an answer:

> how one defines a problem goes a long way in determining the proposed solution . . . . [S]ociopolitical biases influence the questions asked, the research methods selected, the interpretation of research results, the peer review process, judgments about research quality, and decisions about whether to use the research in policy advocacy. (Redding, 2001, p. 206)

Unfortunately, in our field, religion appears to be undervalued and respect for religion must be argued for. A professional must make a case for inclusion of religion as a primary diversity variable, etc., while other assumptions are simply taken to be true and require little if any explanation. Liberal sociopolitical ideology gets a pass in the practice of psychology, despite functioning in much the same way as religious beliefs and values.

Just because someone is not tying their sociopolitical beliefs to religion does not mean they are any less dogmatic about their beliefs. We would do well as a profession to create a context for these principles and formed judgments to be heard and discussed.

Consider Limiting the Role of Psychology to Empirical Data. Psychology moves beyond what it can offer when it moves from empirical data to advocacy, particularly in areas of great public disagreement and in matters of morality. By doing so it often ignores that "is/ought" fallacy, moving from empirical findings to assumptions about moral goods. Psychology can provide valuable data to those who set local, state, and national policy in a range of areas, including matters related to human sexuality and sexual behavior and education. Further, psychology is more relevant to the broader culture when it can understand the perspective of and speak to the concerns of multiple stakeholders, including those who hold formed judgments about sexual behavior informed by religion.

Actively Include the Full Range of Religious Perspectives in Policies. The next step is to include a nuanced understanding of religious interests in policy development. It is not that psychology can speak to religion directly, but when policy is developed that touches on topics of significance to religious persons, an understanding of religious perspectives ought to be accounted for. Again, the preference would be to limit discussions to empirical data and various interpretations of the data rather than advocacy in matters of morality as such.

Unfortunately, what many would anticipate is that only some religious voices will be allowed to be heard; only those who endorse a vision in keeping with existing social agendas. It is not enough to seek out fringe religious groups that endorse liberal expressions of the social issues of our day and claim that religion was represented in policy development.

With the example of same-sex marriage and parenting mentioned above, the working group could have examined the religious dimensions of marriage and family and brought together experts in each of these areas as well as sexual orientation to try to draft resolutions that more accurately reflect what we know (and do not know) about same-sex relationships and parenting. Such a diverse group could also speak to the many stakeholders in these discussions. But it might have been best, given the quality of research conducted thus far, to simply make the research available—pointing out the methodological limitations—but without tying it to a social agenda that is based upon moral visions of gay relationships and families that are beyond the scope of what the behavioral sciences can offer (i.e., the "is/ought" fallacy in philosophy discussed by Redding, 2005, p. 317).

What is particularly interesting is that psychology has been increasingly sensitized to diversity considerations and respect for community standards and experiences (rather than universal norms). We tend to discuss this as taking an *emic* perspective (rather than an *etic* perspective) in working with populations. It is as if the mental health professions do not recognize that the U.S. culture is largely conservative around matters of sexuality and sexual behavior (e.g., Laumann et al., 1994), and preferences for sex education, for example.[4]

In short, as part of policy development, mental health organizations may enhance policies by actively seeking input from representatives of religious organizations. This includes the foundational beliefs and principles of a religion and how these principles and formed judgments impact topics of interest to mental health organizations. One consideration would be "How does this policy affect the religious life of the broader population?"

Enrich Training Programs. Consider ways to enhance training programs to address the unique concerns of religious students. Out of respect for diversity, psychology programs will want to include a wider range of representative sociopolitical perspectives (Redding, 2005). Included among these would be hiring core faculty members who actually adhere to the religions in question. There is a need to encourage the hiring of conservative Catholic, Protestant and Evangelical Christians, as well as conservative Jewish scholars, Mormons, and Muslims. Just knowing that programs are actively recruiting such faculty will be an encouragement to prospective students who want to know if their beliefs and principles will be respected throughout the course of training. Such efforts will also go far in preparing students to work with religious clients.

Related to enriching training programs is the opportunity to proactively protect the constitutional right of religious graduate programs to train students in distinctively religious contexts. At an institutional level is the effort by some within the APA to remove Footnote 4, a provision in the accreditation guidelines that protects religiously affiliated programs by recognizing the right of such programs to hire faculty who can sign with intellectual integrity statements of faith and behavioral codes of conduct consistent with a specific religious affiliation (Smith, 2002). It is sometimes unclear, however, the extent to which Footnote 4 is tolerated out of recognition of recent U.S. Supreme Court rulings on First Amendment rights and concern that the Department of Education might revoke the APA's standing as an accrediting body (Smith, 2002). Interestingly, even in the coverage by Smith, the chair of the APA's Committee on Lesbian, Gay and Bisexual Concerns (CLGBC) is quoted sharing her concerns about the decision, while no one representing the religiously affiliated programs was given a voice in the article so the reader might understand the issues from that diversity standpoint. Is it any wonder some religious persons feel embattled in these discussions? Rather than begrudgingly obey the law, psychologists could actively acknowledge the importance of this constitutional right, move the footnote into the body of the text itself (as is the case with the American Bar Association), and begin to interact with these institutions to gain a better understanding of what religiously-informed understandings contribute to the field of psychology in general and to the study of sexuality in particular.

Conclusion

As these recommendations suggest, mental health organizations such as the American Psychological Association and the American Psychiatric Association becomes more relevant when they appreciate the religious commitments of their own organizations' members and of the broader population served by their organizations. There may be value in developing working groups and task forces in ways that are respectful of religion. This chapter offered suggestions to help mental health organizations identify religion as an important variable in policy formation, so that an accurate and more complex understanding of religion can enhance organizational relevance.

Endnotes

[1] Portions of this section are adapted from Yarhouse, M. A. (2005). Constructive Relationships Between Religion and the Scientific Study of Sexuality. *Journal of Psychology and Christianity, 24* (1), 29-35.

[2] There was an initial Call for Nominations that was later changed to a version that might be read in different ways, one of which would eliminate anyone from consideration who does not agree *a priori* with the Committee on Lesbian, Gay, and Bisexual Concerns. In any case, what was more concerning was that the call for this Task Force appeared to some to already have the conclusions stated before the Task Force was ever formed.

[3] It is also possible that fewer religious students are admitted into graduate training programs by virtue of their Christianity. In Gartner's (1986) study, faculty members in clinical psychology programs rated conservative Christians lower than nonconservative applicants despite having otherwise identical applications (see also, Priester, 2007).

[4] Including an expressed desire by both parents and teens to have parents take more responsibility for sex education (e.g., Miller, 1998; Sommers & Surmann, 2004). Contrast this desire with the recent fiasco centered on a psychologist saying to students at a school assembly: "I am going to encourage you to have sex and encourage you to use drugs appropriately." Followed later by: "Now, what is healthy sexual behavior? Well, I don't care if it's with men and men, women and women, men and women – whatever combination you would like to put together." (http://www.thedenverchannel.com/print/13377661/detail.html)

References

American Psychological Association. (2005). Answers to your questions about sexual orientation and homosexuality. APA Online. Retrieved August 8, 2005, from www.apa.org/pubinfo/answers.html.

Bearman, P., & Bruckner, H. (2001). Promising the future: Virginity pledges and the transition to first intercourse. *American Journal of Sociology, 196,* 859-912.

Beck, S. H., Cole, B. S., & Hammond, J. A. (1991). Religious heritage and premarital sex: Evidence from a national sample of young adults. *Journal for the Scientific Study of Religion, 30,* 173-180.

Bergin, A. E. (1991). Values and religious issues in psychotherapy and mental health. *American Psychologist, 46*, 394-403.

Bidell, M. P. (2005). The Sexual Orientation Counselor Competency Scale: Assessing attitudes, skills, and knowledge of counselors working with lesbian, gay, and bisexual clients. *Counselor Education & Supervision, 44,* 267-279.

Bracher, M., Santow, G., Morgan, S. P., & Trussel, J. (1993). Marriage dissolution in Australia: Models and explanations. *Population Studies, 47*, 403-425.

Brown, S. L., & Booth, A. (1996). Cohabitation versus marriage: A comparison of relationship quality. *Journal of Marriage and the Family, 58*, 668-678.

Bumpass, L. L., & Sweet, J. A. (1989). National estimates of cohabitation. *Demography 26*, 615-625.

Buss, D. M. (2002). Sex, marriage and religion: What adaptive problems do religious phenomena solve? *Psychological Inquiry, 13,* 201-238.

Cochran, J. K., & Beeghley, L. (1991). The influence of religion on attitudes toward nonmarital sexuality: A preliminary assessment of reference group theory. *Journal for the Scientific Study of Religion, 30,* 45-62.

Corey, G., Corey, M. S., & Callanan, P. (2007). *Issues and ethics in the helping profession* (7th ed.). Belmont, CA: Thomson Brooks/Cole.

Crarey, D. (2007, September 20). Group to review therapy stance. *Oakland Tribune.* Retrieved from http://findarticles.com/p/articles/mi_qn4 1 76/is_200707 11 /ai_n19358074

Crooks, R., & Baur, K. (2007). *Our sexuality* (10th ed.). Belmont, CA: Thompson Wadsworth.

DeMaris, A., & Rao, V. (1992). Premarital cohabitation and subsequent marital stability in the United States: A reassessment. *Journal of Marriage and the Family, 54*, 178-190.

Dillon, F. R., & Worthington, R. L. (2003). The Lesbian, Gay, and Bisexual Affirmative Counseling Self-Efficacy Inventory (LGB-CSI): Development, validation, and training implications. *Journal of Counseling Psychology, 50(2)*, 235-251.

Ford, M. P., & Hendrick, S. S. (2003). Therapists' sexual values for self and clients: Implications for practice and training. *Professional Psychology: Research and Practice, 34(1)*, 80-87.

Gallup, G. (2000). *The Gallup Poll: Public Opinion 2000.* Wilmington, DE: Scholarly Resources, Inc.

Gallup, C. (2001). *The Gallup Poll: Public Opinion 2001.* Wilmington, DE: Scholarly Resources, Inc.

Gartner, J. D. (1986). Antireligious prejudice in admissions to doctoral programs in clinical psychology. *Professional Psychology: Research and Practice, 17*, 473-475.

Greeley, A., Michael, r., & Smith, t. (1990). Americans and their sexual partners. *Society, 27*, 36-42.

Grossman, M. (2006). *Unprotected: A campus psychiatrist reveals how political correctness in her profession endangers every student.* New York: Sentinel.

Hart, A. D., Hart-Weber, C. & Taylor, D. L. (1998). *Secrets of Eve: Understanding the mystery of female sexuality.* Nashville, TN: Word.

Hathaway, W. L. (2004/2005, Winter). Same-sex families and relationships resolutions and Division 36. *Psychology of Religion Newsletter, Division 36 of the American Psychological Association, 30(1)*, 13-16.

Hermann, M. A., & Herlihy, B. R. (2006). Legal and ethical implications of refusing to counsel homosexual clients. *Journal of Counseling & Development, 84*, 414-418.

Jones, S. L. (1994). A constructive relationship for religion with the science and profession of psychology: Perhaps the boldest model yet. *American Psychologist, 49,* 184-199.

Jones, S. L., & Yarhouse, M. A. (2007). *Ex-gays? A longitudinal study of religiously-mediated change of sexual orientation.* Downers Grove, IL: Inter Varsity Press.

King, B. M. (1999). *Human sexuality today* (3rd ed.). Upper Saddle Rive, NJ: Prentice Hall.

Laumann, E., Gagnon, J., Michael, R., & Michaels, S. (1994). *The social organization of sexuality.* Chicago: University of Chicago Press.

Masters, W., Johnson, V. E., & Kolodny, R. C. (1992). *Human sexuality* (4th ed.). Needham Heights, MA: Allyn & Bacon.

McCullough, M. E., Hoyt, W. T., Larson, D. B., Koenig, H. G., & Rhoresen, C. E. (2000). Religious involvement and mortality: A meta-analytic review. *Health Psychology, 19,* 211-222.

Miller, B. C. (1998). *Family matters: A research synthesis of family influence on adolescent pregnancy.* Washington, DC: National Campaign to Prevent Teen Pregnancy.

O'Donohuc, W. (1989). The (even) bolder model: The clinical psychologist as metaphysician-scientist-practitioner. *American Psychologist, 44(12),* 1460-1468.

Paglia, C. (1994). *Vamps and tramps.* New York: Vintage Books.

Powell, L. H., Shahabi, L., & Thoresen, C. E. (2003). Religion and spirituality: Linkages to physical health. *American Psychologist, 58(1),* 3 6-52.

Priester, P. E. (2007, August 18). Antireligious bias in admissions to APA-accredited psychology programs. Poster presented at the American Psychological Association's Annual Conference.

Redding, R. E. (2001). Sociopolitical diversity in psychology: The case for pluralism. *American Psychologist, 56,* 205-215.

Redding, R. E. (2005). Sociopolitical diversity in psychology: The case for pluralism. In R. H. Wright & N. A. Cummings (Eds.), *Destructive trends in mental health: The well-intentioned path to harm* (pp. 303-324). New York: Routledge.

Rosenbaum E., & Kandel, D. B. (1990). Early onset of adolescent sexual behavior and drug involvement. *Journal of Marriage and the Family, 52,* 783-798.

Shafranske, E. P. (2000). Religious involvement and professional practices of psychiatrists and other mental health professionals. *Psychiatric Annals, 30,* 525-532.

Shidlo, A., & Schroeder, M. (2002). Changing sexual orientation: A

consumers' report. *Professional Psychology: Research and Practice, 33(3)*, 249-259.
Seeman, T. E., Dubin, L. F., & Seeman, M. (2003). Religiosity/spirituality and health: A critical review of the evidence for biological pathways. *American Psychologist, 58(1)*, 53-63.
Smith, D. (2002, January). Accreditation committee decides to keep religious exemption. *Monitory on Psychology, 33(1).*
Spitzer, R. L. (2003). Can some gay men and lesbians change their sexual orientation? 200 participants reporting a change from homosexual to heterosexual orientation. *Archives of Sexual Behavior, 32*, 403-417.
Somers, C. L., & Surman, A. T. (2004). Adolescents' preferences for source of sex education. *Child Study Journal, 34*, 47-59.
Stanton, G. T. (1997). *Why marriage matters.* Colorado Springs, CO: Pinon Press.
Thomas, M. H. (2000). Abstinence-based programs for prevention of adolescent pregnancies. *Journal of Adolescent Heath, 26*, 5-17.
Waite, L. J., & Gallagher, M. (2000). *The case for marriage: Why married people are happier, healthier, and better off financially.* New York: Broadway Books.
Wincze, J. P., & Carey, M. P. (2001). *Sexual dysfunction: A guide for assessment and treatment* (2nd ed.). New York: The Guilford Press.
Wright, R., H., & Cummings, N. A. (Eds.) (2005). *Destructive trends in mental health: The well-intentioned path to harm.* New York: Routledge.
Wulff, D. M. (1997). *Psychology of religion: Classic and contemporary (2nd ed)*. New York: John Wiley.
Young, K., & Nathanson, P. (2003). Keeping it all in the family. Retrieved September 20, 2007, from http://www. marriageinstitute.ca/pages/keep.htm

Chapter 5

Psychotherapy and Judaism: From a Struggle Between Giants to Reconciliation and Cooperation

Isaschar Eshet, Ph.D.
Translated from the Hebrew by Tami Dumai

Introduction

In this article we will learn about the relations between the Jewish worldview and worldviews offered by some of the psychotherapeutic theories. There are numerous streams in each of these worlds but there are also elements which make it possible to clearly identify a distinct therapeutic world and a religious world. This article will make clear that some groups within each world struggle and compete for dominance of man's soul. Yet there are groups that combine forces, in order to identify man's and the world's enemies together. We will also discover how complex worldviews can emerge out of partnerships; worldviews that contribute to the reduction of injustice, to moderating the harm done to man, fauna, flora and still life, to the reconciliation of extremes, to increasing compassion towards minorities and the needy, and to enhancing world peace.

What is worldview?

Worldview or *Weltanschauung.* According to different dictionaries, it is the comprehensive perception of an individual's or a group's ideas and beliefs about life and about matters of spirituality, morality and society. Worldview contains recommendations or instructions in various facets of life.

Some worldviews allow freedom of choice while others require commitment. Every worldview has a theory of reward and punishment ranging from fixed punishments and an enforcement mechanism, to reward and punishment that are a natural result of fulfilling or failing to fulfill the recommendation or the instruction. Fulfilling the recommendations or the commandments increases the chance of having a good life; in failing to fulfill them, harms life. A good life prevails, according to the worldview, when we survive, are happy and do not fail to live a moral life. Worldview has also the authority to dictate the recommendations and commandments that constitute the instructions. According to Aloni (1998), who studied methods in humanistic education, this authority may be God, science, common sense, social agreement or even I myself.

The basic differences between the two "worldviews"

Out of the large variety of worldviews, this chapter refers to the Jewish worldview set against some of the worldviews that theories of psychotherapy offer. There are a number of fundamental differences between the two worldviews.

A. Source of life and authority: The sources of authority, according to the worldviews offered by various psychotherapies are, for the most part, science and philosophy, which are man-made. Man is entitled to be proud of his achievements and his mission in this world. The source of authority in the Jewish religion is God, who bestowed a worldview upon man and thus man is committed to modesty and to a deep understanding that he is not omnipotent. According to Jewish worldview, divine authority operates whether we choose it or not and it is a force external to us. Ever since the Torah was given to the Jews, religious scholars have studied the practical meaning of the commandments. The source of life according to science is nature, while according to religion, is God.

B. Practical instructions for a recommended way of life: Both views call for man to take upon himself instructions and recommendations. The different psychotherapies are satisfied with recommendations based on scientific research, with man free to choose whether to adopt them or not. A man who does not fulfill the recommendations may harm himself and his environment. The Jewish worldview is based on commandments (Mitzvahs) that compel man. These commandments were driven from God, a supreme, transcendental deity. Failing to fulfill them is a sin, namely, hurting not only man and the environment but the supreme authority as well. According to Jewish perception, there is no direct visible correlation between fulfilling the commandments and happiness. Nevertheless, man must fulfill the commandments as part of a divine plan in which he is committed to his environment, his people and his world.

C. Moral principles: Jewish worldview openly declares the moral principles that refer to the relations between man and himself and with his environment. Most psychotherapeutic worldviews maintain neutrality when it comes to morality and are satisfied with mental health leading man towards a good life. And yet, many researchers, such as Doherty (1995) and others show that still, psychotherapeutic worldviews also assume moral values. Thus, the difference between the views in connection to moral values is the level of commitment to the assorted recommendations and instructions.

D. Guilt and guilt feelings: Failing to fulfill the Torah commandments is a sin. Some commandments govern man's self-conduct, like the proper way to eat. Other commandments deal with the relations between man and his fellowmen, his family and his community—such commandments, for instance, that refer to fair trade or how to conduct family life. There are also commandments that administer man's relationship to God, including the prayers, ceremonies and rituals a Jew is committed to several times a day and on specific dates during the year. These commandments regulate the entire worldly and spiritual life of the faithful, and thus sin does not only harm de facto, but also deviates from the correct path as defined by each religion. The consequence of sin is guilt. Guilt is important in the Jewish way of life inasmuch as it helps man return to the correct path. As a rule, key psychotherapies do not deal with guilt. The conscience, or the Super Ego as Freud defines it, is analogous to the Jewish feelings of guilt. Most psychotherapies recommend that therapists not be judgmental and reproaching, and that they engage as little as possible in moral education. The various psychotherapeutic theories gave a new meaning to the principle "...but the just will live by his faith" (*Habakkuk*, 2, 4) which obliges man to live within the Torah framework; according to them, it is a pluralistic principle allowing man to chose the framework in which "Man will live by his faith!" It seems that the fundamental level of commitment to a worldview determines the intensity of guilt feelings that will ensue.

E. Man and society: Rotenberg (1994) found in his studies that western psychotherapy puts stress mainly on egocentrism, whereas the Jewish worldview sets great store on mutual social responsibility. These different emphases bear on the different messages a rabbi and a psychologist convey to a man who seeks healing for his distress. The psychologist will try to heal the troubled soul. The rabbi, who represents the Jewish worldview, will offer social support and the reinforcement of faith.

F. The value of family: Jewish worldview contends that the value of family is part of man's complete life. Most psychotherapeutic views accept the family as a social datum and study this essence trying to answer questions such as: What makes it possible to live well within a family? Does family life have any better survival value compared to bachelorhood? And so on. Although studies point at family life as being of value to man, few psychologists state clearly that family life is preferable to any other way of life.

In this article we will be introduced to three phases of relationships between Judaism and psychotherapy:

(a) A state of struggle for power and predominance over man's soul, values and his mental health.
(b) A state of mutual respect enabling therapists and patients to have the best of both worlds.
(c) A state of synthesis of opposing assertions and a new creation in which the two worlds go hand-in-hand to combine the two worlds so they can nourish one another.

We will be accompanied by Abraham (alias), a veteran Jewish psychologist. Abraham abides by the Jewish way of life and every so often he encounters, in different aspects of his work, contradictions between his worldview and the psychological theories he follows as a therapist. Abraham will share his thoughts with us and we will see how he has managed to live with these contradictions.

Fathers and Our Father in Heaven

Ehud Manor (1978), an Israeli poet, wrote:

Someone, someone cares for me up there. He has reached out and lit a few stars, and one by one they descend. We follow two divergent ways, all day and night; Tired, hungry, awaiting a sign, over time and dusty paths. We'll meet at the end of roads and queries; we'll meet when many days are gone, when many nights are gone...

In 2001 a group of Jewish Israeli rabbis and religious as well as secular therapists and doctors, decided to give up following two separate paths. The group met once a month for two years and discussed the possibility of merging their efforts to help man, family and society in accordance with Judaism and the various psychotherapeutic theories. Every participant in the group has personally experienced the phases of struggle between the two worlds, as well as the mutual respect. Some participants have started to acknowledge the possible synthesis of opposing assertions in various subjects. They searched their hearts as Moses suggested: "It is not in Heaven...neither is it beyond the sea...But the word is very high unto thee, in thy mouth and in thy heart, that thou mayest do it... (*Deuteronomy*, 30, 12-14).

One of the participants, a veteran therapist named Abraham (alias) was asked by Yitzhak (alias), a young therapist, to advise him in a difficult case of bereavement in the family of Jacob's (alias), who had died untimely. Throughout the counseling process he felt like the Biblical Abraham who was told by God: "Go thee out of thy country and from thy kindred..." (*Genesis* 12, 1-2). He reported that in this particular case he had a sensation as though he himself was told "Go thee from your therapeutic land and from the therapeutic Fathers from whom you had learned to another country where you will be blessed with grace to the benefit of all families of land!"

"They say you know something about Judaism"

Through Yitzhak, the young psychologist, Abraham became acquainted with the story of young ultra-orthodox people. The father, Jacob, passed away and his wife and small son must face the enormous pit they fell into. The parents, grandparents, the whole community, are all shocked. They cry, shout, embrace each other and pray for the glorification and sanctification of God's great name, and for comfort they cry out: "O ISRAEL please listen...O LORD our God, our one LORD...".

"They say you know something about Judaism..." Yitzhak says as he seeks Abraham's guidance.

Abraham offers a scholarly answer, actually from the world of psychotherapy: "Judaism specifies the rules for a time of bereavement, but we have books about man's soul at such moments...read them, and if you meet with any difficulty, I will help you."

Bereavement laws in Halacha (Jewish Law) and in Psychotherapy.

The panic-stricken Yitzhak wishes to talk to Abraham: "Should the ten year old son, Levi, say Kadish (the Jewish mourner's prayer) for his father? It really breaks his heart..."

"I think this is asking too much..." Abraham answers, thinking of the child's tender soul and the need to protect him from the horror. He agrees with Yitzhak: "Perhaps you can convince the mother to wait awhile; science teaches us that children are to be exposed to pain gradually."

Yet the young Levi keeps on saying the Kadish; more expertly with every day that passes. The entire audience responds and agrees: "May His great name be blessed forever and to all eternity." It seems that the social role of the orphan's Kadish protects him no less than gradual exposure, as the theory of psychotherapy claims.

A few days into the Shiva (seven days of mourning after the death of a family member), Yithak calls urgently: "It looks as if Levi is taking charge of the Shiva...encouraging everyone...what do you think?"

"You may want to tell his mother to let him be with himself and with his friends for a while ... to approach the bereavement a little at a time? Science tells us that some children find it comforting to be with their friends at a time like this."

Levi maintains his fortitude, standing next to the rabbi during Morning Prayer. Yithak, the young psychologist, listens carefully for Levi's voice to break, but it never does. Children coming over to express their sympathy know their role. They play among themselves, participate in the prayers and in the study session (Shiuor). It is all written down in the *Shulchan Aruch* (a codification or written catalogue of Halacha, Jewish law). "Mother told me I was entrusted with a gift and now God has taken it away from me," Levi points out confidently.

...Three painful months have passed. Again Yithak meets Abraham urgently: "What do you say, should his mother get married so soon...? She told me it was important that she got married soon so the child would have a father... I've heard that a woman should not remain a widow for too long...perhaps inasmuch as she might be a threat to married men...or maybe because she is young and in need of love...?"

"What...!?" Abraham calls out. "I don't think it is good for Levi... what's the rush?" Abraham is certainly familiar with the values of the Jewish family and with Jewish practice, yet he knows from psychotherapy that a painful experience needs time to be processed.

Not a year has passed and the wife of the late Jacob is again in love. The young woman needs love. She gets married with the approval and encouragement of all concerned. The boy should not be left without a permanent father. In the non-religious society such a move would often be met with an antagonistic reaction.

Only a week has passed..."They've decided that the boy should call him father...now he has two fathers, one in heaven and one down here," Yitzhak, the young psychologist informs Abraham, who is starting to consider the possible integration of psychology and Judaism in matters of bereavement.

"And he has Our Father in Heaven..." Abraham jokes, confused: "...Are you sure this is right...?"

"So it seems," answers Yitzhak both hesitantly and confidently. He, too, is beginning to realize that much can be learned from the bereavement customs of a Jewish family.

The family functions well. The new father is just the right person for the family. Levi feels close to his father who is in heaven. They all cry and mourn; they all have fears – but together. Yitzhak and Abraham stay perplexed and astonished.

Belonging to Two Worlds

"On the first anniversary of Jacob's death they called me up to the reading of the Torah in the synagogue in honor of the deceased..." Yitzhak tells Abraham over a cup of tea. Itzhak is no longer completely secular. Abraham envies him.

The mother thanks Yitzhak profoundly for his help: "You have been there for me..." Clearly, the religious mother greatly respects scientific and medical books. She says that, for her, they are like "Help Meets for Him" (*Genesis* 2, 18) "I believe that science is a gift from God," she adds. Yitzhak indicates genially that he had learned from her and from the community numerous significant lines of conduct that will, in his opinion, find their way to scientific and psychotherapeutic books.

On a cool evening Yitzhak and Abraham read the Kaddish, the orphan's mourning prayer carefully and discover other versions of: "He and only He who makes peace in His Heights will make peace for us and all Israel and the people of the world." They find out that many years of cultural affiliation are required to internalize the power latent in the Kaddish... "One does not even need to be very religious in order to be strengthened," says Abraham and thus adds another bond between the Jewish spirit and the worldviews that the different psychotherapies offer.

It is late and Yitzhak leaves. Abraham clears the tea cups and puts them in the sink, cleans cake crumbs off the table. He goes to bed, embraces his wife, and with a sense of belonging, his sorrow is somewhat diluted by his tears. Their devastation did lead Jacob's family to a long exile from the land of joy, yet solace and redemption are already there. Here comes another night of relatively undisturbed sleep.

A. Power struggle and control/dominance

From the end of the 19th century to the beginning of the 20th century, the worldview of religion and tradition conflicted with that of science and progress about the basic values of human existence. In this chapter we will see how this negation may cause collisions between extreme therapists and extreme rabbis.

From the end of the 19th century to the beginning of the 20th, big ideologies, or worldviews, proposed new ways, other than religion, to achieve a "worthy life." Science replaced religion as a tool for reinforcing control and reassurance in the world. In his 1882 book *The Gay Science* Nietzsche (1882/1975) announced God's death and asked where would human culture proceed from then on? Etzion (1966) claims, that the admiration of man during that period was based mainly on the belief in science, progress, social laws and human morality. In 1902, in his book *Altneuland* Herzl (1902/1947) posits passionately that if you will something it is no dream.

In opposition to admiring a socially organized man who controls the world, Judaism keeps bending its head in front of God's might and the wisdom of the Torah He bestowed onto us. Ecclesiastes summarizes the essence of man's being according to Judaism, namely, life in face of the supreme authority and its commandments: "Let us hear the conclusion of the whole matter: Fear God, and keep his commandments: for this is the whole duty of man" (*Ecclesiastes*, 12, 13).

The spiritual movement of western society found its way also to Jewish society. Rosenak (2005) points out that the Jewish Enlightenment movement, at the time adopting the enlightenment values, encouraged Jews to integrate into the society around them. The enlightened Jew is inclined to focus on man's well being and his freedom. No more will society determine man's life, but rather his will and his wisdom

Against this background, Freud, the father of western psychotherapy, presented his worldview through psychoanalysis. He asserted that science was designated to research man's soul. Freud (1928), who did not denounce his Jewish identity, claimed in a book published in 1927 that both psychoanalysis and religion address man's soul and its aggravations. But whereas religion tries to heal through illusion, psychotherapy seeks to help man acknowledge reality as it is. Freud called religion the "neurosis of the masses." When his psychoanalyst followers immigrated to Israel, collectivist Zionism encountered the pessimistic Freudian perception of the individual; this encounter gave rise to cooperation, but none the less to fights, which Rolnik (2007) describes in his book.

Warnock (1989) mentions other psychologists who decidedly oppose religion. Frederic Skinner, for example, refers to religion solely as conditioning, while Ellis (1958) asserts that religious faith increases mental distress. Incidentally, Ellis (2004) had changed his attitude as a result of research, and later claimed that believing in God has a positive impact on one's health.

The conversation in the treatment room hardly ever involved God, faith and moral values. Instead, the conversation evolved about emotions, frustrations, despair, self-esteem, free choice and man's freedom. Personal and family past replaced national past and culture.

Freud's followers, humanists and existentialists were not satisfied with studying man's soul as an object, and felt the urge to find ways to express man's spirit as well, but free of God. Maslow (1971), Rogers (1951), Yalom (1989), to name a few researchers, believed that man seeks meaning and self actualization, not only survival. Seligman (2005) proposed to fight existential void by means of a positive approach to man and to life. In contrast, Jewish worldview loyalists keep on chanting in front of the Torah in the synagogue, that the Torah is: "...a tree of life to them that lay hold upon her: and happy is every one that retaineth her" *(Proverbs*, 3, 8).

In Israel, most of those engaged in psychotherapy belong to the secular, leftist intellectual group. Many scholars have described the characteristics of the extremists in this social group with regard to Jewish religion and tradition. Alexander (2002) and others claim that the extreme secular person in Israeli society often finds himself alienated from Jewish origins on numerous levels and in various subjects. This group declares it endeavors to find ways to mold the life of the country as a normal country, just like any other, and not necessarily as a Jewish state. The extreme secular thinks that mental salvation will ensue only from democracy, the rights of the individual, freedom of speech, rich cultural life, medicine and psychology. Yizhar (1974) passionately proclaims that since each person has their own truth, values and morality are not to be taught. If a non-religious person seeks spirituality, he will find it in alternative medicine and in eastern spirituality. Alexander (2002) calls this process "the intellectuals' betrayal." This fight extracts from Professor Schweid (1975) a warning, namely: "if the People of Israel estranges itself from its culture, it may cease to exist physically" (p. 73). Thus, for example, can Elizur (2006), a secular Israeli, Jewish therapist write of an awakening heart and a new vision, following Buddhist coaching. Sartre (1948) claimed that democracy would safeguard the Jew as a man, but would destroy him as a Jew since democracy acts as a barrier between the Jew and his religion and culture. This opinion, too, is not manifested in this extreme group.

Opposing them are the extreme Jews who fight to protect the Jewish worldview from the secular alternative worldview that is gradually crystallizing. Mahler & Mahler (1998) cite what Rabbi

Karelitz (known as the Hazon Ish) told David Ben Gurion, Israel's prime minister in 1950: "Your kind of Jews are an empty cart!"

Orthodox extremists warn that the values of psychotherapy negate the Jewish worldview. Seeman (1999) finds the expression "There is no subconscious, there is only God," (p. 437) in one of the ultra-orthodox Pashkevils (Yiddish for Jewish religious poster), cautioning against the sin of believing in free will. According to Judaism, man's main motive is to seek God and not to pursue subconscious motives. Rotenberg (1994) who relies, among others, on Max Weber, points at a significant contradiction between western psychotherapeutic theories whose base is Christian, Calvinist or Protestant, and a Jewish-based psychology. This Christian stream extols the survival of the more gifted as a superior value, whereas Jewish, as well as Japanese psychology, is based on mutual social responsibility. Rotenberg further claims that in contrast with the Christian pessimistic psychotherapy which offers man no salvation in this world, Jewish psychology is optimistic, open to positive interpretations of the past, to judging parents on a scale of merit, and of the present—giving ourselves a chance to self-rectify in this world by means of forgiveness and atonement.

This, then, is how these two worldviews are perceived by the extremist on both sides. Their war takes place in the academic world, in treatment rooms, on the street, and inside man's soul. For the most part, the struggles highlight the many dangers embedded in them. Merv Osher, an emotional religious therapist, describes it well in Bareket (2003):

> For me, Yitzhak Rabin's assassination clearly marks the beginning of the process of bonding emotional therapy with Judaism. The palpable sense that there are different sectors in the public and that mistrust, animosity and antagonism between them is increasing, had reached unbearable magnitude with the assassination and the severe emotional reactions that followed. We began to experience and see what was called "the breach in the nation." (p. 14)

A mental health professional identifying with those extreme

groups may find himself reacting with basic non-acceptance, alienation, and at times even animosity and disregard towards a patient or towards a therapist with a Jewish and religious affinity. An extremist rabbi, for example, who denies emotional therapy to a religious woman suffering from postnatal depression, may cause her and her family immense damage.

Abraham

Abraham is already an old-hand, an experienced clinical psychologist and family therapist. Until the age of forty, his Judaism had been manifested by living in the state of Israel, serving in the army, settling in a kibbutz, choosing to live in the periphery for the sake of settling the land, and using the Hebrew language. For him, the kibbutz and socialism are a denomination in Judaism. To a certain extent, the kibbutz is kosher approved by Ha'Cohen Kook (1967) in his 1906 article *Maamar Hador (The Words of the Generation)* in the book *Beikvei Htzon (Following the Flock*) where he appreciates the endeavor of the kibbutzim members even though they do not live by the Halacha.

God's presence in Abraham's life began after he reached the age of forty. Jewish identity and even the religious facet are realized in his way of living and in his spiritual world. Occasionally, he finds himself arguing with his colleagues: "You are trying to make us repent," claim some of them. "What's the use of God?" others ask scornfully. "You force your ideas upon us," he sometimes hears from critical visitors. "Rosh Hashanah (New Year's Day)? Yom Kippur (Day of Atonement)? Tisha Be'av (Day of Fasting)? What's all that got to do with our professional discussion?" ask some members of his group. His family, too, fears that he might become an extreme repentant. Some family members fight with him, even raising their voices, demanding that he treat the family "as you used to." And indeed, Abraham often expresses extreme ideas. Sometimes he sounds like a person who makes others repent and on other occasions he sounds like a psychologist ignoring his Jewish identity. At times Abraham feels threatened by his inner extremity and by the reactions of the surrounding. He is afraid of professional rejection, of losing his livelihood. At times he feels lonely. He himself finds it difficult to merge the two worldviews, yet his Jewish identity takes hold of his mind. He keeps going and so do the conflicts.

B. Mutual respect

Fifty years of psychotherapy and of a religious world within a free world and scientific progress, give rise to more moderate therapeutic approaches and religious streams. In this chapter we will find out how more flexible approaches make it possible for the two worldviews to live in mutual respect.

Psychotherapeutic research of recent years shows the growing weight placed on values that are proposed by a religious worldview in general and by the Jewish worldview in particular. Miller, Hubble and Duncan (1997), and Seligman (2005) find in studies that the power of life experience, inner power, social support, faith and spiritual hope, community belonging, family support and more affect people's lives. Psychologists relying on such findings find it easier to respect tradition and religion. And indeed, Wendel (2003) claims that in the last ten years, faith and spirituality have become a "hot topic" in psychotherapy.

The psychoanalytical approach too, is undergoing changes, as Stephen and Margaret (1995) point out. In some circles, the approach is far less scientific and tends to think more of human relations and sensitivity to the other. Thus a psychologist who follows these approaches can respect the Jewish worldview which encourages caring for fellowmen through mutual social responsibility and charity. Elizur (2006) argues that the psychoanalyst's interpretation of the patient's world-component is basically similar to the Midrash interpretation of the Bible's verse. Both caretaker and preacher pursue deep meaning. The psychologist looks for deep meaning in the components of a man's life, and the preacher pursues the Torah verses for deep meaning of the Jew's life. Ankori (1991) finds similarities between the Hassidic stream representing Judaism, and Carl Jung's psychology. Jung, like the Hassidic stream, believes man was created in God's image; the potential each of us has to open up to the divine spark or to deny it, affects self-realization according to Jung, and recognition of man's mission according to the Haasidic stream. The analyst Erlich (2003) asserts that psychotherapy is a way of repairing the soul, and repairing the individual will bring about the reparation of the world just as every Jewish public prayer ends: "To repair the Almighty kingdom" Elitzur (2006) cites key Jewish psychologists like Viktor Frankl who brought into notice studies about the Holocaust and contributed to the understanding of Jewish worldview. Efforts to bring the worldviews closer make it easier for interested psychologists to respect the Jewish life worldview.

Heilman and Witztum (1997) propose that the psychologist should be sensitive to the patient's beliefs. Duairy (1998) suggests utilizing the patient's cultural strength. These scholars claim that the therapist is not supposed to solve only psychological problems, but help the patient to integrate in his culture. With this in mind, the therapist should adapt the treatment method to the patients' culture, their beliefs and their moral values. In Bilu and Witztum's (1993) view, when a therapist treats a religious Jew, he must be sensitive to the Jewish religion. These researchers claim that it is feasible to bridge the gap between the two worlds using therapeutic means and with help of the community.

Two central therapeutic approaches in the world of psychotherapy today have elements similar to the Jewish worldview. The psychologist who follows them can better understand and respect the Jewish approach. The cognitive-behavioral therapeutic approach as described by Garfield and Bergin (1986) highlights the molding of adaptive beliefs and creating behavioral change processes in therapy. According to Caspi (2002), in Jewish language this means repairing one's characteristics, and removing oneself from pagan worship of idols that are extreme principles promising ready-made happiness. The family in family therapy, according to Hoffman (1981) is the one that has the strength to do right or to harm. Jewish worldview too, amplifies the importance of the family as a significant power, strengthening the individual and human society.

In the religious traditional world we will also find flexible denominations and the willingness to be assisted by science for the benefit of man. There is no contradiction between science and religion, asserts Levi (1983). Judaism and science are prompted by wisdom and complement one another. Jewish religious scholars and mental health experts pursue ways to cooperate. In the

"Rabbinate and Psychology, Will They Walk Together?" conference at the Shilo Institute (2004), Rabbi Meir Lao says there is no contradiction whatsoever between psychology as a science and Jewish outlook, but psychologists must be cautiously attentive when their beliefs and their moral values are in danger of clashing with religion's values and beliefs. Rosenhiem (2003), a religious Jewish psychologist thinks there is Jewish psychology in Jewish worldview, and in many areas it can live in peace with psychology's worldview.

Two Jewish streams: The Movement for Progressive Judaism and The Movement for Conservative Judaism offer a pluralistic Judaism that does not denounce science. Secular Jewish seminars open their gates to Jewish spiritual worlds and enable secular people to get acquainted with the Jewish world.

It seems that flexibility on both sides has a positive effect on the world of psychology and the Jewish world, enabling them to live side by side in peace. The opposition between those two worlds is no reason to give up cooperation between the two worlds. A rabbi and a psychologist ready to make concessions find ways to help each other. The psychologist is able to respect traditions whereas the rabbi can be helped in research-based therapeutic processes.

Abraham

A growing number of colleagues accept Abraham's Jewish identity. He, too, keeps learning about Judaism and discovers its pluralism. He reads the "*Education Book*" that asserts the Torah is of seventy faces, meaning that there are many different ways to interpret the Torah, each interpretation being a different face of God.

His family relaxes, often expressing interest and curiosity as to where he is going next. He finds out how to respect the other and realizes that others respect him no less. "Rabbi Abraham, what does Judaism say about...?" friends ask, in good friendly humor. The "We shall do and we shall hear..." (*Exodus*, 24:7) that the Children of Israel declared in facing the Mount Sinai revelation sounds like a guideline from a book of cognitive behavioral therapy. The value of family becomes more important and is even reinforced scientifically.

He is already building a dictionary which translates the ancient religious Jewish language into modern Hebrew and vice versa, and by doing so, he in fact translates the Jewish mindset into a psychological mindset. Charity is benevolence; a commandment is an obligation to be followed; an idol is an extreme principle misleading us to believe that only if we follow it and act upon its guidelines, will we obtain happiness and security; change is a process of repentance, back to the healthy, secure and valuable way; a prayer is self suggestibility, encouraging the identification of wishes towards their realization, and so on.

C. Unity of opposite assertions and new creations

Alongside those who fight between them, and those who respect the other, there are approaches in both Judaism and psychotherapy that offer worldviews integrating religious elements in general, and Jewish elements in particular, with elements of the psychotherapeutic world. In this chapter we will examine a number of attempts to build worldviews that combine some of the differences.

Some psychotherapeutic approaches give much space to those elements that otherwise seem to distinguish the word of psychotherapy from that of Judaism.

Religious belief and God's presence: Contrary to Freud and others, God's presence is significant for some therapists. For Jung (1938), God is present; man was created in a Godlike image and the experience of God's presence is affected by personal experience and by culture. Warnock (1989) cites key psychologists who refer to God. Erich Fromm refers to religion as if it were human love. In his article *Sabbath Ritual,* Fromm (1951) claims that the Sabbath rest, giving up control of the world for a short while, is a moment of freedom enabling a peaceful and calm life with the other and with nature. Erik Erikson asserts that religion is an extra genetic feature. William James studies religion as a powerful personal experience. According to Abraham Maslow, religion is man's highest stage of development. For Fritz Perls in Walker (1971), religion has the capacity to bond with the creative energies of the universe. These therapeutic approaches have the potential to build a worldview and a therapeutic worldview in which

God's presence is central.

Emphasis on personal responsibility and not only on self-awareness: Existential psychotherapists such as Yalom (1989) gives extra weight to man's accountability for his choices in face of human existence. According to Garfield and Bergin (1986), behavioral psychotherapies emphasize change and self-help. Family therapy, stresses Hoffman (1981), highlights the personal responsibility of spouses in creating family communication channels, retaining a framework, parental authority and so on. These three therapeutic approaches allow not only for mutual respect between religion and psychotherapy, they also put a therapeutic stress on responsibility and obligations as a kind of personal commandment similar to that in religion.

Clear-cut moral values: Doherty (1995) and others assume that it is impossible to neutralize the therapist's values and thus they propose he should be careful not to enforce his values. They think that in certain cases the therapist should openly declare his values on a specific topic. For example, with regard to the importance of family, Doherty recommends that the therapist openly declare to couples seeking therapy, what extent family values are important to him and let the patients decide if his values are compatible with their own. Morality is of greater importance in the treatment room, not as an enforced moral value but rather as a legitimate psychological issue.

Guilt: According to Yalom (1989), existential psychotherapy appropriates much space for guilt as part of the therapeutic process. Buber (1957), the existential humanistic philosopher, who left an impact on many therapists, says in an article he wrote for *Psychiatry Magazine* that guilt is a doorway to personal growth and is essential to man's life. According to him, man lives by his "do" and "don't do" commandments. Upon identifying this guilt, the therapist may guide the patient up to the moment he meets his destiny and his direction in life. Similarly, we find in the *Mishna*, tractate *Kidushin*, page 40: "Man must always see himself as if half of him is guilty and half is innocent." From here, it does not take much to bond Judaism and psychotherapy on the concept of guilt.

Mutual social responsibility: Many ethical codes in different countries emphasize the psychologist's social responsibility and recommend that he be involved in social issues and enhance them. Just as is written in *Safra*, a Hallacha interpretation of the book of *Deuteronomy*: "All of Israel are Arevim (responsible) for one another." The two similar trends in Judaism and in psychotherapy make it possible for the rabbi and the therapist to propose behavioral and emotional therapeutic procedures allowing the patient enough space for his commitments to others in his various life circles.

Family: Studies in recent years, such as Wall, Browning and Doherty (2002), show that marriage does indeed improve a couple's quality of life, and if the partners commit themselves to their togetherness, and the togetherness is positive, marriage contributes to the well-being of body and soul. The utmost value that Judaism ascribes to marriage gives power to both therapist and rabbi to design the therapy so that it supports marriage.

In Judaism, too, there are voices that call for the integration of opposites. As early as 1906, Rabbi Ha Cohen Kook (1967), who served as Chief Rabbi in Eretz Israel in the beginning of the 20th century, wished to unite opposite assertions. Against the declaration voiced in the Zionist Congress that Zionism has nothing to do with religion, in his 1906 article *Maamar Hador,* he expresses his deep sympathy for secular Zionism. "Ours is a wonderful generation; darkness and light intertwined. It is lowly and humble—majestic and lofty. It is absolutely guilty and at the same time altogether innocent." He proposed to create a Jewish school of thought that touched upon man's heart and his emotions (p. 108).

Some Jewish trends see science as a component integrated with faith. The Masorti Movement (Conservative) explains on its website (www.masorti.org) that there is no contradiction between religious faith and science. Religion deals with values, norms of life and morality. Science deals with establishing facts and interpreting them. The Movement for Progressive Judaism, on its website (www.reform.org), invites people to listen to the integration of voices: historical, spiritual, traditional, persistent, and the voice of creation and that of human wisdom, of scientific research and of criticism.

Schweid (2000) asserts that with the completion of the secularization of the Jewish people, it has become obvious that there is material abundance and control over nature. Yet at the same time, the need for spirituality has increased as a consequence of social distress. He proposes that representatives of the religious and secular movements launch a discussion in order to make a joint creative life possible. And indeed, over the past few years, alongside wide usage of psychological theories including those from the East, Judaism as a worldview has returned to nest in the hearts of some secular Jews. In their studies, Itzhaki (2000), Malkin (2004) and others argue that the secular Jew believes in life on earth, in the meaning he gives his life, and in striving towards social justice and improving life through science. But the secular Jew need not estrange himself from his Jewish identity and he can draw values of morality, ways of life, culture, rituals and contemplation from Hebrew sources. According to the Panim Association (www.panim.org) reports, nearly 200 study centers for Jewish culture have been opened in recent years. This activity is also expanding through annual conferences. Orly Kenneth (personal communication), an activist in civil organizations for the progress of a pluralistic Jewish identity, considers this activity a mission aiming to make secular Jews feel at home with their own culture, as well as be its modern interpreters, develop it and adapt it. These organizations compose a modern Jewish-Israeli *Shulchan Aruch,* the written catalogue of *Halachah*, the Jewish law. Even a new version of worship houses are established in various places in Israel; for example, the Song of the Heart Congregation (www.hamidrasha.org) in the north of Israel and the Israel House of Worship (www.guru4rent.com) in Tel Aviv.

Jewish clergymen and mental health providers seek ways to cooperate. This is the objective of the Rabbinate and Psychology, Can They Walk Together? Convention organized by the Shilo Institute (2004) at Bar Ilan University. During the convention, Bar Ilan University president, Prof. Moshe Karev, proposed to establish a center for the integration of Rabbinate and psychology. Rabbi Rafi Feurstein noted the lack of auxiliary literature for rabbis, written by psychologists. And Eliyahu Rosenheim, a professor and religious psychologist from the psychology department at Bar Ilan, answered the question of whether a rabbi and a psychologist can walk together unequivocally: "They have no choice!"

Research is also taking place to develop a Jewish psychology. Rotenberg (1994, 1997) is working out a Jewish psychology with the narrative approach, stressing Jewish roots. Caspi (2007) is collecting psychological tools from Hebrew sources for developing a sense of purpose, and social and personal commitment to fix the world while God is watching. Caspi offers a clear distinction between the man who stands in front of his Creator, and the man who sees himself as the center of his world:

(a) When the world belongs to God, humans thank God for giving them space in it. When man conquers his place in the world he is in no hurry to share it with others.
(b) In a world administered by God, man is invited to take part in a great endeavor of self-reparation and the reparation of human society. A self-administered man will dictate his own truth to the world.
(c) He who has no God has only his own perception of what is right and wrong. He who acknowledges the Creator's authority finds out that accepting His boundaries grant him a existence free of the disposition of evil, of social pressure and fear of death.
(d) When only God knows what is going to happen in the future, man knows he should be prepared for unexpected hardships his Creator may place before him. For a man who believes he is in absolute control of his future, unexpected crises are an intolerable threat.
(e) A man who strives for greatness doesn't appreciate his own limitations. When God is the Almighty, man may experience pain and great misery; he is allowed to be limited and ask for what is beyond his power.

Schweid (1975) proposes that the Jew strengthens his Jewish identity through various statements of commitment to the sources, and his free choice of attitude to, and interpretation of, those sources. Twerski (1993) is considered both a rabbi and a therapist. Adahan (1987) offers a Jewish mental maturity guide; an approach considered to be a Jewish cognitive therapy based on the Torah, the first five books of the Bible. As in cognitive treatment, Adahan encourages man to see every occurrence as God's grace and a gift as well as an opportunity for personal growth; to look forward with hope and faith since there is meaning to life in every situation. Yemima (1977) and her followers teach how to cope with everyday burdens by integrating a cognitive behavioral approach with religious elements. For Yemima, the here and now mental setup affects interpersonal relations. Man's attention should be directed to his own uniqueness, and at the same time to the space in which he lives. This is the space in which he must act in order to actualize his mission, while showing consideration for others within the same space.

Caspi (2007b) summarizes this activity of uniting opposites with a daring vision. Psychotherapeutic worldviews are not Judaism's big enemy. Jewish worldview's fight is with progress that has brought about an extreme trust in science, or in other words, in human wisdom, in inquiry processes, in freedom of thought. Psychotherapeutic worldviews are a relatively small factor in the army of science threatening Jewish worldview, and it reflects what most secular people think about this question. In this sense, Freud well expressed the spirit of his time. There is much to say for the two worldviews' mutual criticism and, to a large extent, both are right.

Science is right to establish that Judaism rendered man too small and God too big. The extreme orthodox world, in fighting science, ascribes everything to God. One need not work or serve in the army since God will provide and God will set up a miracle and abolish the Iranians. This, to be sure, is paganism in the name of religion. Here, science and progress can act as God's army coming to cleanse Judaism from its paganism.

Jewish worldview is right to say that science and progress made man too big, almost as big as God, while man lost his appropriate place. Or in other words, narcissism is the spirit of the times. Some individuals are severely damaged by narcissism, but we all have caught the "illness." Jewish worldview is an efficient remedy from narcissism: Bringing man back to stand before God's authority and his commandments.

Abraham

Abraham is not the kind of religious Jew who observes the six hundred and thirteen commandments of the *Pentateuch*, yet most of the time he experiences God's presence and His wisdom, as manifested in Jewish sources. The study of psychology is also an essential component in his life. Whom should he believe when a contradiction between the two worlds occurs? The empty space between antipodal worlds is filled up with compromises and a variety of combinations.

When a religious married homosexual who does not want a divorce comes for therapy, Abraham well knows that according to APA instructions he should not engage in "conversion treatment" aiming to change the man's sexual tendency. Yet the Jewish religion finds it hard to accept the homosexual. Together with the two spouses, they look for a way for the man to be able to turn to a homosexual fantasy-world when the need arises, even during intimate marital relations, in order to preserve the family framework. It seems that a homosexual fantasy does not negate the Halacha.

Every March 8th Abraham marks International Women's Day as a day of obtaining full rights for women. He wants to integrate the quest for personal freedom with the trend for women's modesty, like not being allowed to be called to the podium to read from the Torah in the synagogue in front of an audience. If a woman is interested in higher education, he will offer the husband the option of "canceling Torah study" for the sake of his wife, who is in need of spiritual development as a "life-saver" (Pikoah Nefesh), and of pursuing personal development in the name of keeping her mental health.

The "Brith Mila," the Jewish rite of circumcision, is an intrusive act with no pronounced scientific health advantage, but likewise, with no proof of any health damage. Abraham is open to discuss the Brith as integral to Jewish identity and affiliation. Every so often a family would not circumcise their son; however the discussion touches upon the deep affiliation and identity experience of that particular family, as a basis for near future rethinking on this critical subject.

According to Judaism, abortion is a crime in the sense that it takes away life. At times, the birth would take away a woman's soul as well as her body. Abraham will make do with providing the rabbi with a professional opinion that under certain circumstances he should allow an abortion and also the use of contraceptives.

Honoring one's parents; mourning customs; the value of a stable family; guarding the tongue (against slander), have become valuable therapeutic tools. Abraham has acquired textbooks of literature dealing with such topics. Transference and counter-transference are key tools in psychotherapy and serve the idea that your attitude to the other is affected not only by the other but by your inner world as well. These are scientific translations of similar circumstances described by Judaism, such as: "It takes one to know one," "Practice what you preach," and more.

Abraham cannot say: "It's by the Halachah," because for a psychologist this is an ethical offence of enforcing his values. On the other hand, he cannot dismiss the Halachah because for him, that would count as heresy. He learns how to find solutions integrating research and Halacha. He has a strong hope in trusting Rambam [Moshe Maimonides] that "The Sages said that the perfectly righteous people cannot stand in the rank of a penitent" (*The Laws of Repentance*, 7, 4).

Conclusions

Life is made of opposites. "See, I have set before thee this day life and good and death and evil." (*Deuteronomy*, 30). The good Lord gave us a Torah and "She is a tree of life to them that embrace her: those who lay hold of her will be blessed. Her ways are ways of pleasantness, and all her paths are peace." (*Proverbs*, 3). This Torah proposes instructions, or in Jewish language commandments—about how to live in this world of oppositions. It offers paths for survival, roads to a meaningful life in a peaceful moral way.

This Torah is not unattainable, "It is not hidden from thee, neither is it far off" (*Deuteronomy*, 30). This Torah is imprinted in our hearts, it can be orally expressed and one can live by it: "But the word is very nigh unto thee, in thy mouth and in thou heart that thou mayest do it" (*Deuteronomy*, 30). Yet the human brain can obtain divine wisdom only to a certain degree. We learn this from Moses who pursued this Torah. "Show me now thy way that

I shall know thee" (*Exodus*, 33). God answerd that this knowledge is only partially possible: "Thou canst not see my face; for there shall no man see me and live...and thou shall see my back parts; but my face shall not be seen" (*Exodus*, 33).

I believe that the evolving psychological therapy in recent years can also provide us with tools to unravel hints from the divine worldview imprinted upon us, teaching us how to unite oppositions. Those tools help us develop mechanisms of listening, understanding and processing. Melanie Klein in Stephen and Margaret (1995) and followed by others, says that possessing the knowledge that the other is sometimes good and sometimes evil, makes reasonable mental health possible. The Rambam (Moshe Maimonides) (1180) said that for man to be whole in his body, he ought to be in the intermediate state, which is the in-between path connecting right and wrong. Thus increases the chance that the worldview we yield to will lead us to a balanced mental state, and from here the road is paved to identify the role God has designated for us in this world, at this moment in the historical succession of the creation of the universe.

A Summary of the History of the Jews in Light of World Peace According to Jewish Sources

This summary is an attempt to describe, in a nut shell, something of the history of the Jewish people as the people assigned the responsibility of God's mission. Their mission aspires to promote world peace by living according to the worldview given to the Jews by God. Free use of several sources was practiced in writing this summary: (Eisenberg; Caspi, 2006; Dror, 1997))

The Jewish people were chosen to spread God's worldview among mankind.

The history of the Jewish people began somewhere in the eighteenth century B.C. The Creator of the world and of man revealed Himself to Abraham who is considered the father of the Jewish people. According to the Biblical report, it seems to be the first time in human history that God was conceived as a superior, supernatural and absolute power who gives human beings a worldview in order to make it possible to obtain a peaceful life on earth. This worldview contains commands that direct man on how to administer positive relations with God, his fellowmen and with reality as a whole. No more belief in numerous idols but rather faith in one God who rules the world. It is no more possible to appease this idol or that but only to refer to oneself, to reality and to God bowing to the commands of His exclusive authority. Man has great wisdom, yet he is limited, and understanding God's words is difficult. Therefore, man is obliged by God to administer his life in the framework of the commands, free to interpret and understand the commands.

According to Jewish sources, God chose Abraham and his offspring, the Jewish people, to be the emissaries whose role is to bestow His worldview on all humans. God also promises the Jewish people the Land of Israel, with borders approximately the same as those of today's Israel. This would be an exemplary land, a model for how God commands humans to conduct their life. Some six hundred years passed from the moment of revelation to Abraham until, approximately in the 12th century B.C., Moses unified Abraham's offsprings to become the People of Israel, the Jewish People. By God's command he freed them from a long period of slavery in Egypt and lead them to the Promised Land—the Land of Israel. On the way, at Mount Sinai, the entire people witnessed a Divine revelation and experienced something of the worldview God designated for humans. The People of Israel received directions to establish the Temple, a spiritual center in Jerusalem. The People of Israel are also commanded to observe the Sabbath as a day free of any kind of work, a day when one gives up self-management in order to deeply experience God's absolute rule of the world.

The Jewish People attempt to live up to God's mission in the Land of Israel.

According to Jewish sources and partial historical evidence, the People of Israel conquered the Land of Israel and managed to always retain a territory albeit full of crises, wars and even exile for some, up to the second century A.D. The kingdom also underwent inner struggles while carrying out God's mission. The other cultures and faiths of the region offered tempting idols, covered with gold, and the joys of life. The difficulty of living under one commanding supernatural God, and the wish to integrate into neighboring peoples, caused groups inside the People of Israel to import faiths and cultures from the peoples in the surrounding area. For example, there was a good deal of Hellenization of large groups during the third and second centuries B.C. Throughout this period, there was a continuous nucleus of Jews who lived by God's worldview and who, in different ways, spread His worldview all over the world.

The Jewish people attempted to live up to this mission throughout the entire world.

Around the first century A.D., the Temple was destroyed by the Romans and has never been rebuilt. The People of Israel were scattered among the nations. Large Jewish centers existed in Spain, Persia, Eastern Europe, North America and more. Up to the 20th century these Jewish communities existed, grew and some were destroyed. Eventually, the Land of Israel and the Temple as unifying factors, were replaced by three main components:

a. **The synagogue as a community center and a place of ritual:** the People of Israel keep their hold on the Torah and the commandments through investing in groups of scholars who delve deeply into the Holy Scriptures and add to them crystallized material that is theoretical and, according to the Hallachah, suites a period when the People are scattered and in exile. The Torah and the words of the prophets are read to the crowd in the synagogues time and again, every Sabbath, and they learn updated versions of the Jewish worldview. Still, the Jews do not forget to mention in their prayers the affinity to the Land of Israel, to Jerusalem, to the Temple and to the Messiah who would redeem the nation.

b. **Family framework:** Beginning in the 10th century, the family unit, as well as women's status, was strengthened as a consequence of the prohibition to marry more than one woman.

c. **The belief in the continuation of life after death:** Beginning about the 2nd century, the belief that man's life continues after death gives the Jews, persecuted in exile, some solace and hope in face of the fear of death and existential suffering. A widespread mystic literature, with the Zohar Book as its center, developed describing those upper worlds.

Instead of spreading God's Torah among humans, the mission of the People of Israel becomes survival, facing new faiths and worldviews. In the 3rd century A.D. Christianity, also based on Holy Scriptures and one god, spreads out. In the 6th century Islam—another religion that believes in an absolute single God and is based on Scriptures—spreads out. Both Christianity and Islam claim a new revelation of God— the only one and the more developed. In the 19th and 20th centuries the belief in man, his mind and his right of freedom develops along with Communism, Liberalism, Capitalism and Nazism. The new beliefs and new worldviews consider Judaism, in one way or another, a substantial enemy and, at different periods, various communities suffer persecution, pogroms, exile, restrictive laws and ultimately an attempt at genocide during the Holocaust. Only in developed countries on the American continent, where many Jews arrived while fleeing, were they allowed to develop their religion and their way of life. The worldviews of the Far East, too, have no overt schism with Jewish worldviews.

The establishment of the State of Israel; the attempt to administer the mission in Israel.

During the 19th century, accelerated secularization processes took place within the Jewish Community. This movement, named the Enlightenment Movement, cultivated a wide Zionist movement with a firm socialist basis, aiming to solve the problems of the persecuted Jews by establishing a Jewish state in the Land of Israel. Additional persecutions, with the Holocaust at their peak and the annihilation of a third of the Jewish people, caused the nations of the world to declare the establishment of a national homeland for the Jews, which occupies part of the territory of the

Land of Israel. The Arabs who lived in the area opposed the decision, and up to the present the two peoples have engaged in a bloody conflict, including terrorist acts against Jewish citizens in the Land of Israel and the conquest of territories by the Israeli army, beyond the United Nations decision, aiming to stabilize secure conditions. At the root of the conflict lays the Arab misgiving about the right of the Jewish People to their own independent homeland.

The secularization processes in Israel have accelerated. In Jewish communities the world over, assimilation processes have increased to a large extent. Often even a religious Jew is fully occupied with survival and finds no time or energy to engage in his divine mission. The State allocates the minority of religious Jews the budget to safeguard the Torah's commandments and to develop the understanding of those commandments. Some State laws—such as marriage laws, observance of the Sabbath and other holy days, keeping kosher, burial laws—are based on God's given Torah. Yet the State of Israel has not turned into an exemplary enlightened country. There is no mutual support, no social justice. The gaps in income grow only larger. The attempt to establish small exemplary societies in the form of Kibbutzim, founded on mutual communal support, failed. The modern Israeli gets further and further away from his Jewish identity roots. "To denounce the Diaspora and its customs!", "Here, a new Jew will emerge!" cry out the State's founders. "Our state will be like any other!" cry out the nation's leaders who follow them. The existence of the State of Israel is based primarily on military power, an amazing economic momentum and a western-style cultural life.

The State of Israel today and in the future: will we become emissaries?

At present, the State of Israel is considered a Jewish "Home." The Law of Return makes it possible for every Jew in the world to settle in Israel and gain citizenship. A number of symbols emphasize the State's Jewishness: the Hebrew language, the army securing the Jews, the Sabbath, kosher laws, people observing common special days and holydays such as Passover, Yom Kippur, Independence Day, Holocaust Memorial Day, etc. Families observe customs such as the Brith, Bar Mitzvah, marriage and mourning rituals; there is a synagogues everywhere, the state finances various religious needs; the Western Wall, a last remnant of the Temple in Jerusalem is well kept and maintained.

In today's Israel there are groups who seek to return to the Jewish sources attempting to offer a life of mutual support, social justice, smaller gaps in income and protection of the environment, thus enhancing the notion of an exemplary nation. Efforts are made to integrate and bring together the Western, secular lifestyle and far Eastern faiths that take root in the country, with the Jewish way of life—out of believing in one single God. The fight for the mere existence of the Jewish People in the State of Israel created political processes that brought about peace agreements with Egypt and Jordan. Yet there are still external and internal threats. There are those in the Arab nation, that have not yet given up on the idea of kicking the Jews out of the Land of Israel. Some groups within the Jewish People in Israel and in Jewish communities in different places call for a new answer to the question: who is the secular Jew? According to this approach, a Jew has an affinity mainly to the Jewish culture and not necessarily to God who teaches the Jewish way of life.

Where are the Jews headed in the 21st century? Will the day come when emissaries of the Jewish People will, in some manner, fulfill the mission of spreading God's words among all people of the world for harmony among humans and for world peace?

References

Adahan, M. (1987). *EMMET: A step by step guide to emotional maturity established through Torah.* Jerusalem: Feldheim.

Alexander, E. (2002, September). *Israel: Betrayal of the intellectuals.* (Written in Hebrew) *Nativ, 15(4-5).* Retrieved from http://www.nativ.cc/September2002/alexander.htm

Aloni, N. (1998). *For human sake: Ways of humanistic education.* (Written in Hebrew) Tel Aviv: Hakibbutz Hameuchad.

Ankori, M. (1991). *The heart and the spring: Hasidism and analytical psychology.* (Written in Hebrew) Modan.

Bareket, N. (2003, August). Belief inside the therapy room: Isaschar Eshet and Osher Merv, psychotherapists, integrating their belief with their work. (Written in Hebrew) *Al Hagush, 214,* 14-15.

Bilu, Y. & Witztum E. (1993, June). Working with Jewish ultra-orthodox patients: Guidelines for a culturally sensitive therapy. *Culture, Medicine and Psychiatry, 17(2),* 161-299.

Bubber, M. (1957, May). Guilt and guilt feelings. *Psychiatry, 20(2),* 114-29.

Caspi, Y. (2002). *Inquiring of God.* (Written in Hebrew) Tel Aviv : Yediot Aharonot.

Caspi, Y. (2006). *Exemplary society.* (Written in Hebrew) Retrieved from http://www.notes.co.il/yair/17104.asp

Caspi Y. (2007a). *Revealing myself through knowing God.* (Written in Hebrew) Retrieved from http://www.notes.co.il/yair

Caspi, Y. (2007b). *Uniting opposites, a daring vision.* (personal communication)

Doherty, W. (1995). *Soul searching: Why psychotherapy must promote moral responsibility?* New York: Basic Books.

Dror, Y. (1997). *Renewal of Zionism.* (Written in Hebrew). Hassifria Haziyonit- the Zionist Library.

Duairy, M. A. (1998). *Cross cultural counseling: The Arab Palestinian case.* New York: Haworth Press.

Eisenberg, Y. (Ed.). *Jewish encyclopedia for Israeli cultural subjects and Israeli sources.* (Written in Hebrew) Retrieved from http://www.daat.ac.il/encyclopedia/index.asp

Elitzur, A. (2006). *Liberators of the mind: Jews and Judaism within the psychoanalytic movement.* In Y. Yovel (Ed.), *New Jewish times: Jewish culture in secular times.* (Written in Hebrew) Jerusalem: Ketter.

Elizur, E. (2006, July-August). A journey into the Buddhist practice. (Written in Hebrew) *Sihot, 20(3)*, 280-290.

Ellis, A. (1958). *Sex without guilt.* New York: Hillman.

Ellis, A. (2004). *The road to tolerance: The philosophy of rational emotive behavior therapy.* Prometheus Books.

Erlich, H. S. (2003, April). *Klein an we – on Tikkun (Repairing the World).* [Conference lecture; in Hebrew.] Tel Aviv: Tel Aviv University and the Israel Psychoanalytic Society.

Etzion, I. R. H. (1966, Winter). The psychology of atheism and the psychology of faith. (Written in Hebrew). *Niv Hamidrashia*, 52-66.

Freud, S. (1928). *The future of an illusion.* New York: Liveright.

Fromm, E. (1951). *Forgotten language: An introduction to the understanding of dreams, fairy tales, and myths.* New York: Rinehart and Co.

Garfield, S. L. & Bergin, A. E. (Eds.) (1986) *Handbook of psychotherapy and behavior change: An empirical analysis.* (3rd edition). New York: Wiley.

Heilman, S.H., & Witztum, E. (1997, Fall). Value-sensitive therapy: Learning from ultra-orthodox patients. *American Journal of Psychotherapy, 51(4)*, 522-541.

Herzl, T. (1941). *Old-new land: Altneuland.* New York: Bloch Publishing Co. and Herzl Press.

Hoffman, L. (1981). *Foundation of family therapy.* New York: Basic Books.

Israeli House of Worship. (2004). Retrieved from http://www.guru4rent.com/index.asp?site_lan=he

Itzhaki Y. (2000). *Uncovered Head.* (Written in Hebrew) The University of Haifa: Zmora Bitan.

Jung, C. G. (1938). *Psychology and religion the Terry lectures.* New Haven: Yale University Press.

Kenneth, O. *Modern "Shulchan Aruch," the written catalogue of halacha, the Jewish law.* (personal communication)

Kook, A. I. HaCohen (1967). *Eder hyakar.* (Written in Hebrew). Je-

rusalem: Mossad Harav Kook.
Levi, Y. (1983). *Torah and science: Their interplay in the world scheme.* New York: Association of Orthodox Jewish Scientists and Feldheim Publishers.
Mahler, S., & Mahler D. (1998). *The soul's hunters: An answer to the "Teshuva."* (Written in Hebrew). Tel Aviv: Zmora Bitan.
Malkin, Y. (2004). *Judaism without God, Judaism as culture, the Bible as literature.* (Written in Hebrew). Ketter.
Manor, E. (1978). *Mishehoo ("Somone", a Hebrew song).* Retrieved from http://www. shiron.net/homepage.aspx?homep=1
Maslow, A. (1971). *Farther reaches of human nature.* New York: Viking Press (Esalen Series).
Masorti (Conservative) Movement in Israel. Retrieved from http://www.masorti.org
Miller, S.D., Hubble, M.A., & Duncan, B.L. (1997). *Escape from Babel: Toward a unifying language for psychotherapy practice.* W. W. Norton & Company, Inc.
Movement for Progressive Judaism. Retrieved from http://www.reform.org.il/Eng/Index.asp
Nietzsche, F. (1975). *The gay science.* (Written in Hebrew). Tel Aviv: Shoken.
Panim Association. Retrieved from http://www.panim.org.il
Rambam (1180). *The Mishneh Tora, a comprehensive code of Jewish law, De'ot: general proper behavior A' D'* (Written in Hebrew)
Rogers, C. (1951). *Client-centered therapy: Its current practice, implications and theory.* London: Constable.
Rolnik, J. E. (2007). *Freud in Zion: History of psychoanalysis in Jewish Palestine/Israel 1918-1948.* (Written in Hebrew) Am Oved.
Rosenak, M. (2005). *The birth of the modern Jew—the history of the Jewish Haskala Movement.* (Written in Hebrew). Hakibbutz Hameuhad.
Rosenheim, E. (2003). *My heart goes out to you.* (Written in Hebrew) Tel Aviv: Ydiot Achronot.
Rotenberg, M. (1994). *Christianity and psychiatry: Theology behind psychology.* (Written in Hebrew). Jerusalem: Israel Ministry of Defense.

Rotenberg, M. (1997). *Jewish psychology and Hasidism.* (Written in Hebrew) Jerusalem: Israel Ministry of Defense.

Sartre, J.P. (1948). *Anti-Semite and Jew.* (Written in Hebrew) Paris: Schocken Books.

Schweid, E. (1975). *The lonely Jew and Judaism.* (Written in Hebrew) Tel Aviv: Am Oved.

Schweid. E. (2000, November). The "post secular" era. (Written in Hebrew). [Letter] *Jerusalem Viewpoints, 440 H.*

Seeman, D. (1999). Subjectivity, culture, life-world: An appraisal. *Transcultural Psychiatry, 36(4),* (1 p. 3/4), 437-445.

Seligman, M. (2005). *Authentic happiness.* (Written in Hebrew). Modan.

Shilo Institute (2004). *Rabbinate and psychology, will they walk together?* (Written in Hebrew) Retrieved from http://www.mshilo.co.il/site/siteHomePage.asp

Song of Heart Congregation (2003). Retrieved from http://www.hamidrasha.org.il

Stephen, A.M., & Margaret, J.B. (1995). *Freud and beyond: A history of modern psychoanalytic thought.* Basic Books.

Twerski, A. J. (1993). *I am I: A Jewish perspective - From the case files of an eminent psychiatrist.* New York: Shaar Press.

Walker, J. L. (1971). *Body and soul: Gestalt therapy and religious experience.* Nashville, TN: Abingdon Press.

Wall, J., Browning D., Doherty W. J., & Post, S. (2002). *Marriage, health and the professions.* Eerdmans Pub.

Warnock, S. (1989). Rational-emotive therapy and the Christian client. *Journal of Rational Emotive and Cognitive Behavior Therapy, 7(4),* 263-273.

Wendel, R. (2003, Spring). Lived religion and family therapy: What does spirituality have to do with it? *Family Process, 42(1)*; 165.

Yalom, I. D. (1989). *Existential psychotherapy.* New York: Basic Books.

Yemima, A. (1977). *Cognitive thinking, Yemima Method.* (Written in Hebrew) Retrieved from http://www.yemima.co.il

Yizhar, S. (1974). *On education and values education.* (Written in Hebrew) Tel Aviv: Am Oved.

Chapter 6

The War on Catholicism

William A. Donohue, Ph.D.

The uneasy, and at times acerbic, relationship between Catholicism and psychology was evident from the start. In the 19th century, the Catholic Church in Europe was still reeling from the social fallout of the French Revolution, making it wary of secular schools of thought. But thanks to Edward Pace and Thomas Verner Moore at Catholic University, Catholic institutions of higher education became increasingly receptive to the empirical work that marked the "new psychology." When Pace opened the first psychology laboratory on a Catholic campus—it was one of the first on any American campus—it "placed him and the Catholic University of America on the cutting edge of American psychology, at least for a short period of time." (Gillespie, 2001, p. 163)

In the 20th century, the post-war period saw an explosion of interest in the behaviorism of B.F. Skinner, a determinist whose ideas regarding human nature and free will were antithetical to the teachings of Catholicism. Psychoanalysis was also greeted with skepticism by the Church, but by the time Vatican II began in 1962, the Church was open to all kinds of ideas. So much so that its embrace of humanistic psychology would later come back to haunt it. Abraham Maslow and Carl Rogers were troubled souls, and it was their work that eventually wreaked havoc in the Catholic Church; their teachings made their way into seminaries and convents. More about this later.

It may be that the Catholic perspective on the human condition does not neatly comport with the prevailing assumptions of most psychologists, but it is quite a leap to maintain that there is something inherently problematic about the relationship between the two orientations. There is not. Nonetheless, there is no denying that many psychologists—including the most influential among them—have harbored an animus against Catholicism. If it is true that "The social sciences are the refuge of many who are anti-religious," as Jean-Francois Orsini (1994) contends, it is even easier to verify Paul Vitz's observation (2002) that "the hostility of most psychologists to Christianity is still very real."

Vitz does not exaggerate. When Scripture is blamed for "supporting aggression and hostility to others," including the Holocaust, (Ellens, 2007, pp. 12-14) as well as today's ecological problems (White, 1967), there is more than mere disagreement at work. The anti-religious bias is also evident in psychotherapy (Field, 1989), and has even affected Alcoholics Anonymous with its strong anti-Catholic cast (Judge, 2003). Some, like Fraser J. Field, say the bias is ubiquitous: "Evidence of anti-religious bias, for example, has been documented in the areas of the licensing and hiring of psychologists; accreditation; and graduate-school admissions" (Field, 2001).

Things are so bad in academe that in 2003 the Catholic League was asked to intervene in the case of a Hunter College professor of psychology who was asked the most intrusive questions about her religion simply because her specialty was Catholic mysticism. The professor, who received the highest recommendations from her department, was denied tenure. It was later revealed to the tenure committee that the professor was not Catholic after all—

she was Jewish (Catholic League, 2003). The professor told me that anti-Catholicism was rampant in her department.

In a 1969 Carnegie Commission survey, it was found that "Compared to the faculty in the physical sciences, psychologists and anthropologists are almost *twice* as likely to be irreligious, to never attend church, or to have no religion" (emphasis in the original) Stark, Iannaccone & Finke, 1996). More recently, Harvard's Neil Gross and George Mason's Solon Simmons found that "Psychology and biology have the highest proportion of atheists and agnostics, at about 61 percent (Gross & Simmons, 2006)." Now if psychologists are more given to atheism and agnosticism than other professors, and Roman Catholicism is viewed unkindly by professors in general, it stands to reason that anti-Catholicism is more likely to surface in psychology than in other fields. Whether this is because there are more psychologists who suffer the consequences of a "defective father," as Vitz has shown (1999), or whether there is something intrinsic to contemporary modes of psychological inquiry that account for its anti-Catholic bent, need not detain us. What matters is that an animus exists.

As Vitz (1986) showed in the 1980s, and Diane Ravitch (2003) detailed more recently, school textbooks—from kindergarten through college—are relentlessly anti-religious. But it would be a mistake to say that all religions are hated equally: there is a special hatred for Christianity, in general, and Roman Catholicism, in particular. When it comes to Islam, however, it is treated as "tolerant and egalitarian," despite overwhelming evidence to the contrary (Ravitch, 2003). At best, Christianity and Islam are treated by many psychologists as moral equals. Not only is the Christian concept of "just war" seen as analogous to the barbarism of Islamo-fascism (Davis, 2007), conservative Christians are branded as having more in common with Islamic terrorists than with other Christians (Ellens, 2007, p. 16). Moreover, Buddhism and the religious beliefs and practices of American Indians also fare well, making it plain that the bias against Catholicism is visceral (Vitz, 1986). Particularly disturbing is the finding by Elizabeth Lehr and Bernard Spilka (1989) that there was a sharp increase in the negative treatment of religion in psychology textbooks between the 1950s and the late 1980s.

To cite one contemporary example, take David M. Wulff's treatment of the medieval practice of witch-burning. In his widely used textbook, *Psychology of Religion* (1997), he says that "the Catholic Church's orthodox scholars reified their own incestuous interests by projecting them into the figure of the witch, who inherited all the attributes of women incompatible with the imago of the virgin mother;" this is accompanied by a sketch of three women being burned as witches.

Quite frankly, this is the kind of nonsense found in Dan Brown's *The Da Vinci Code* (2004). It is preposterous to claim, for example, that witch-burning led to 5 million women being killed by the Catholic Church. The fact is most scholars say the number is somewhere between 30,000-50,000. Not all were women and, more important, most were not killed by the Catholic Church—they were murdered by civil authorities (Donohue, 2006). Worse still is Wulff's desire to project base motives to Catholic scholars. This is reminiscent of Norman Cohn's failed attempt to employ a Freudian psychohistory of witch-burning. Sociologist Rodney Stark cut to the quick by saying, the "application of psychohistory to the witch-hunts amounts to explaining one fantasy with another" (2003, pp. 223-224).

Cohn learned from the master, and what he picked up was evident. "Not only was Freud antireligion," writes Pamela Paul, "but the behaviorists who came afterward were extremely eager to avoid religion in order to establish psychology as a respected science" (2005). Freud, of course, described himself as "a godless Jew," "a wicked pagan," and "totally non-religious" (Meng & Freud, 1963). But he was more than that—Freud candidly said that "my real enemy" was "the Roman Catholic Church" (Rempel, 1997). Even Wulff readily admits of Freud that "religion seems to have inspired in him an active hatred of it, or at least Roman Catholicism…."(p. 276). It is not only logical—it is predictable—that Freudian interpretations of Catholic beliefs and practices would inexorably be anti-Catholic.

Michael P. Carroll (1986) believes he can account for Marian apparitions in strictly Freudian terms. In his mind, apparitions are hallucinations; Mary, of course, symbolizes sexual denial. "These apparitions occur to males because such apparitions are sublimations of the male's sexual desire for his mother," he contends. As for females, apparitions occur "because they provide these females with a way of identifying with Mary and thus enjoying the ultimate Oedipal fantasy" (Dart, 1985).

But if it is true that all apparitions are nothing but hallucinatory exercises, why is there any need to wax Freudian by assigning a sexual nature to them? Unless, of course, we are to believe that all hallucinations smack of sexual repression. Not surprisingly, Carroll's explanations were found persuasive by Donald Capps of Princeton's Theological Seminary. Capps would later contend that Jesus was not the son of God, but the result of an illicit sexual encounter between his mother and a Roman soldier. This is the kind of gossip that might be attractive to those who read the tabloids, but not to serious scholars. It does not speak well for the Society for the Scientific Study of Religion of which Capps was once president.

Wulff is not buying all of this Freudian stuff. In his textbook, he tells college students that Carroll's Freudian interpretation of praying the rosary makes sense "if the ritual is understood as a disguised fulfillment of repressed anal-erotic desires." Fortunately, Wulff is honest enough to offer a contrary view. He cites a Jesuit psychologist from the 1920s who emphasized the devotional and psychologically soothing elements of saying the rosary. Wulff allows that "the peculiar qualities of the rosary may be attractive to persons of an 'anal' disposition," but it is also true that "this experience seems directly accessible to empathic understanding, requiring no appeal to unconscious infantile desires" (1997, pp 317-318). Wulff is too kind: if a social phenomenon can adequately be explained without indulging in speculative notions regarding unconscious infantile desires, why give credence to the fatuous? Besides, shouldn't it be the task of the social scientist to weigh reality from the actor's perspective, and not impute motives to him?

Jungian psychology has also had a problematic record in dealing with Catholicism. Jung was so obsessed with Catholicism that he found it necessary to write an essay explaining why he never joined the Catholic Church (1980). More important, he also found it necessary to speculate on the meaning of the Trinity. For Jung,

(1969a) the Trinity was incomplete without a fourth element, namely, the principle of evil. In other words, while Jung was not prepared to accept the biblical interpretation of the Trinity, he could not resist maintaining that without Satan—the fourth element—the whole story makes no sense. Similarly, Christians get it wrong when they say that Christ died to make men free: when Christ suffered, we are advised, so did his Father; it is analogous to the king who dies to save his people from famine (Jung, 1969b). So once again, Christianity makes sense only when revised to fit the lens of secular psychologists.

"Jung's entire life and work were motivated by his detestation of the Catholic Church," writes Richard Noll (1997), "whose religious doctrines and moral teachings he considered to be the source of all the neuroses which afflicted Western man." Noll cites Jung's *New Paths of Psychology* as his definitive work on the subject. "Jung wrote that the only way to overthrow the neuroses inducing Judeo-Christian religion and its 'sex-fixated ethics' was to establish a new religion—the new religion of psychoanalysis," he writes. This explains why "Jungians understand that they must do everything in their power to eliminate the traditional understanding of Roman Catholicism."

God only knows they have tried. So did the founders of psychotherapy. Rollo May said Christianity was for "weaklings" (Field, 2001) and Eric Fromm made palpable his animus in *The Dogma of Christ* (1955).

All of this raises the question: What exactly is it about Catholicism that so many psychologists abhor? Surely part of the explanation can be found in the need of modern psychologists to validate their discipline as a science. Hence, the quest to distance psychology from religion, a process that has frequently resulted in distorting history for the sake of establishing scientific legitimacy. In this regard, no religion has been used as the whipping boy more than Catholicism. How ironic the choice given that Catholicism is, by all fair accounts, the womb of science.

"For the last fifty years," writes historian Thomas E. Woods, Jr. (2005, p. 4), "virtually all historians of science—including A.C. Crombie, David Lindberg, Edward Grant, Stanley Jaki, Thomas Goldstein, and J.L. Heilborn—have concluded that the Scientific

Revolution was indebted to the [Catholic] Church." These scholars are fully appreciative of Descartes contention that the search for natural laws must be based on grounds that such laws must exist because God is perfect and therefore "acts in a manner as constant and immutable as possible" (Stark, 2005, p. 16). It is for reasons like this that sociologist Rodney Stark has been able to conclude that the rise of science "was the natural outgrowth of Christian doctrine: nature exists because it was created by God" (2005, p. 22).

Yet despite all the evidence to the contrary, many psychologists persist in the mythology that there is some inherent contradiction between science and religion. Without bothering to defend their position, they simply drop the dreaded name Galileo, not knowing that Cardinal Bellarmine, as well as Pope Urban VIII, welcomed Galileo's research; they presented him with medals and gifts. It was only after Galileo persisted in promoting his hypothesis as fact (this was the heresy, not the claim that the earth revolved around the sun) that trouble ensued. He was never tortured, never imprisoned and stayed at a Vatican apartment for 20 days, all because he drew conclusions that at that time had yet been scientifically verified (Woods, 2005; Thavis, 2003).

If there is one area where psychology and the teachings of the Catholic Church collide it is in their contrary perspectives on human nature. Where Catholicism emphasizes the inherent limitations of the human condition, psychology (especially humanistic psychology) posits a more optimistic rendering. Where Catholicism places a premium on the interests of the collective, psychology is drawn to the interests of the individual. Indeed, as Vitz has said, "psychology's deep commitment to narcissism, egoism, self-worship, the individual, isolated self...has been thoroughly demonstrated." He, and others, call it "selfism" (2002, pp. x-xi).

On this level, the disjunction between Catholicism and psychology seems plain enough, but even here there are some psychologists who impute a narcissistic motive to practicing Christians. So it was that Rokeach (1969) and Pruyser (1991) understood the Christian belief in salvation to be a self-serving quest to save one's own soul. But in the Catholic tradition, salvation is not possible without faith *and* works, i.e., only by "doing unto others as one would do unto oneself" is it possible to be saved. There is nothing narcissistic about this—quite the opposite. That is why it is intellectually dishonest to pretend that Catholic missionaries, for example, had narcissistic intentions. Anyone who knows anything about the self-sacrifice that these men and women endured—all for the good of others—knows that to call them narcissists smacks of either ignorance or malice.

Let's consider this one step further. It was not self-centered men and women who gave their lives to rescue Jews during the Holocaust—it was those who had a clear, strong commitment to others who did so. And as Samuel and Pearl Oliner (1988) recounted in their classic, *The Altruistic Personality*, it was those rescuers whose religious commitment emphasized the commonality of all peoples that were most likely to help Jews. Moreover, as Kristen Monroe (1996) has demonstrated, it is slanderous to continue the fable adopted by people like Hobbes, Freud and Darwin that altruism can be read as self-interest. Yet this is exactly what the anti-Catholic practitioners of psychology do when they assign egocentric motives to Catholics who have given of themselves for others.

More accurate is the assessment of Father Benedict Groeschel (personal communication), a clinical psychologist with abundant first-hand knowledge, that problems of "selfism" mark psychology—not Catholicism (Gillespie, 2001). Indeed, the Christian concept of suffering is unintelligible from the standpoint of selfist psychology, so insufferably individualistic has it become (Vitz, 2002). This is particularly true of humanistic psychologists, the crown princes of selfism. Not surprisingly, the most prominent among them were virulently anti-Catholic.

In 1962, Abraham Maslow took his self-actualization tour to Sacred Heart College in Newton, Massachusetts, proselytizing in a way that would make any Bible-thumping preacher blush. Except for one nun who was not fooled, he succeeded. Most revealing of all is what he wrote in his journal: "They [the nuns] shouldn't applaud me—they should attack. If they were fully aware of what I was doing, they would" (Milton, 2002, p. 139). He was right.

Maslow sought to upend their world, turning it topsy-turvy, much the way he felt his own life had unfolded. His mother, whom he hated with a passion, and his father, a passive figure, were first cousins, something Abe found worthy of mimicking: he fell in love with his first cousin when she was a teenager and married her (Milton, 2002, p. 40-43). A utopian and a sexual libertine, Maslow would eventually hook up with Carl Rogers, another humanistic psychologist who preyed on nuns.

In 1965, Rogers began shopping his ideas of self-actualization to any institution willing to be seduced. The notion that each person is the arbiter of his own truth, and only by acting on our feelings can we be truly human, was right out of the 1960s. It was also contrary to every Catholic belief. Unfortunately, the Sisters of the Immaculate Heart of Mary (IHM) in Los Angeles welcomed Rogers, and his assistant Bill Coulson, into their lives, allowing them to conduct a two-year experiment designed to free them from their "artificially induced psychological shackles." They were instructed to bare their innermost feelings in public and allow their psyches to unwind.

It didn't take long before every aspect of their lives was put under a microscope and found wanting. By participating in encounter groups, the sisters liberated themselves from all the norms they had committed themselves to and proclaimed themselves emancipated. In actual fact, they collapsed: the result of this "grand opening" was the destruction of the IHM community. Some of the nuns began to experiment sexually—many became lesbians—and most left the order. Fortunately, Coulson saw the light, dropped his Rogerian connections and went on to become a distinguished Catholic psychologist. But not before more damage was done.

When an order of priests, St. Anthony's Franciscan Seminary in Santa Barbara, approached Rogers to employ his madness, they also paid a big price: a quarter century after being "liberated"—seminarians were told they could visit friars' rooms whenever they wanted to—the priestly order was making headlines around the world for its notorious pedophilia ring. To make matters worse, when the St. Anthony's story hit the newspapers in 1993, Father Stephen Rosetti, a psychologist who treats wayward priests at a Maryland clinic, blamed what had happened at the seminary on the Church's "repressive" ideas about sexuality.

Thus did he buy into the very Rogerian view that gave rise to the problem in the first place. In fact, it was the wholesale rejection of restraint, and the total celebration of hedonism, that created the problem of predatory priests. Had the priests acted on their vows, instead of their id, there would have been no scandal (Milton, 2002).

The canard that Catholicism is repressive, and generates authoritarian personalities in its subjects, was made popular by Adorno (1950) in the 1950s, but subsequent scholarship has undermined his thesis. It is true that most studies of tolerance show that those who are religious are more intolerant than secularists, but it is also true that it is easier to offend those who hold to a strong core of moral values. For example, in one of the more famous studies, moral objections to infidelity were scored as intolerant. But is it really a badge of enlightenment to greet adultery with aplomb? More to the point, if moral relativism tends to anesthesize moral outrage, what exactly is there to cheer about? No matter, the bottom line is, as a more refined study of tolerance found, most Americans are intolerant of some groups. It is therefore bogus to claim that those who are religious are any more intolerant than anyone else (Donohue, 1991).

Similarly, it used to be thought that Intrinsic-Extrinsic (I-E) research yielded an accurate measurement of a person's true attitudes. That has since been disputed. More important, the idea that the I-E scale offers a good way of measuring positive and negative types of religious sentiments is now regarded as "a too simplistic good-versus-bad formulation of religion" (Paloutzian, 1996). Dogmatism can be found across the board. No matter, in Wulff's textbook, students learn a different lesson. They are told that in an earlier work by Allport and Ross that used the I-E scale that intrinsic-typed Catholics appeared less prejudiced than the extrinsic type, but—and this is the key—they are also instructed that this should be treated as an anomaly! "Unfortunately," he says, "it is not unusual for statistical trends inexplicably to reverse themselves" (Wulff, 1997, pp. 232-233). Which is another way of saying to the reader: Be wary of data that challenge Catholic stereotypes.

When Milton Rokeach (1960) published his Dogmatism Scale

in 1960, everyone's worst fears of Catholics were confirmed: they were closed minded. Ten years later, Arthur G. Cryns (1970) used Rokeach's methodology to study Catholic clergy and ex-clergy and found that those who stayed in active ministry were more dogmatic than those who had left. Again, however, was it dogmatism that was being measured, or sensitivity to cherished values? In other words, why is it surprising that those who abandoned their vocation would appear open minded? For example, in the late 1990s, when radical Catholics who had rejected many of the Catholic Church's teachings learned that rank-and-file Catholics wanted nothing to do with their dissident agenda, they exploded in a rash of elitist invective. The leader of the malcontents, Sister Maureen Fiedler, said progressive Catholics had "overestimated Catholic theological maturity, and underestimated the pietism of the Catholic laity" (Morrison, 1997).

The simplistic assumptions that color much of this kind of research were blown apart in 2001 when the findings of a major study of 802 fifteen- and sixteen-year olds in the United Kingdom was published. Both the Rokeach Dogmatism Scale and the Francis Scale of Attitude toward Christianity, together with the Junior Eysenck Personality Inventory, were used to determine if those who are religious are more or less open-minded than others. "This review makes it abundantly clear," writes Leslie J. Francis (2001), "that there is no simple empirical consensus to support the popular accusation that religious faith and the closed mind go hand in hand."

Much has been made of those studies that purport to find a link between Catholicism and any number of psychological maladies. But as Raymond Paloutzian (1996) has accurately observed, the Catholic understanding of Confession, to take one example, "may appear to the nonparticipant as bizarre; that is, as abnormal and consequently symptomatic of pathology." He hastens to add that there is nothing inherently abnormal about the practice. Furthermore, he says there is no necessary link between religion and abnormal personalities. But perhaps he is being too kind. Could it not also be said that there is something bizarre, if not abnormal, about the practice of total strangers baring their souls in therapy and then whipping out their credit cards to pay for it?

Moreover, since bartenders are good listeners, too, and they cost a lot less, is it not irrational to go to a shrink?

"Not surprisingly," say Stark, Iannaccone and Finke (1998), "the most extreme claims of religious psychopathology have been the most thoroughly debunked." As Stark found, those diagnosed as mentally ill were far less likely to attend church or to score high on an index of orthodox religious belief. He also found no evidence of a link between religiosity and authoritarianism. In recent years, there have been many reports, in the U.S. and abroad, showing the positive effects of religion on the psychological and physical well-being of men and women. Perhaps more to the point, the record amassed by Catholic charitable organizations in servicing the psychological and physical needs of the public, especially the indigent, is far more impressive than the good works done collectively by psychologists.

Harvard professor of public health, Edward C. Green, credits Catholic Relief Services with implementing an AIDS preventive education program in Zimbabwe that "has greatly improved the quality of life for PLWHAs [people living with AIDS], assured dying parents their children will be cared for, and brought support and comfort to families and communities afflicted by AIDS" (2003, p. 288). In fact, the Catholic Church provides for nearly 27 percent of HIV/AIDS services worldwide (Ramirez, 2006), though it rarely gets any credit for doing so. And, of course, there is the work of Mother Teresa and her army of sisters who have provided for the poor all over the world. So beloved was she that when she died she was dubbed "a second Mohandas Gandhi" by the prime minister of India and afforded a lavish state funeral (Morella, 1997).

Even among those psychologists who are willing to concede these points, there remains the stubborn notion that Catholics have allowed fear and guilt to pervert their sex lives. It is the old bugaboo about sin—a concept many psychologists find incoherent—that under girds the discussion.

In the 1970s, psychologist Karl Menninger (1973) was able to ask, "Whatever became of sin?" A decade later, an answer was forthcoming from Pope John Paul II: He advised us to consider "the errors made in evaluating certain findings of the human sciences. Thus on the basis of certain affirmations of psychology, concern to avoid creating feelings of guilt or to place limits on freedom leads to a refusal ever to admit any shortcoming" (1984). How different the pontiff's words are from those of Oskar Pfister (1948) and Roy Lee (1949), two Protestant ministers whose psychological training allowed them to speak in the 1940s of the "neurotic" qualities and the "rubbish" that Christianity teaches about atonement. Following Freud, they insisted that real freedom lay in casting off such baggage.

When it comes to ripping Christianity, especially Catholicism, none of these psychoanalysts/ministers are any match for Raymond L. Lawrence, another sage with dual credentials. In 2007, he published a remarkable book, *Sexual Liberation: The Scandal of Christendom*, the title of which says it all. He's got a stellar resume: Lawrence is Director of Pastoral Care at New York Presbyterian Hospital, Columbia University Medical Center, General Secretary of the College of Pastoral Supervision and Psychotherapy, and Director of Pastoral Care at the New York Council of Churches. And after all that training, what he came up with is equally stellar. Make that astounding.

For Lawrence, not only has "sexual pleasure" been "profoundly devalued" by Christianity, it has been "perversely demonized" (2007, p. xvii). It was the Catholic Church, of course, that did it. By the 4th century, he instructs, the Church had adopted "a sex-phobic Platonist posture toward sexual pleasure" (2007, p. xvii). Nowhere does he commend the sexual reticence that marks Catholic teachings for its commitment to family solidarity and the protection of women. That's because he's too busy speculating on the sexual life of Jesus, and too busy advancing the "Da Vinci Code" (Brown, 2004) hoax: Jesus wasn't celibate, he insists, and indeed he was married to Mary Magdalene.

Like Dan Brown, Lawrence has no evidence to support his claim. What we do know is that Paul the Apostle was celibate, as was John the Baptist, and so were the Essenes—the Jews who produced the Dead Sea Scrolls. None of the Gospel accounts say anything about Jesus being married to anyone, yet Lawrence is prepared to believe the speculative account found in a text written long after the accepted Gospels. Indeed, even Lawrence does not say that the Gnostic gospels held that Jesus and Mary Magdalene married—he simply says they "suggest" it may have happened (2007, p. 1).

It may be asked, "What does this have to do with anything?" Plenty. Lawrence wants the reader to believe that Jesus believed in free love and saw marriage as a control mechanism. Thus did the Catholic Church get it wrong from the get-go. He argues that Jesus "affirmed the joy of sexual pleasure as a gift from God while at the same time being critical of the institutional forms—marriage, for example—by which culture seeks to control sexual behavior." (2007, p. 6).

At the end of his book, Lawrence reveals that the "joy of sexual pleasure" knows no boundaries. He is adamant in his conviction that "the notion that an average 16-year-old boy would be marred for life by a homosexual experience with an adult should be examined with skepticism." Want more? "Man/boy love has never been my cup of tea, but in recent times its harmful effects on personality development have been exaggerated beyond reason or evidence" (2007, p. 147). It would hard to find a more thorough-going defense of child rape than this. Indeed, it reads like a tract published by the North American Man/Boy Love Association. This is reminiscent of the famous words of Paul Shanley, the ex-priest who committed monstrous sex crimes against kids. In 1977, he said that when an adult and a child have sex, "the adult is not the seducer—the kid is the seducer" (Donohue, 2002). Shanley, of course, is in prison. Lawrence is treating patients and advising the faithful.

As mentioned in the beginning, there is nothing inherently anti-Catholic about the discipline of psychology. That it has evolved this way is indisputable. It is time for responsible psychologists, preferably practicing Catholic men and women, to challenge the conventional wisdom and set a new course. In short, psychology needs to be rehabilitated.

References

Adorno, T. W. et al. (1950). *The authoritarian personality.* New York: Harper and Row.

Bartlett, T. (2006, October 20). Professors are more religious than some might assume. *Chronicle of Higher Education.*

Brown, D. (2004). The Da Vinci code. New York: Doubleday.

Capps, D. (2000). *Jesus: A psychological biography.* St. Louis: Chalice Press.

Carroll, M. P. (1986). *The cult of the Virgin Mary: Psychological origins.* Princeton, NJ: Princeton University Press.

Catholic League 2003 annual report on Anti-Catholicism, p. 21.

Cryns, A. G. (1970, Fall). Dogmatism of Catholic clergy. *Journal for the Scientific Study of Religion, 9*, 239-243.

Dart, J. (1985, July 27). Sexual repression theory applied to sightings; Visions of Mary: Hallucinations? *Los Angeles Times, Part 2*, 4.

Davis, C. T. III. (2007). The Qur'an, Muhammad and jihad in context. In J. H. Ellens (Ed.), *The destructive power of religion* . Westport, CT: Praeger.

Donohue, W. (2002, July/August). When guidelines are not enough. *Catalyst.*

Donohue, W. (2006, May). Da Vinci Code peddles lies. *Catalyst.*

Donohue, W. A. (1991, March). Tolerance and consensus. *The World and I.* 541-553.

Ellens, J. H. (2007). *The destructive power of religion.* Westport, CT: Praeger.

Field, F. (1989). Anti-religious bias in psychotherapy: Implications and challenges. [Master's Thesis] University of Victoria.

Field, F. J. (2001, December 1). Psychology II: Religion and psychology. *Catholic Insight,* 31.

Francis, L. J. (2001, Spring). Christianity and dogmatism revisited: A study of fifteen and sixteen year olds in the United Kingdom. *Religious Education.*

Fromm, E. (1955). *The dogma of Christ and other essays.* New York: Holt, Reinhart and Winston.

Gillespie, C. K. (2001). *Psychology and American Catholicism.* New York: Crossroad Publishing Company.

Green, E.C. (2003). *Rethinking AIDS prevention.* Westport, CT: Praeger.

Gross, N., & Simmons, S. (2006, October 5). How religious are America's college and university professors? [Working Paper]

Judge, M. G. (2003, November 23). Recovery: It can be so addicting. *Washington Post,* B1.

Jung, C. (1969a). A psychological approach to the dogma of the Trinity. *The Collected Works, Volume 11* (2nd edition). 107-200.

Jung, C. (1969b). Transformation symbolism in the Mass. *The Collected Works, Volume 11* (2nd edition). 201-296.

Jung, C. (1977). Why I am not a Catholic. *The Collected Works of C. G. Jung. Volume 18.* (R.F.C. Hull, Trans.) Princeton, NJ: Princeton University Press, 645-647.

Lawrence, R. J. Jr. (2007). *Sexual liberation: The scandal of Christendom.* Westport, CT: Praeger.

Lee, R. (1949). *Freud and Christianity.* London: James Clark.

Lehr, E., & Spilka, B. (1989, September) Religion in the introductory psychology textbook: A comparison of three decades. *Journal for the Scientific Study of Religion, 28(3),* 366-371.

Meng, H., & Freud, E. L. (Eds.) (1963). *Psychoanalysis and faith: The letters of Sigmund Freud and Oskar Pfister.* New York: Basic Books.

Menninger, K.A. (1973). *Whatever became of sin?* New York: Hawthorn Books.

Milton, J. (2002). *Malpsychia: humanistic psychology and our discontents.* San Francisco: Encounter Books.

Monroe, K. (1996). *The heart of altruism.* Princeton, NJ: Princeton University Press.

Morella, C. (1997, September 9). Mother Teresa's touch left imprint. *USA Today,* p. 6A.

Morrison, D. (1997, November 7). We are church: It seemed like such a good idea. *Our Sunday Visitor*, p. 21.

Noll, R. (1997, May-June). Jungian psychology as Catholic theology. *St. Catherine Review.*

Oliner, S. & Oliner, P. (1988). *The altruistic personality: Rescuers of Jews in Nazi Europe.* New York: Free Press.

Orsini, J. F. (1994, April 9). Why religion is so despised by America's ruling class. *Washington Times,* p. D2.

Paloutzian, R. F. (1996). *Invitation to the psychology of religion.* (2nd ed.) Needham Heights, MA: Allyn and Bacon.

Paul, P. (2005, May/June). With God as my shrink. *Psychology Today.*

Rempel, M. (1997, Winter). Understanding Freud's philosophy of religion. *Canadian Journal of Psychoanalysis*, 236.

Pfister, O. (1948). *Christianity and fear: A study in history and in the psychology and hygiene of religion.* (W.H. Johnston, Trans.) London: George Allen & Unwin.

Pope John Paul II. (1984, December 2). *Reconciliation and penance.*

Pruyser, P. W. (1991). Narcissism in contemporary religion. In H. N. Maloney & B. Spilka (Eds.), *Religion in Psychodynamic Perspective: the Contributions of Paul W. Pruyser* (pp. 66-82). New York: Oxford University.

Ramirez, M. (2006, July 13). Catholics seek unity at AIDS forum. *Chicago Tribune: Metro*, p. 1.

Ravitch, D. (2003). *The language police.* New York: Alfred A. Knopf.

Rokeach, M. (1960). *The open and closed mind.* New York: Basic Books.

Rokeach, M. (1969). Religious values and social compassion. *Review of Religious Research, 11*, 24-39.

Stark, R. (2003). *For the glory of God.* Princeton, NJ: Princeton University Press.

Stark, R. (2005). *The victory of reason: How Christianity led to freedom, capitalism and western success.* New York: Random House.

Stark, R., Iannaccone, L., & Finke, R. (1996, May). Religion, science and rationality. *American Economic Review, 86(2)*, 433-437.

Stark, R., Iannaccone, L., & Finke, R. (1998, July). Rationality and the "religious mind." *Economic Inquiry.*

Thavis, J. (2003, August 27). Vatican official says stories about Galileo often oversimplified. *Catholic News Service.*

Vitz, P. (1986). *Censorship evidence of bias in our children's textbooks.* Ann Arbor: Servant Publications.

Vitz, P. (1999). *Faith of the fatherless: The psychology of atheism.* Dallas, TX: Spence Publishing Company.

Vitz, P. (2002). *Psychology as religion: The cult of self-worship.* Grand Rapids, MI: William B. Eerdmans Publishing Company.
White, L. (1967). The historical roots of our ecological crisis. *Science*, pp. 1203-1207.
Woods, T. E. Jr. (2005). *How the Catholic Church built western civilization.* Washington, DC: Regnery.
Wulff, D. M. (1997). *Psychology of religion.* (2nd ed.) Hoboken, NJ: John Wiley & Sons.

Chapter 7

Psychology's War on Protestants Is One Size Fits All

Nicholas A. Cummings, Ph.D., Sc.D.
and Janet L. Cummings, Psy.D.

In 2008 the Penn State University *Collegian* (Dooley & Weisler) reported that the Reverend David Arthur Code had filed a religious discrimination complaint with the Pennsylvania Human Relations Commission. Code, an Episcopal minister and graduate student in the Penn State doctoral program in counseling psychology, was educated at Yale, Princeton, and La Sorbonne Universities. Up until the time of his dismissal, he was a straight A student. The Penn State faculty had jumped to the conclusion that he was a "right-wing family values minister," and therefore must be anti-gay and anti-feminist. Ironically, Code is liberal and highly supportive of gay and feminist issues (personal communication). Yet as an Episcopal minister with years experience as a family counselor, he was quickly stereotyped and ordered to desist from all of his ministerial activities, or leave the doctoral program. He refused and was dismissed.

The Reverend Code's "sin" was his work and subsequent publication of research on marriage and parenting in conjunction with a medical school professor (Sherry & Code, 2008). Based on studies now being conducted by neuroscientists, primates are herd animals and if their family structure were to break down, their rapid extinction could be anticipated. There is currently neuroscience research suggesting that the breakdown of the family unit in chimps could pose the same or a similar problem for humans. Science progresses by debate and replication, and an attitude of freedom of inquiry should prevail in science departments in our universities. Has psychology, however, predetermined the outcome of this and similar issues?

How can such a flagrant intrusion into an individual's religious freedom occur on a major American university campus in the 21st century? In a January 2008 article in the *New York Times,* Nicholas Kristoff (2008) writes how, on campuses across America, it has become fashionable to scorn people for their faith. Psychology's war on religion is mainly directed toward Christianity. Buddhism is espoused and renamed "mindfulness." Zen has many adherents within psychology, Hinduism is prominently featured in humanistic psychology, and Islam gets a free pass based on multiculturalism and political correctness. Judaism, for centuries the recipient of widespread anti-Semitism and now bathed in our guilt-ridden memories of the Holocaust, also gets a free pass (see Chapters 2 and 12 this volume). Not so for Christianity, regarded as part of the establishment and therefore exempt from the political correctness which largely benefits disadvantaged minorities. It is the brunt of stereotypy, the hallmark of bias. This chapter will address the plethora of Christian sects, numbering several hundred in the United States alone, with beliefs ranging from "born again" fundamentalism to extreme liberalism, while psychology continues to stereotype Protestants into one-size-fits-all and reacts to them accordingly.

Protestantism: One Size Fits None

There are many shades of thought in the Catholic Church, but this religion has one ultimate authority, the Vatican. Hence its basic tenants are subject to direct attack. Not so for Protestantism. It has literally hundreds of different denominations, each with its own hierarchy and basic tenants which cover the gamut from fundamentalists, evangelicals, moderates (e.g., Methodists, Congregationalists, Episcopalians), to Universalist/Unitarians who are indistinguishable from secular humanism. Attacking Protestantism is like objecting to the color of the rainbow: you pick the one color you dislike and attribute your objection to the entire rainbow.

This colorful panoply we call Protestant is largely an American phenomenon, reflecting our freedom, individualism and diversity, all melding to produce a different denomination to reflect each of our myriads of often only slightly differing religious thought. European countries may have several Protestant faiths residing within their borders, but never to the plethora found in America. Let us look at what is called Protestant in America, noting that a number bearing the appellation appeared centuries after the Protestant Reformation in Europe in the early 1500s and are really not part of that movement and era.

- Protestant refers to the protest toward the centuries of the near religious monopoly of the Catholic Church, a movement that occurred as a part of the European renaissance. It includes the Lutheran Church (Martin Luther) in Germany, Methodist (John Wesley) in England, Presbyterian (John Calvin) in Scotland, and on through such mainstream Protestant denominations as Episcopal, Baptist, Congregational and so forth.

- A number of these have divisions within their own ranks. As two of many examples, the Missouri Synod comprises the more conservative branch of the Lutheran Church just as Southern Baptists are far more fundamentalist and have a different governing structure than their Northern brethren.

- The Roman Catholic and Greek Orthodox religions were the original *one* Christian church with roots in the Middle East and Asia Minor, the so-called "cradle of Christianity." It eventually spread to Rome with the conversion of the Roman emperor Constantine, and a rift leading to separation occurred centuries ago over the infallibility and authority of the Pope, whose office at the beginning was that of the Bishop of Rome. Whereas Catholicism has remained firm in opposing divorce, birth control and abortion, Greek Orthodoxy in America is liberal toward all three. It has retained all of its rituals but has modernized into a more Protestant than Catholic message. It is characterized by full attendance every Sunday while the Catholic mass suffers a sparse attendance, which would be even less were it not for Hispanic immigrants.

- A number of large denominations often included under the rubric Protestant first appeared in America long after the Protestant Reformation. Seventh-day Adventist (Ellen G. White) arose in the 1800s, as did also the Church of Jesus Christ of Latter Day Saints (LDS or Mormon; Joseph Smith and Brigham Young, see Chapter 8 this volume). Jehovah's Witnesses (Judge Rutherford) was a 20th century creation. One must also consider Christian Science (Mary Baker Eddy), founded in the 20th century and grew to enjoy a very large following before it began its recent decline. It should be noted that Christian Science held to the belief that all illness is caused by faulty thinking long before psychology began to explore the connection between stress and physical illness. These and several other established denominations have in common that they are American innovations, but as will be seen below, the similarity stops there.

- The Pentecostal movement certainly has its roots in the early New Testament description of the disciples who were said to be "speaking in tongues." But, as a modern religious thrust, it is markedly an American innovation. It had a remarkable growth during the 1920s, and now the Pentecost faiths, which share much in common, reflect a number of separate entities.

The stereotype of Protestantism shared by many in psychology is that of Sinclair Lewis' *Elmer Gantry,* a 1920s novel portraying a fiery but hypocritical, and perhaps even psychopathic evangelist. This stereotype is fueled, as are all such biases, by the several but exceptional fallen radio and TV evangelists of more recent times. It is surprising and unfortunate that it is necessary to challenge such a stereotype among ostensibly liberal psychologists, but here are a number of other glaring contradictions to the one-size-fits-all mentality.

- Some so-called Protestant faiths have tenants that are more suggestive of Judaism than Christianity. Seventh-day Adventists (SDA) worship on the Jewish Sabbath (Saturday) and, in their diet, observe the Old Testament code of Leviticus that prohibits the eating of pork and all animals that "do not split the hoof and chew the cud." We recently met a Seventh-day Adventist lay minister who has retained his ordination as an Orthodox Jewish Rabbi but who believes in the authenticity of Jesus Christ. When asked why he chose SDA to reflect his Christianity, he replied that he would not have to change his Kosher diet or his day of worship.

- Jehovah's Witnesses subscribe only to the Old Testament and regard Jesus Christ as just another prophet among many. The daily Bible readings expected of all faithful Jehovah's Witnesses generally minimize the importance of the New Testament, thus side-stepping the writings upon which Christianity is founded (i.e., the Four Gospels, Acts of the Apostles, Epistles of St. Paul, Revelations of St. John, etc.)

- Psychology views Protestants as anti-feminist because most sects will not ordain women, yet a number of very large religions were founded by women. Mary Baker Eddy founded Christian Science, Ellen Gould White was the prophet and guiding light of Seventh-day Adventists, and Amy Semple McPherson and her Four Square Gospel was pivotal in Pentecostal growth.

- A number of denominations ordain both women and gays. We have two lesbian minister acquaintances who are married to each other and have separate lesbian and gay congregations. Another lesbian minister of a solely lesbian congregation shared the name Dorothy Cummings, the wife of one author and the mother of the second, whose parishioners often called our home by mistake and were startled into silence when Nicholas Cummings identified himself as Dorothy's husband.

- Some denominations permit same sex marriage vows or ceremonies, and regard homosexual behavior as not only acceptable, but also natural. Although most would not, invariably they teach compassion and acceptance of gays, although they might require abstinence from same sex activity. This latter formality is seldom enforced on a seemingly unwritten don't ask, don't tell policy. In other words, Protestant Churches, despite the bias to the contrary, are not permeated with "Gay Police," and the issue seldom arises without in-your-face confrontation from militant gays.

- An overwhelming number of Protestant denominations, including the evangelicals, are becoming more moderate (Wallis, 2007), and the Elmer Gantry stereotype of hell-fire-and-brimstone is egregiously way off the mark for the vast majority. The theory of evolution is essentially accommodated, birth control is near universal, but faith persists as it has the right to do.

- Because Protestant congregations are becoming more moderate, people who have the need for a stricter gospel either gravitate to the more conservative denominations or splinter off into their own ways. Even a somewhat less-than-mainstream denomination such as Seventh-day Adventist had its David Karesh who led many fellow SDAs to defect into what he termed the Branch Davidians, where they subsequently died in the inferno that destroyed their own compound at the hand of the government forces that surrounded it.

- In spite of the title "Church of Jesus Christ of Latter Day Saints," Mormons are subjected to discrimination by a large number of evangelicals that do not regard them as Christian (see Chapter 8 by Dr. Byrd in this volume).

- It is very difficult to ascertain where the Church of Scientology should fall. In the late 1940s L. Ron Hubbard, a science fiction writer, developed a treatment approach he named Dianetics. Its specially trained practitioners, called "auditors," began to flourish in the early 1950s, two of whom had offices just down the hall in the same medical building in which the senior author of this volume practiced. When Dianetics had difficulty obtaining tax exemption, Hubbard founded the Church of Scientology and qualified it as a tax-exempt church. It is believed that Dianetics is still practiced within Scientology. Though shrouded in some mystery, it is believed by some authorities that Hubbard had been treated, over his objections for a mental illness, and his subsequent enmity accounts for Scientology's strong anti-psychiatric and anti-psychological stances. Movie actor Tom Cruise's famous televised rant is only one example of this hostility.

Many other examples could be given to illustrate the amazingly variant nature of Protestant Christianity, but when one examines its plurality, the mystery is how do militant secular progressives arrive at their stereotype? The answer can only be that it is promulgated and continued as all stereotypes are: on ignorance and bias.

The Politics of Protestantism

For most of the first half of the 20th century Protestant churches lived by the dictum that religion and politics did not mix, and accordingly refrained from direct involvement in the political process (e.g., running for office, promoting and endorsing candidates or political parties). They fiercely participated in the debate over the Scopes "monkey trial" of the 1920s, and certainly this had political overtones, but it stopped far short of attempting to directly influence elections. All this changed circa 1970 when Christianity began to feel attacked by secular forces, particularly the American Civil Liberties Union (ACLU) which seemed bent on removing all semblance of religious symbols and artifacts from public property and national holidays. With a rapidity and intensity that took the political scene by surprise, the Moral Majority, or what secularists like to call the Christian right, became a potent political force that has influenced every national and state election since its launching (Walvin, 2007). So much has this been so, the Democratic Party, which in the recent past has alienated the religious forces, has diligently set out in the 2008 election to make amends by prominently attending churches and courting the religious voter.

Not frequently discussed is why the original U.S. Constitution and its Bill of Rights did not equally apply to women and slaves. It led to the need for Protestantism, and especially the Southern churches, to justify the existence of slavery. They promulgated an egregious, but religious "justification" for slavery, a flawed belief that survived the Civil War and later fueled the separate-but-equal doctrine.

Unto the Children of Noah's Sons

The framers of the United States Constitution were educated men who patterned our republic after the democracy of ancient Greece. Although the ancient Greeks at the time of Pericles were remarkably enlightened, we must remember that self government in ancient Greece was the right of male citizens only; it did not apply to women and slaves. In denying women the vote and in accepting slavery, our constitution codified two profound exceptions to freedom that were thus engraved, and required centuries to rectify. In the meantime, both of these exceptions needed justification, and so-called Biblical scholars rose to the occasion. The belief that women were secondary to men had both a long religious and cultural history and was, therefore, less surprising than the flimsy justification for slavery that emerged, especially after serious opposition gained momentum, first in England and then the United States.

According to the Old Testament book of Genesis, Noah had three sons from whom the entire earth was repopulated after everyone but his family had perished in the flood (Wallis, 2005). These sons, Shem, Ham and Japheth, were ostensibly the progenitors of the Semitic, Negro and Caucasian races. This was the first invention, as Chapter 10 of the Book of Genesis does not make such a specification. The story goes on, in the words of the New King James Version:

> And Noah began to be a farmer, and he planted a vineyard (verse 20). Then he drank of the wine and was drunk, and became uncovered in his tent (verse 21). And Ham, the father of Canaan, saw the nakedness of his father, and told his two brothers outside (verse 22). But Shem and Japheth took a garment, laid it on both of their shoulders, and went backward and covered the nakedness of their father. Their faces were turned away, and they did not see their father's nakedness (verse 23). So Noah awoke from his wine, and knew what his younger son had done to him (verse 24). Then he said:
>
> Cursed be Canaan!
> The lowest of slaves
> will he be to his bothers (verse 25).

From this sketchy genealogy in the Old Testament a quantum leap was made. Ham, through his son Canaan, was the progenitor of the Black race that was cursed to forever be the slave of the white descendants of Japheth (verse 27). The architects of this fallacy do not explain how Shem and Japheth, both white, had a black brother. But then this is the least of the quandaries stemming from a fabrication used from the pulpit for centuries to justify slavery, and then the notion, after their emancipation, that African Americans were inherently inferior to whites.

Again it should be noted that this belief was solely an American invention, conjured to justify an inhuman practice that was flourishing in the southern half of the United States when it had waned world-wide. It never had credence in European Protestantism, and it was never a tenet of either the Roman Catholic or Eastern (Greek) Orthodox Churches. That it survived as long as it did before fading in everyone's memory is a testimonial to the insidiousness of racism.

Protestants, Abolitionists, and the Civil Rights Movement.

Paradoxically, Christianity, and especially Protestant Christianity, was a pivotal force in both the abolition movement of the 18th and 19th centuries, as well as the Civil Rights movement of the 20th century. All of this existed coincidentally with the misapplication of the story of Noah and his three sons, again underlining the fallacy that Protestants are all alike when it comes to basic beliefs.

Notable is the career of William Wilberforce (1759-1833) in England, who was elected to Parliament at an early age, but did not become the leader of the antislavery movement until after his conversion at the age of 28 to evangelical Christianity. An intense reformer, an avid Christian, a fine singer who popularized the hymn "Amazing Grace," and an electrifying public speaker, he worked tirelessly with a group of anti-slave advocates. With the help of his friend Prime Minister William Pitt, he saw the passage of the Slave Trade Act of 1807, forbidding British ships from engaging in slave trafficking. Since British ships were the primary transporters of slaves, this only diminished the slave trade, as some British ship captains ignored the new law, and ships of other nations (including the United States) took up some of the slack. It was not until the Slavery Abolition Act of 1833 resulted in the complete abolition of slavery in the entire British Empire that worldwide slavery appreciably diminished everywhere but the Southern United States (Piper, 2006). This was decades before President Lincoln's Emancipation Proclamation which paved the way for the end of American slavery, but ushered in a prolonged era of segregation and the separate-but-equal doctrine in the South public schools.[1]

The American abolition movement, like its counterpart in Britain which was its inspiration, was in large measure a religious movement of the Protestant churches, especially in the North. "Underground railroads" were created, with a series of "safe houses," that made possible the steady escape of Southern slaves to the North. In these endeavors those who facilitated the escape risked their lives, along with the escapees, as detection of either brought swift reprisal in the South, if not always by the authorities, at least by local militants. It was the religious dedication of northern Protestants that kept the pressure of the American abolition movement until it became the law of the land.

The Civil Rights Movement that began in the 1950s is still fresh in everyone's mind, and the pivotal role of Protestant churches, and especially the black churches, is well known and highly respected (Walvin, 2007). It spawned a generation of African American religious/political leaders from the martyred Martin Luther King, Jr. to the present Rev. Jesse Jackson and Rev. Al Sharpton. It is only at the beginning of the 21st century that we are seeing a new breed of political leadership emerging. The offspring of the Civil Right Movement's accomplishments, it emphasizes going forward and beyond the 1960s monumental achievements with its limitations, and is seen in such figures as President Barack Obama, Juan Williams, and the older but ever-prescient Bill Cosby. The presidential campaign of 2008 exposed the existence of black anger in churches like that of Rev. Jeremiah Wright's Trinity United Church of Christ, and the more subtle white anger that exists in white churches, particularly in the South. It has initiated a dialogue about both white and black anger that has the potential to address insidious racial issues on both sides that, as Obama has said, "... have prevented us from achieving a more perfect union."[2] Again, much of the dialogue will take place at the Protestant pulpit.

Protestants Are Moderating

Catholics may comprise more than a quarter of the U.S. population, but only about a third of Catholics actually practice their faith, according to Robert Royal, president of the Washington, D.C. –based Faith and Reason Institute (Miller, 2008). Other authorities place the number as low as one-fifth if one were to exclude the Hispanic immigrants who are more fervent in their religious observance. This has given rise to the term "cafeteria Catholics," the nominal believers who pick and choose from among the Church's teachings, take ample helpings of what they like, and pass over whatever is not to their liking. (Miller, p.55)[3]

This type of religious moderation is matched by Protestants, but in a much different fashion. The term Roman Catholic denotes one Church with a central authority vested in the Vatican, while in contrast the term Protestant is applicable to an array of separate denominations with a plethora of beliefs, tenets, practices and requirements. Rather than a cafeteria, a Protestant is confronted more by a vast "automobile row" in which denominations are a seemingly endless procession of auto dealerships all displaying their wares in competition with each other. These differing sects are held together by the designation Protestant through a common belief in the divinity of Jesus Christ, a history of having been founded after the Protestant Revolution, and of harboring distaste for Papal authority. Beyond that, the common ground gives way to a variety of greater or lesser differences in manner of worship that is reflective of American's fierce individualism. Thus a Protestant can express moderation or its opposite by gravitating to a church of his/her choosing.

Trends toward moderation.

The instances of moderation in Protestant churches, largely a phenomenon of the past three or four decades, are numerous and only a few representative examples ranging from trivial to important will be included here.

Not long ago in many Protestant churches a divorced person was scorned. Although it seldom rose to the level of expulsion, divorced members were made to feel so uncomfortable that they often chose to leave the church. Today in these same congregations divorce is common and hardly noticed.

Underscoring this change in attitudes toward divorce is the now common sponsorship of singles groups. Startling is the emergence of so-called Christian computer dating that not only underscores the changes in post-divorce dating, but also the actual participation by the church in getting singles members together.

Attitudes toward reproductive issues have changed dramatically. Birth control is no longer an issue. The churches that initially opposed infertility treatments as unethical when they first appeared no longer object to them. Even the churches that strongly oppose abortion choose to look the other way if a member chooses to end her pregnancy because of rape, incest, or a life-threatening condition.

Dancing was once forbidden in many Protestant churches, prompt-ting the old joke that asked why Southern Baptists are opposed to fornication? The answer, "Because it might lead to dancing." Now these same churches sponsor evenings of dancing, especially for their teenagers who otherwise might lose interest in the church.

The status of women in the church has changed dramatically. Several Protestant denominations now ordain women, and of those that do not, the lay ministry is often dominated by women. In large congregations that have several pastors, women lay ministers, although not ordained, attend meetings with the pastors and receive the same salary. In many churches the parish or church council is composed of more women than men.

Equally dramatic is the change in attitudes about homosexuality. Some denominations ordain homosexuals, and even the most conservative congregations accept homosexuals as members. In these latter, the orientation may not be a sin, but the lifestyle would be.

The attitudes toward race have not only changed, but the fabricated Biblical justification of segregation is all but forgotten. The most dramatic change has been by Mormons who now accept African-Americans as members, and no longer imply they are ineligible to go to heaven.

At one time Protestantism was the backbone of the American temperance movement which forbade even the slightest imbibing in alcohol. All but the most conservative Protestant churches now regard moderate drinking as acceptable.

Seemingly trivial is the acceptance of make-up and jewelry by fundamentalist churches that once fiercely forbade it, but it has made a difference in the complexion of the congregation. For example, if one were to attend a Seventh-day Adventist service fifty years ago the women, regardless of how well dressed, reflected the austerity of no make-up or jewelry. In contrast today one would no longer observe such Puritanism.

The Mega-church

Solely an American Protestant phenomenon, the so-called mega-church with as many as 20,000 or more members is now found in most metropolitan areas. Some areas, like Los Angeles or Phoenix, have several. There are no Catholic mega-churches, even though

24% of Americans identify themselves as Catholic. Truly the mega-church is an outgrowth of American Protestantism, and is flourishing.

The mega-church is more than just a congregation; it is an entire community. It not only attends to its members spiritual needs, it also offers an extensive social life for children and adults, psychological and other counseling, educational opportunities, and an atmosphere so complete that, if it were bound by geography, it could be considered a village.

Change versus losing ground.

The *U.S. Religious Landscape Survey* conducted by the Pew Forum on Religion and Public Life (2008) revealed rapid changes that have occurred in just the last two decades in the United States. It was immediately interpreted by the press that religious affiliation is waning, with moderation in belief increasing to the extent that the stricter religions would be catering to smaller numbers. The findings included:

- Nearly 20% of all men and 13% of all women are unaffiliated, as are also 25% of all adults under 30.
- One in ten Americans identify themselves as former Catholics.
- Two-thirds of Americans who grew up in Jehovah's Witness homes have left that faith.
- Nearly three in four Buddhists in America are converts, primarily from Christianity. These Buddhists are equally divided among Zen, Theravadan, and Tibetan schools.
- Major Protestant denominations are losing members rapidly, while only the non-denominational churches are growing.
- Fluidity is the order of the day, with 44% of Americans responding that they have either changed their denomination, or have joined a denomination after having been raised in a non-religious home.

The Pew Foundation released this `report on February 26, 2008, while a second one was released just days later (March 1, 2008). Rather than showing religion is declining, this second report clearly revealed that "astonishing declines in one direction may be replaced by astonishing growth elsewhere" (God's Country, 2008). Here are some of its findings. They confirm what religious scholars have been saying for years, and they contradict conventional wisdom, such as outspoken critics of faith such as Christopher Hitchens (2007), who would say religion in the United States is declining as it has in Europe:

Religions that demand the most of people are growing the fastest. "The mainline Protestant churches—with their less exclusionary views of salvation, looser rules for sexual conduct, and sermons about social justice—have lost membership, especially since the 1990s. The more traditional evangelical churches keep growing" (God's Country, 2008). One third of converts have simply gone from one Protestant congregation to another. The additional statistic, that a third of respondents are married to someone of a different faith, suggests to the Pew researchers that religion has become more a matter of individual conscience than of continuity and tradition.

Evangelical congregations refer to themselves as "inter-denominational" or "non-denominational." Thus the surveys showing that membership in the more liberal, established denominations is declining has been misinterpreted as meaning all Protestantism is declining.

Remarkable is the statistic that half of all Americans who grew up without any religious affiliation adopted one in adulthood. Clearly "...Americans are not giving up serious worship to adopt New Age platitudes" (Pew, p. A8). Eighty-four percent of Americans claim affiliation with one of hundreds of established faiths, a figure that has remained steady for decades.

It bears comment that the remarkable feature of such religious diversity is that it exists in an atmosphere of quiet religious tolerance, where in so many parts of the world differences in faith spark violence and ostracism. America so honors the principle of religious tolerance that it has brought it into the home. The Pew Foundation concludes that the statistics about church-switching may be less a sign of spiritual flakiness than an emblem of freedom. The incidences of religious intolerance come largely from militant secularists, as will be discussed below.

Church historian Diana Butler Bass, in reviewing the Pew survey as well as a number of others that reveal the so-called shifting sands of faith, sums it up. "The Protestant worldview is deep in our political and literary cultures. There's a Protestant ethic of individual conscience that will stick around a while longer, even if people are not identified with a particular faith" (Grossman, p. 78).

This strictly American "Protestant worldview," which began with our nation's founders, has defined America for centuries. It embodies, first and foremost, a religious freedom that has its roots in the Protestant Reformation's rebellion against European government's tyranny and the Catholic Church's oppression of freedom to worship in accordance with one's conscience. With it came a work ethic that was part of our Puritan heritage. In contrast to medieval distrust of science, it promoted freedom of scientific inquiry beginning with Harvard College and every institution of higher learning that came thereafter. The religious prohibition of the dissection of cadavers in medical schools was not only defied, but the authorities were lax in its enforcement. Visit, for example, the original buildings at Johns Hopkins University. Baltimore in colonial days had a somewhat greater Catholic influence and the anti-cadaver laws were more likely to be enforced. The benches upon which the medical students sat had wooden lids that swung open to hide the cadavers on the rare occasions that the police made their loudly heralded, but infrequent raids. No cadavers were ever found, no students or professors were ever arrested.

This sense of freedom pervaded business, encouraging the rise of capitalism far beyond what Adam Smith had ever envisaged. It is not surprising that entrepreneurship is largely an American institution that is not only the envy of the world, but has been imported by such diverse emerging countries as India, Malaysia and the Arab Emirates. It has been espoused paradoxically by the Chinese Communists who, in just one generation, have lifted their nation out of going-nowhere socialism to vibrant capitalism. The shaping of America by a Protestant ethic codified in our Constitution and its Bill of Rights has fascinated scholars and economists, alike (Wills, 2007; Keller, 2008).

Secularism, Religious Intolerance, and Psychology

A recently published cartoon portrayed the secularist, or even relativist view of religion and spirituality.[4] It shows a determined but exhausted longhaired, bearded man on a treadmill, feverishly but ineffectively walking with hiking stick in hand toward a sign pointing ahead and reading "Truth." That secularists, and particularly militant atheists, vigorously point only to the negative aspects of religion, which certainly exist, is an attitude that seems to permeate most of American psychology.

Protestants, and particularly evangelicals, are content to practice their own religion, attending to matters of worship within their own faith. They remain comfortably tolerant of religious diversity, and would remain content if it were not for the incessant attacks from the militant secularists in our society who seem determined to remove all signs of faith from our culture. For example, they are willing to share Christmas trees and manger scenes in the public square with menorahs, Islamic symbols, or any other faith, but are aroused to battle when the ACLU or other secular forces attempt to eradicate all signs of worship from the public scene. They are incensed when public schools are allowed to teach the meaning of Ramadan, but not Easter. Rabbi Aryeh Spero (2002) has dubbed these attacks on Christmas, Hanukah, Easter, etc. as the "seasonal hostility virus." In essence, the secular-religious war is constantly fueled mostly by one side that seems determined that religious tolerance means absence of religion. In fact, were it not for Protestants being attacked, today there would be no Moral Majority, Judicial Watch, or "Christian right."

The main flashpoints, not necessarily in order of importance, are (1) creationism, (2) abortion, (3) pornography, (4) gay marriage, (5) religious symbols in government buildings or public areas, and (6) and the right of students not be ridiculed or scorned for their faith by teachers or professors. The APA has weighed in with a number of proclamations that have been more disputatious than authoritative, and because the public has essentially ignored them, they have not been effective. Nonetheless, they have had the effect of convincing the American public that psychology is inhospitable —if not hostile—toward religion, and has contributed to the decline of psychotherapy because many Americans are wary that their faith will not be respected in the treatment process.

Creationism. Most Protestant sects have long ago accommodated to the scientific evidences of evolution, and only the most fundamentalist sects adhere to a literal 6-day creation of the universe. Intelligent design, compatible with the thinking of many scientists, including Albert Einstein (DeWall), has every right to be part of our dialogue. However, after several proclamations denouncing the teaching of creationism, in 2007 the APA proclaimed that intelligent design should be included in its list of prohibitions. This has had an immediate alienating effect, as well as discouraging an open dialogue within psychology. Religion as a universal phenomenon should be an intense province of inquiry and research by psychologists, but this has been inhibited by antireligious bias within the profession (Dembski, 1999).

Abortion. This is an area that would have been settled long ago were not each extreme side so unyielding. Religious Protestants are rankled by such stances as: the refusal to ban late term abortion; giving teenage girls access to abortion without parental knowledge or consent; refusal to include the teaching of abstinence as one way of reducing teenage pregnancy or the spread of sexually transmitted diseases; distribution of condoms instead; banning pre-abortion counseling or offering adoption as an alternative; and the insistence on taxpayer supported abortion. Were it not for this political militancy, most Protestants would decide the issue for themselves, and accord all other adult women the freedom to make a personal choice. Much of the contentiousness stems from the fact that well-funded organizations on both extremes owe their existence to continuing the battle. The APA has strongly supported a women's right to choose in a number of press releases or proclamations, and unfortunately has inhibited research into the psychological implications of ending a pregnancy in such instances where a woman goes against her own religious convictions, learns later in life that she is infertile and cannot again become pregnant, or otherwise suffers from a later onset of guilt-ridden depression.

Pornography has grown to where it has engulfed the internet. The APA has issued no proclamations on the subject, but through the years has demonstrated a liberal stance, regarding pornography as freedom of speech, and implying it is harmless without encouraging or sponsoring research on its possible deleterious effects, especially on children.

Gay marriage is one of the most militant stances within the APA, strongly implying that anyone who might be in opposition is homophobic. Culturally, marriage has been defined as a union between a man and a woman for thousands of years and in every civilization. Most Americans don't care with whom one wants to mate, but want to preserve the traditional institution of marriage. We are convinced that had gay militants accepted civil unions with all the rights of marriage (i.e., all but the name), Protestant opposition would have quickly ameliorated. The issue is complicated by militant gays who insist on marriage or nothing, and after so much militancy many people who are sympathetic with gay rights but wish to preserve the institution of marriage are now suspicious that civil union is a sneaky way of opening the door to gay marriage.

Eradicating faith from government buildings and public areas baffles most Americans who see it as a total waste of time. One only needs visit the Washington Monument, Lincoln and Jefferson Memorials, and scores of public buildings throughout Washington to realize that our founders believed our government was "endowed by our Creator." Just enter the building of the Supreme Court, which is the ultimate determiner of separation of church and state. Prominently displayed are the Ten Commandments. Most Americans regard this as part of our heritage, history and culture, and see no infringement of government on religion. Separation of church and state means to them freedom to worship as they please, not the removal of "in God we Trust" from our currency or "under God" in our Pledge of Allegiance. Thus, they regard these attacks by secular progressives as irrelevant, irritating and unnecessary. The APA has not officially weighed-in on the subject, but throughout publications such as the *Monitor on Psychology,* it is obviously sympathetic to the eradicators.

The rights of religious students to be free of scorn for their faith is not an issue the APA would openly oppose. However, of all the complaints filed against egregious professors who have belittled students for their faith, not a single one resulted in reprimand or sanction. On the other hand, racist or sexist attitudes on the part of professors are swiftly addressed and punished. Most appalling is the lack of action toward offending doctoral programs that are APA approved, such as that of the expulsion of Rev. David Code by Penn State University's doctoral counseling program.

Faith versus Science

In all facets of science, from physics to psychology, repeatedly it is stated that science is the most reliable form of knowledge because it is based on testable hypotheses. Religion, on the other hand, is based on faith. Until rather recently the laws of physics, upon which all science is based, have been regarded as immutable and off limits. According to this traditional view, the job of the scientist is to discover the laws and apply them, not inquire into their provenance. In recent years, however, this mood has shifted considerably (Davies, 2007a), particularly as biologists inquire into the emergence of life in the universe and astrophysicists realize that these laws vary from place to place on a mega-cosmic scale. Paul Davies, the director of Beyond, a research center at Arizona State University, likened them less to immutable laws and more to "local bylaws" as they vary in the cosmos, yielding a "multiverse theory." He goes on to state (Davies, 2007b, pp. 3, 4):

> Isaac Newton first got the idea of absolute, universal, perfect, laws from the Christian doctrine that God created the world in a rational way. Christians envisage God as upholding the natural order from beyond the universe, while physicists think of laws as inhabiting an abstract transcendent realm of perfect mathematical relationships.

As seen in a previous chapter, Albert Einstein himself questioned the ability of pure science to answer this fundamental question of how these laws came to be and how they can differ in the cosmos (Isaacson, 2007). Although not a deist who believed in a personal God, Einstein left open the question of an intelligent force designing these laws. As hard scientists enlarge and continue this debate, some in the APA, representing a soft science at best, would attempt to close it by proclaiming that intelligent design should be banned in the schools and colleges—a stand both unfortunate and embarrassing.

Some Beginnings in Psychology

Flickers of progress toward understanding the ubiquitous need by humans for religious explanation, or its reaction formation perhaps revealed in a compelling need to reject religion, have begun to be seen in research psychology. Reported in previous chapters is that this need may have an evolutionary explanation and has been adaptive. Also reported in a previous chapter is the research showing the deleterious effect of the early sexualization of girls, a subject that heretofore had been taboo because of its resemblance to a long-standing religious view favoring chastity.

Now comes a recently reported psychological research that suggests religion is a source of hope. DeWall and Baumeister (2008) seeded the minds of undergraduate subjects with thoughts of their own mortality by asking them to contemplate their own death. In the meantime, another group of undergraduates were asked to contemplate pain rather than death, by imagining excruciatingly painful, but not fatal, dental procedures. Then the researchers asked both groups to play simple word games. It was found that the mortality-hounded students were more apt to select cheerier words than the students who were asked to contemplate painful dental drilling and other non-fatal procedures. For example, a mortality-haunted student was more likely to turn the prompt "jo" into joy rather than job. The investigators concluded that the unconscious mind automatically copes with the prospect of death through a kind of "psychological immune system" that is like a built in mechanism isolating and neutralizing the memories and threat of death. These results defied the students' own intuitions inasmuch as none of them thought the contemplation of their own ultimate demise would invoke an unconscious need to always look on the brighter side of life. The speculation, of course, is that throughout the millennia primitive and advancing cultures survived insecurity by invoking religious beliefs that went beyond death, such as a life hereafter.

Summary and Conclusions

Christianity is the main object of psychology's war on religion, with Judaism less in the cross hairs as it can engender accusations of anti-Semitism. With Catholicism, the church is criticized for its bygone activities, such as the suppression of science (e.g., Galileo) or the Spanish Inquisition, incidents that took place centuries ago. The implication is that the Catholic Church is still doing these things; therefore we need tenure for university faculties and other safeguards to protect against religious incursion or even persecution. As disputatious as this argument is, it pales in comparison to the absurdity of viewing the Protestant faiths and their over 250 separate denominations, which range from strict fundamentalism to a social gospel, as one unitary monolith. The Protestant churches would politically still be a sleeping giant engrossed in religious issues within its own particular sect had not it felt suddenly attacked and even persecuted by secular progressive forces. Perceptions of Protestantism curtailing the freedom to not believe are based on bygone days, just as they are in the centuries-old and no longer existent practices of Catholicism. If there was a religious war by Protestants, it essentially was directed toward Catholicism and reflected a deep-seated distrust of Papal authority, a hangover of the Protestant Reformation. It should also be noted in all of this that Islam is treated as a cultural phenomenon and gets a free pass on the religious debate, thanks to misapplied multiculturalism and political correctness.

American psychology has revealed its anti-religious bias in a series of gratuitous proclamations that inhibit and even suppress open research into questions of faith, paramount of which is the fact that religion has been universal in every known civilization. Whether there is a human need to protect against fears of mortality and vulnerability, as well as a drive to explain the otherwise inexplicable, religion is ubiquitous and fulfills needs that need to be explored by psychology. In all of this, serious inquiry is stymied by psychology's hostility toward religion, fueled in part by the strong gay movement in psychology that regards Christianity as a threat to gay and lesbian civil liberties.

Psychology is beginning to explore the ubiquitous nature of faith as possibly being an adaptive response with genetic implications. This is in keeping with its obligation to understand human behavior, not prejudge it.

End Notes

[1] Of interest also are the following: Belmonte, K. (2002). *Hero for humanity: A biography of William Wilberforce.* London: Navpress. Also: Henell, M. (1950), *William Wilberforce, 1759-1 833, the liberator of the Slave.* London: Church Book Room. And also Metaxas, E. (2007), *Amazing grace: William Wilberforce and the heroic campaign to end slavery.* New York: Harper.

[2] Barack Obama's speech in March 2008 following the fall-out from his twenty year relationship with Rev. Jeremiah Wright, former pastor of the Trinity United Church of Christ (not connected with the national sect named Church of Christ) was widely covered in the media. Lost in the heat of a highly political and volatile presidential campaign were his comments on the need to reconcile both black *and* white anger. This important, but largely avoided point will doubtlessly be revisited once the partisanship of the presidential campaign subsides. He essentially opened for dialogue undercurrents that have been largely avoided in our national debate because of the sensitivity to the question of race.

[3] Miller's "The last great crusade" was written in anticipation of the April 20, 2008 celebration in Yankee Stadium by Pope Benedict XVI, and outlines the many challenges confronting the Roman Catholic Church.

[4] The cartoon appeared in the Comments section of *Forbes,* February 11. 2008, p. 22.

References

Davies, P. (2007a). *Cosmic jackpot: Why our universe is just right for life.* Phoenix: Arizona State University Press.

Davies, P. (2007b, November 24). Taking science on faith. *New York Times*, Op-ed, pp. 3-4.

Dembski, W. A. (1999). *Intelligent Design: The bridge between science and religion.* Downers Grove, IL: Inter Varsity Press.

DeWall, C. N. & Baumeister, R. F. (2008, March). From terror to joy: Automatically turning to positive affective information following mortality salience. *Psychological Science,* as reported in *The Atlantic, 301(2),* 32.

Dooley, T. & Weisler, A. (2008, January 25). Rev. files complaint. *The Daily Collegian Online.* Retrieved from http://www.collegian.psu.edu/archive/2008/01/25/rev_files_complaint.aspx

God's Country. (2008, March 1). *Wall Street Journal.* A8.

Grossman, C. L. (2008, February 26). Shifting sands of faith. *USA Today,* pp. 6B-7B.

Hitchens, C. (2007). *God is not great.* New York: Twelve (Hachette Book Group)

Isaacson, W. (2007). *Einstein: His life and universe.* New York: Simon and Schuster.

Keller, T. (2008). *The reason for god.* New York: Dutton (Penguin Group).

Kristof, N. D. (2008, February 3). Evangelicals a liberal can love. *New York Times.* Retrieved from http://www.nytimes.com/2008/02/03/opinion/03kristof.html ?em8ex=

Miller, B. (2008, April). The last great crusade. *NewsMax.* 52-63.

Pew Forum (2008). *U.S. Religious Landscape Survey.* Pew Forum on Religion and Public Life. Retrieved from www.PewForum.org.

Piper, P. (2006). *Amazing grace in the life of William Wilberforce.* Wheaton, IL: Crossways Books.

Sherry, D. & Code, D. (2008, January 21). Put kids in their place, for good. *Philadelphia Inquirer.* Retrieved from http://www.philly.com/philly/opinion/20080121_Put_kids_in_their_place__for_good.html

Spero, Rabbi A. (2002, December 25). Seasonal hostility virus. *Washington Times*. 6.
Wallis, J. (2005). *God's politics*. San Francisco: HarperCollins).
Walvin, J. (2007). *A short history of slavery*. London: Penguin.
Wills, G. (2007). *Head and heart: American Christianities*. New York: Penguin.

Chapter 8

Psychology's Assault on Religion: A Case for Mormonism

A. Dean Byrd, Ph.D.

"It is a fly-on-the wall account of how the Mormon religion completely takes over lives... 'the Church is a corporation ... with no heart'... It is a must-see film for any psychologist interested in mind control, brainwashing, and self-esteem issues."

—Sponsored by APA Ad Hoc Committee on Film and Other Media APA National Convention held in Hawaii, 2004 (APA, July 2004)

Introduction

What do Congressmen Harry Reid, Gordon Smith, Orrin Hatch, Bob Bennett, Chris Cannon, Rob Bishop, presidential candidate and former Massachusetts governor Mitt Romney, NFL superstar

Steve Young, hotel magnate J. Willard Marriott, journalist Jayne Clayson, author Orson Scott Card, entertainers Donny and Marie Osmond, and megastar Gladys Knight have in common with the real Dennis the Menace (Jay North) and 13 million other people? They are members of The Church of Jesus Christ of Latter-day Saints (also referred to as the LDS Church or the Mormon Church).

What else do these millions of people have in common? The American Psychological Association (APA) has declared them all members of a church that is a corporation with no heart, and has indicated that their faith tradition is characterized by mind control and brainwashing.

When? In APA's official convention program, specifically sponsored by the APA Ad Hoc Committee on Films and Other Media, in Hawaii on July 31, 2004. The offensive language was included in the written description of a film that was shown during the convention (APA, July 2004).

It is hard to believe that the largest national organization of doctoral level mental health professionals would engage in such actions of blatant religious bigotry. Even more alarming are the responses of APA when confronted by its Mormon membership.

Shortly after the APA-sponsored program aired, APA member and church member Dr. Gary L. Groom sent a letter to Diane F. Halpern, APA President, in which he indicated that he was seriously considered resigning from APA, comparing the libelous language in this APA-sponsored film to the prejudices of the KKK.

In his letter to Dr. Halpern, Dr. Groom concluded, "With the endorsement of APA perhaps hundreds of uninformed college and university teachers during the next few semesters will show this film under the guise of psychological science and spread such prejudice to hundreds of thousands of students." (Groom, August, 2004)

Dr. Groom further noted the irony in this particular APA convention which "incorporated the inclusive Hawaiian spirit including rituals, prayers and suggestions of reaching up to a 'higher power' and drawing closer to others." He concluded that "the ad hoc Committee's choice to feature the anti-Mormon film was a decidedly sour note in an otherwise harmonious conference."

More surprising than the endorsement of this film by APA was Dr. Halpern's patronizing letter to Dr. Groom with its concluding last sentence: "I do not know what was depicted in the film and I cannot promise a satisfactory outcome, but I do appreciate that you wrote about your dissatisfaction" (Halpern, August 2004). Concern over religious bigotry is simply viewed as dissatisfaction?

Where is her outrage? Where is Dr. Halpern's consistency with her voiced concern about "Prejudice in Any Language?" Would her response have been any different had this been an anti-gay film?

Dissatisfied with APA's response to this egregious action, Dr. Groom solicited the help of Dr. Chauncey S. Adams, APA member and fellow Mormon. Dr. Adams wrote a five-page letter to Dr. Halpern indicating that "conference attendees were misinformed with prejudicial material," and strongly urged APA to contact conference attendees and "make an official response to this mistake" (Adams, September 2004).

Further response to Drs. Groom and Adams added insult to injury.

Dr. Michael L. Haley, Chair of the Board of Convention Affairs (BCA), responded in a letter to Dr. Groom, "BCA is always interested in feedback, both positive and critical. ... Your comments and concerns have highlighted a significant omission that we are now taking steps to correct."

Dr. Haley further informed Drs. Groom and Adams that the Ad Hoc Committee previews each film and chooses the films to be shown at the convention. Then incredulously, Dr. Haley notes, "What your letter has highlighted is the omission of a disclaimer statement (Hayley, September, 2004).

In essence, Dr. Haley offers no apology for the religious bigotry portrayed in the film but rather regrets the omission of a "disclaimer." How can one sponsor and disclaim a film at the same time? One could make an argument that Dr. Haley cares more about covering the APA's liability than he does about the lasting effects of prejudice, bigotry and discrimination on a minority group.

After several more letters, Dr. Halpern invited Dr. Groom to prepare a 300-word letter to be published in APA's Monitor on Psychology (Halpern, November 2004). A 300-word letter was ostensibly adequate to address the religious bigotry of APA?

Drs. Groom and Adams, dismayed and dissatisfied with APA's responses, began a Web site, www.biasfire.com, which included information and exchanges regarding this appalling ordeal.[1]

The response from the local media and the Utah Psychological Association (UPA) was swift.

Dr. Stephen B. Morris, former UPA president, stated,

> I am frankly appalled by the APA's tepid and patronizing response to the concerns, which I fully share. Nothing less than a published apology by the APA will begin to be sufficient. I believe we also have a right to know who is/are directly responsible for the inclusion of the damaging language in the convention program (Morris, 2005).

Dr. Debbie Quackenbush, UPA Board member noted, "I have reviewed most everything on the biasfire site and perhaps have not reviewed enough but have to admit that APA seems pretty dismissive. Do they not think that Mormons represent a large enough group of people to be more responsive?"(Quackenbush, 2005).

Dr. Tom Wallace, UPA president-elect, concluded:

> I don't believe most psychologists want to pay dues to a professional organization to promote or degrade individual beliefs, or to promote the biases of those who are in the driver's seat at the time. Most of us are intelligent people who don't need people who are afraid of Jews or Mormons or Baptists or Catholics or whatever, doing our thinking for us, just because they are in an influential APA position to do so.

He further noted,

> I just read the www.biasfire.com link to the APA program. How did something like that get into print?! For an organization that promotes diversity and better understanding of minority groups, they blew that one, didn't they!!! That document must have been edited several times. How did it get through, unless APA does have an ax to grind with the Mormons (Wallace, 2005).

Dr. David Ranks, another Utah psychologist, offered the following:

> I think the BEST thing for APA to do is send a letter to all members with an official apology, a statement that this film and the actions of the committee that put the introduction in the program do not represent the views of APA, and that such bias and attack on any specific group is harmful to all and a violation of APA ethics (Ranks, 2005).

The local *Deseret News* carried the story as the leadership of the Utah Psychological Association attempted to resolve the issues. Reporter Carrie A. Moore headlined the news article, "Psychology group calms Utahns over film on LDS. Film claims church methods were like 'brainwashing'"(Moore, 2005).

APA's response to its Utah membership? Not much until an official delegation of UPA leadership (8 members: Past-President Janet Warburton, President-elect Tom Wallace, Great Divide Chair Mark Owens, Diversity Chair Janiece Pompa, Federal Advocacy Coordinator Chris Wehl, APA Council Representative Nanci Klein, President Cheri Reynolds, and Past-President Stephen Morris), traveled to Washington, D.C., and met with APA President Ron Levant, CEO Norman Anderson, and President-elect Gerald Koocher.

According to UPA President Cheri Reynolds, APA agreed to do the following:

1. Write a retraction regarding the film's introduction—they will disavow any connection between the introduction and APA.
2. Write an apology to be distributed through the listserv and the APA Monitor.
3. Review their process of reviewing material printed in APA programs, bulletins, etc.
4. And, most importantly, they volunteered to visit Utah, speak with psychologists, and participate in our Great Divide Program (Reynolds, 2005).

The following statement appeared on page iii of the 113th Annual Convention Program, held in Washington, D. C., August 18–21, 2005:

> The Board of Directors of the American Psychological Association (APA) wishes to apologize for the offensive description of the Church of Jesus Christ of Latter-day Saints that appeared in the 2004 APA Convention Program describing a film that was shown during that meeting. The Board rejects the characterization of the Church used in the program and regrets any harm this caused. The language used in the film's description does not in any way reflect the policies of the Association. In response to this unfortunate occurrence, APA is taking steps to protect against the use of offensive language in the convention program in the future and, more generally, is working to ensure openness to religious diversity throughout the Association (APA, August, 2005).

So after 10 months, numerous letters from APA members, the creation of a bias-free website and a visit from a UPA delegation, the APA finally offers a letter of apology. It is interesting that the APA offers no condemnation of the film, and offers no apology to the Church.

The Board "regrets" and "rejects," but does not condemn religious bigotry.

The Board indeed wants to "protect against the use of offensive language" and wants to "ensure openness to religious diversity." But when does the Board condemn religious bigotry as it has repeatedly condemned anti-gay bigotry?

The APA's assault on the LDS Church is not limited to this incident but rather can be found in the history of its antagonism toward the Church and the Church's theology. Such antagonism has served to perpetuate myths about the LDS Church and the beliefs of its members. Such myths include the erroneous belief that the LDS Church is a cult. To the contrary, the LDS Church is a worldwide religion with nearly 13 million members, more than half of whom live outside the United States (Watson, 2007). Other myths include:

1. **The Church subjugates women.** Church doctrine values the complementary nature of men and women. Indeed, men and women cannot receive the blessings of heaven unless they are "together and equally"(Nelson, 1999). From the earliest days, both men and women participated in church matters when presented to the membership for vote (Smith & Thomas, 1992) In fact, Utah was the third state with equal voting rights for women to join the Union (Madsen, 1992)!

2. **Mormons are not Christian.** This myth carries with it a kind of irony because the official name of the church is The Church of Jesus Christ of Latter-day Saints. Jesus Christ is center stage of all that which Mormons believe including the belief that all things are predicated on the atonement of Jesus Christ, the Savior of the world.

3. **Mormons are racist.** There was a time in Mormon history where the priesthood was not extended to men of color. That practice is no longer in place and the priesthood is now extended to any worthy male, regardless of race (Kimball, 1978).

4. **Mormons practice polygamy.** Polygamy was practiced for a time in Mormon history. The practice was not so dissimilar to the patriarchs of biblical times. The practice was abandoned in 1890 by official declaration (Davis, 1992).

5. **Mormons do not believe in the Bible.** Mormons fully embrace the Bible, both Old and New Testament as holy scripture. They also include the Book of Mormon, the Doctrine and Covenants as well as the Pearl of Great Price. Together these scriptures provide a witness that Jesus is the Christ, the Son of God.

6. **Mormons vote as a block as directed by the Church leaders.** The Church does not endorse any political candidate but rather members are encouraged to study the issues and to fully participate in the political process as citizens.

7. **Mormons do not practice birth control.** Having children is

considered a highly personal and sacred matter. The Church takes no position on birth control. Members of the Church are advised to make such decisions jointly as husband and wife. Elective abortion is condemned.

8. **Mormons do not allow divorce.** The Church encourages healthy marriages and healthy families. Divorce is viewed as a last resort, when all other efforts have failed. But the Church does recognize divorce.

9. **Mormon temples are used for secret rituals.** Mormon temples are considered sacred edifices where ordinances are performed that are important to families. Such sacred ordinances as eternal marriages and sacred sealings unite families not only in this life but in the eternities.

   It is perhaps worthy to note that the Mormon sense of family, community and life-style has been the subject of much research. The emphasis on family and healthy living through a health code that precludes the use of alcohol, tobacco, coffee, tea and elicit drugs has been associated with longer and healthier lifespans. For example, practicing Mormons have one of the lowest death rates from cancer and coronary heart disease—about half that of the general population (Enstrom, 1989).

Such myths perpetuated by the the APA's antagonism to the Church and its doctrines can be readily found in APA's activities regarding the Church's moral positions on a number of issues including the Equal Rights Amendment, Footnote 4, abortion, human sexuality, and the traditional family among many others.

In all of the issues noted below, not only were the APA's attacks blatant, they were in direct violation of the APA's own policies. In all cases, the APA has falsely presented as "scientific" positions, statements where it has no more expertise than the average citizen. The evidence below speaks for itself.

APA's Political Prostitutes Assault Mormonism: Support of the Equal Rights Amendment

The APA's support of the Equal Rights Amendment (ERA) was a direct violation of the Leona Tyler Principle, which had been fully embraced by APA and never rescinded. The principle, offered by APA President Leona Tyler in 1973 mandated that when psychologists are speaking as psychologists, their "advocacy should be based on scientific data and demonstrable professional experience. Absent such validation, psychologists are free to speak as any concerned citizen, either as individuals or collectively" (Wright & Cummings, 2005).

What's even more astonishing is the admission by the APA that it had no data, no research, and no science to justify its position on the ERA. And yet the APA, as a scientific organization, knowingly took a political position, claiming justification.

Clearly stated in its own publication, the APA concludes, "Psychological theories and research should have no bearing upon the desirability of the Equal Rights Amendment, which is a matter of human rights rather than of scientific fact." The APA admits their position has no scientific foundation but still "resolves to support the passage of the Equal Rights Amendment" (Wright & Cummings, 2005).

So in this instance the APA, which has repeatedly attempted to define itself as a scientific organization, knowingly took a position for which it has no expertise? Perhaps some would characterize this as "not guilty by reason of insanity." A better characterization might be "guilty but insane!" A scientific organization knowingly takes a political, non-scientific position on an issue having nothing to do with its science or expertise?

To further add to this political insanity, the APA extended an invitation to Sonia Johnson, Mormon dissident, to present a paper at its annual meeting in New York City in 1979. The title of her delivered paper was "Patriarchal Panic: Sexual Politics in the Mormon Church," which can only be characterized as a gross misrepresentation of the Church's actual position, tainted with radical feminist rhetoric.

Consider the following descriptions of the Church and its alleged actions from Johnson's delivered address:

1. "Saturated as it is with the anti-female bias that is patriarchy's very definition and reason for being ..."
2. "covert and oppressive activity....murky political activities of the political purposes.
3. "the recent profound disenfranchisement of Mormon women by Church leaders."
4. "mass renunciation of individual conscience"
5. "covert activity"
6. "the usual trick of enlisting women to carry out men's oppressive measures against women, hiding the identity of the real oppressors and alienating women from each other."
7. "Encyclicals from the Brethren....seriously harmed women's self-esteem, lowered our status, made us bootlickers and toadies to the men of the Church" (Benson, 2005).

Johnson's rhetoric continued in this political speech under the banner of the APA with no invitation from the Church or APA members who were members of the Mormon faith to respond. There was no dialogue, no panel discussion, and no exchange.

One could reasonably interpret the APA's sponsorship of Johnson, a nonscientist, to address a non-scientific issue (for which APA has no expertise) attacking a faith tradition, as an example of support for religious bigotry and religious discrimination. Certainly, the sponsorship of such individuals does not bode well for the APA's commitment to religious diversity.

The APA should have known and should have acknowledged that the LDS Church takes very few stands or positions on public issues. (LDS Church history demonstrates that this is the case.) The exceptions are those topics that involve moral issues on which the Church is compelled by its doctrine to speak out. The Church makes very few position statements and does not endorse political candidates. Members of the Church, however, are encouraged to speak out in the public forum as citizens. In fact, a parallel version of the Leona Tyler Principle is operative in the Mormon Church. "It is customary for the Church at each national election to issue a letter to be read to all congregations encouraging its members to vote, but emphasizing the Church's neutrality in partisan political matters" (italics added) (LDS Newsroom, 2007). Perhaps APA could learn from this practice.

The Church indeed opposed the ERA—on moral grounds. Consider the Church's reasons for opposing the passage of the ERA:

> While the motives of its supporters may be praiseworthy, ERA as a blanket attempt to help women could indeed bring them far more restraints and repressions. We fear it will even stifle many God-given feminine instincts. It would strike at the family, humankind's basic institution. ERA would bring ambiguity and possibly invite extensive litigation. Passage of ERA, some legal authorities contend, would nullify many accumulated benefits to women in present statutes. We recognize men and women as equally important before the Lord, but with differences biologically, emotionally, and in other ways. ERA, we believe, does not recognize these differences. There are better means for giving women, and men, the rights they deserve (First Presidency, 1976).

In fact, the Church provided a 20-page question-and-answer insert in the *Ensign* (the Church's official magazine) of March, 1980, carefully explaining the morality of the Equal Rights Amendment and why the Church was taking its position. The Church's reasoning focused on gender complementarity and the importance of mothers and fathers to the healthy development of children, and the potential dangers of misguided radical feminism, positions that interestingly find much support in the scientific literature. In fact, there is no better summary of this research than Christina Sommers' book titled *The War Against Boys* (2001).

The Mormon Church did not oppose equal rights for women. Rather, it objected to the ERA as a vehicle for doing so (as apparently did enough Americans to prevent ratification). In fact, the Church's stated position and accompanying reasons reflected a greater understanding of the science than did APA! Is it too late for APA to issue an apology to the Mormon Church for religious discrimination regarding this issue? If it took 10 months for APA to "remedy" its endorsement of a film supporting religious bigotry, one wonders how long it might take to remedy its endorsement of a symposium that supports such religious bigotry?

Proposal to Eliminate Footnote 4: An Attempt to Remove APA Accreditation from Church-owned Brigham Young University?

The APA is recognized by the federal government as the only accrediting agency for psychology programs in the United States, and the Secretary of Education lists APA accordingly. APA-accredited programs ostensibly certify that the graduates of such programs meet high standards. Historically, the APA, in its accrediting process, has assessed a particular category known as Domain D: Cultural and Individual Differences and Diversity (The Becket Fund, 2001a).

In this regard, the APA has always recognized that religious institutions, in order to support their missions, could give preference to those who share their religious views. Footnote 4 specifically allowed accreditation of programs "having a religious affiliation or purpose ... so long as public notice of these policies have been made and the policies do not contravene the intent of other relevant portions of this document or the concept of academic freedom" (APA Guidelines).

In February, 2001, APA published a notice of proposed changes in the Guidelines and Principles for Accreditation of Programs in Professional Psychology, which included the elimination of Footnote 4.

The Becket Fund for Religious Liberty took the lead in inviting academic institutions in the United States to express strong opposition to the elimination of Footnote 4 during the comment period. The Becket Fund viewed the proposed elimination as an attack on religious autonomy that would tear down the wall of separation between church and state and require schools to ignore the faith perspective of their students and faculty, as well as those whom their graduates will counsel as psychologists.

The illegality of this effort to remove Footnote 4 was succinctly noted by the Becket Fund as they cited case after case where this elimination would discriminate against colleges and universities whose hiring, admission standards, and educational mission are based in part on faith requirements. The attorneys for the Becket Fund clearly noted that the Free Exercise Clause of the First Amendment and the Equal Protection Clause of the Fourteenth Amendment strictly prohibit discrimination based on religious belief or exercise, as well as burdens upon that exercise. This Free Speech Clause also forbids discrimination against religious speech, viewpoints, and associations. Additionally, the constitutional and statutory laws of many individual states also forbid such behavior by APA (The Becket Fund, 2001b).

In the end, APA decided to leave Footnote 4 alone, for now. The Committee on Accreditation (COA) conceded to the analysis of the Becket Fund and noted that it "considered recent Supreme Court decisions that showed an increased deference to First Amendment interests over anti-discrimination statutes and the Committee's role as an accrediting body recognized by the U. S. Department of Education" (The Becket Fund, 2005).

But what really persuaded the COA? Perhaps the Becket Fund with its legal muscle helped. But it is likely that the letter from the U. S. Department of Education, threatening the APA, had a greater influence. The final paragraphs of this carefully disguised threat likely caused the COA to retreat (and very quickly).

> Therefore, if the APA were to deny accreditation to a religious institution for following its religious tenets in admission or hiring, the Department of Education's recognition of the APA could have the effect of barring an individual who attended that religious institution from serving in those agencies solely because the individual graduated from a religious institution that was acting in accordance with its Constitutionally protected religious freedom. In this way, the Department could effectively be interfering with both the student's choice regarding attendance at a religious college and with the religious communities' selection and education of their current and future leaders: the people we serve now, or are being trained to serve later, as ministers, pastoral counselors and psychological educators. Such a situation not only would be contrary to the APA's current policy under Footnote 4, but it would raise serious questions under the

> Religious Freedom Restoration Act (RFRA), as recently amended, which prevents the Department of Education from 'substantially burden(ing) a person's exercise of religion...

For these reasons, I urge APA to retain Footnote 4" (Hansen, 2001).

Picarello, from the Becket Fund, concluded:

> The APA has done the right thing, for the right reasons and because this decision will ensure a continued flow of people from many faith traditions into the field of psychology, it will actually promote the very diversity the members of APA are concerned about. This is good for the profession, and good for the many people of faith who prefer to seek help from psychologists who share their faith. Diversity, and constitutional guarantees of religious liberty are both well served by the APA's decision (Becket Fund, 2005).

The APA indeed did the right thing. But for the right reasons?

It doesn't take an academic to know that the reason for retaining Footnote 4 was not that the COA had a change of heart and really understood the error of its ways about its attempt to remove the religious exemption in the first place. Rather, the APA decided to retain Footnote 4 because the "Fear of God" was instilled in them as they were about to lose their own accreditation with the U. S. Department of Education!

As reported in the Monitor on Psychology by D. Smith:

> Also affecting the committee's decision was the U.S. Department of Education (DOE), which suggested that, if the footnote was removed, it would be forced to consider revoking APA's recognition as an accrediting body by DOE to accredit professional psychology programs, that would have left all psychology students in a lurch—ineligible for some types of federal funding and, in some cases, unable to gain licensure (Smith, 2002).

Journalist Maggie Gallagher succinctly summarized as she cited

Judith M. Glassgold's intent to remove Footnote 4. Glassgold, who was a member of the APA's Committee on Lesbian, Gay, and Bisexual concerns, concluded that the student conduct codes at some evangelical Christian universities (which forbid nonmarital sex), were invasive and punitive.

Gallagher concluded:

> The APA beat a quick retreat. At its November meeting, the Committee on Accreditation unanimously voted to retain Footnote 4 and the respect for religious schools it provides. In the statement announcing its decision, the APA noted, "recent Supreme Court decisions that show an increased deference to First Amendment interests over anti-discrimination statutes and the Committee's role as an accrediting body recognized by the U. S. Department of Education." Proving that even in America, the price of religious liberty, no less than any other kind, is eternal vigilance. Good thing for us, the Becket Fund is at post" (Gallagher, 2001).

Church-owned Brigham Young University (BYU) was center stage and a precursor to this debate. The COA representatives visited BYU in 1998. The accreditation committee's visit was positive, and no particular difficulties were noted. Therefore, BYU was quite surprised when accreditation was delayed. Subsequent to several inquiries, special APA site visitors were dispatched to BYU. The special visitors were open in admitting that the Committee was responding to groups or persons who had issue with the religious tenets of the sponsoring institution, particularly in regard to sexual orientation. This issue was never raised in the original site visit. The majority of the inquiry was centered on gay and lesbian issues. It appeared clear that the special site visitors were not interested in science and clinical practice but rather issues clearly outside the scope of the COA. They were interested in sexual orientation diversity but quite uninterested in religious diversity. BYU officials were firm in their stances. And the program was subsequently re-accredited (Carpenter, 2007).

The Family, Abortion, and Human Sexuality: Differing Views, but None Based in Science

The traditional family—mother, father, and children—is central to the doctrines of The Church of Jesus Christ of Latter-day Saints (as it is to most faith traditions). In one of the very few proclamations issued by the Church, the Church doctrines concerning the family were clearly defined in such a way as to not be misunderstood. The issuance, titled *The Family: A Proclamation to the World,* stated the following beliefs of the Church:

1. Marriage between a man and a woman is ordained of God, and that the family is central to the Creator's plan for the eternal destiny of His children.
2. Gender is an essential characteristic of individual premortal, mortal, and eternal identity and purpose.
3. God has commanded that the sacred powers of procreation are to be employed only between man and woman, lawfully wedded as husband and wife.
4. We affirm the sanctity of life.
5. Children are entitled to birth within the bonds of matrimony, and to be reared by a father and a mother who honor marital vows with complete fidelity.
6. Successful marriages and families are established and maintained on principles of faith, prayer, repentance, forgiveness, respect, love, compassion, work, and wholesome recreational activities.
7. Fathers and mothers are obligated to help one another as equal partners.
8. Disability, death, or other circumstances may necessitate individual adaptation. Extended families should lend support when needed.
9. We warn that individuals who violate covenants of chastity, who abuse spouse or offspring, or who fail to fulfill family responsibilities will one day stand accountable before God.
10. We call upon responsible citizens and officers of government everywhere to promote those measures designed to maintain and strengthen the family as the fundamental unit of society.

(The First Presiency, 1995)

Certainly, this proclamation is not a scientific document, nor was it intended to be. The document is a clear statement of the doctrine of The Church of Jesus Christ of Latter-day Saints pertaining to families and issues of human sexuality, including abortion and homosexual relationships. However, it is likely that many tenets of Mormon doctrine noted in this document could find support in the scientific literature (Baumrind, 1994; Biller, 1993; Blankhorn, 1995; Popenoe, 1996; and Pruet, 1993).

Now, compare this to the statements, resolutions, and positions taken by the APA regarding abortion, human sexuality, and the family.

First, the APA has offered a resolution on abortion. Without any data, the APA has declared the following: "The APA Council of Representatives decries the uninformed movement in many state legislatures to recriminalize abortion or limit access to the full range of reproductive options" (Adler, 1989).

By what authority does APA claim that the elected representatives of the American people are uninformed about abortion, which is not an issue of science but one of opinion? Ironically, "the APA does not cite any—yet alone compelling—evidence that suggests its position on this divisive issue is the obviously 'informed' and correct one" (p. 48). The point is that the APA has not been able to "offer strong evidence for asserting its position," but has instead taken a politically motivated position where no conclusive evidence supports them. Certainly, members of the APA (more accurately, a rotating few members of the APA) are not a representative sample of the American public. The APA should indeed know something about sampling and generalizability from a scientific perspective.

The APA has no scientific data to support its position because this is not a matter of science but rather a matter of opinion. In fact, faith traditions are as entitled to such opinions as is the APA. Moreover, leading the public to believe that somehow the APA is informed by science on abortion is an ethical violation of the grandest proportion, the consequences of which include "the possibility of error and attendant harm; the impression of an epistemological irrationalism or dogmatism by failing to cite or search for evidence that bears on the question; and the failure to educate" (O'Donohue & Dyslin, 2005).

O'Donohue and Dyslin appropriately suggested the following:

> Unless the APA has extremely compelling data to show the utter illegitimacy of the anti-abortion stance, it might be prudent not to take a position on this divisive issue, both out of respect for the diversity of opinion surrounding this issue and to avoid placing member-psychologists in an unnecessarily difficult situation.

Society, especially American society, is embroiled in a huge debate on issues regarding sexuality, with homosexuality accompanied by issues of homosexual marriage and parenting by homosexual couples occupying center stage. There are strong arguments on both sides of the issue. But what has become increasingly clear is that such issues are political, moral, and ethical issues, not scientific issues. However, APA has entered the debate ostensibly as a scientific organization and offered what amounts to activism masquerading as science. Political correctness has gone awry in the APA, and even the APA's members who disagree with the its narrow politicism are regularly intimidated (p. 51).

The Mormon Church's doctrine is really quite clear and straight forward on the matter of homosexuality and homosexual relationships. Of homosexual relationships, The First Presidency of the Church has declared,

> The Lord's law of moral conduct is abstinence outside of lawful marriage and fidelity within marriage. Sexual relations are proper only between husband and wife appropriately expressed within the bonds of marriage. Any other sexual contact, including fornication, adultery, and homosexual and lesbian behavior, is sinful (The First Presidency, 1991).

Of homosexual marriages, The First Presidency issued the following statement:

> The principles of the gospel and the sacred responsibilities

> given us require that The Church of Jesus Christ of Latter-day Saints oppose any efforts to give legal authorization to marriages between persons of the same gender.
>
> Marriage between a man and a woman is ordained of God to fulfill the eternal destiny of His children. The union of husband and wife assures perpetuation of the race and provides a divinely-ordained setting for the nurturing and teaching of children. This sacred family setting, with father and mother and children firmly committed to each other and to righteous living, offers the best hope for avoiding many of the ills that afflict society (1994).

However, the Church does not condone any disrespect or unkindness toward self-identified homosexuals. The Church offers the following on their Web site:

The Church teaches that all of us are sons and daughters of God and should be honored and respected as such. We reach out to assist people with all of the challenges of life. Those with same-gender attraction are certainly not excluded from the circle of love and fellowship the Church hopes to provide.

President Gordon B. Hinckley (the current leader of the Church) has said,

> Nevertheless, and I emphasize this, I wish to say that our opposition to attempts to legalize same-sex marriage should never be interpreted as justification for hatred, intolerance, or abuse of those who profess homosexual tendencies, either individually or as a group. As I said from this pulpit one year ago, our hearts reach out to those who refer to themselves as gay and lesbians. We love and honor them as sons and daughters of God. They are welcome in the Church. It is expected, however, that they follow the same God-given rules of conduct that apply to everyone, whether single or married (Hinckley, 2007).

This is a succinct summary of the Church's theology on homosexuality, homosexual marriage, and homosexual parenting. The Church claims no scientific authority, relies on no scientific evidence, but rather focuses clearly on its theology. In fact, Elder

Oaks of the Quorum of the Twelve Apostles has declared, "The Church does not have a position on the causes of any of these susceptibilities or inclinations, including those related to same-gender attractions. Those are scientific questions—whether nature or nurture—those are things the Church doesn't have a position on" (Oaks & Wickman, 2006).

Interestingly, O'Donohue and Caselles (2005), both acclaimed academics, provide secular arguments regarding the immorality of homosexuality based on natural law, concluding, "Ethical arguments exist that take homosexuality to be morally wrong and that are not obviously unsound."

Such argument parallel the LDS Church's position, and support that notion that the Church's doctrine, too, is obviously not unsound.

The APA's history with homosexuality is an interesting one, guided more by activism than by science. In 1973, the American Psychiatric Association, by a vote of 5,854 to 3,810, removed the diagnostic category of homosexuality from the Diagnostic and Statistical Manual of Mental Disorders (DSM) (Bayer, 1981). In subsequent years, Dr. Nicholas Cummings introduced resolutions in the Council of Representatives stating that homosexuality was not a psychiatric condition and that there should be no barriers to employment for homosexuals. Associated with these resolutions was the proscription that there was need for appropriate research to substantiate these decisions. The following describes Dr. Cummings' consternation at the APA's lack of scientific evidence:

> Cummings watched with dismay as there was no effort on the part of APA to promote or even encourage such required research. The two APAs had established forever that medical and psychological diagnoses are subject to political fiat. Diagnosis today in psychology and psychiatry is cluttered with politically correct verbiage, which seemingly has taken precedence over sound professional experience and scientific validation (Wright & Cummings, 2005).

The APA seems to have followed such political correctness and activism in addressing homosexuality in recent years including addressing individual rights to psychological care for unwanted homosexual attractions, resolutions on homosexual marriage, and on homosexual parenting. For example, there have been repeated attempts to declare the treatment of homosexuality unethical even if the patient willingly seeks treatment. Many individuals who seek psychological care to diminish homosexual attractions are motivated by their faith tradition and desire to bring their sexuality in conformity to their faith tradition. Such value systems (Mormonism is a good example) should not be dismissed, judged by the therapists to be improper, or overridden through therapeutic manipulation. In fact, Dr. Douglas Haldeman, a member of the Council of Representatives and Division 44, and a self-identified gay man offers the following:

> A corollary issue for many [clients] is a sense of religious or spiritual identity that is sometimes as deeply felt as is sexual orientation. For some it is easier, and less emotionally disruptive, to contemplate changing sexual orientation, than to disengage from a religious way of life that is seen as completely central to the individual's sense of self and purpose. However we may view this choice or the psychological underpinnings thereof, do we have the right to deny such an individual treatment that may help him adapt in the way he has decided is right for him? I would say that we do not (Haldeman, 2000).

Although APA has no definition of competence in practice, and best practices really do not exist in organized psychology, efforts were made in the mid 1990s to ban the practice of re-orientation therapy even when requested by the client. The efforts rose to the level of a resolution (Wright & Cummings, 2005).

Former APA president Robert Perloff persuaded Council Members not to infringe upon the client's rights to autonomy and self determination in spite of the efforts of the gay lobby (Perloff, 2003). The resolution was narrowly defeated.

Unfortunately, the issue of banning re-orientation therapy has re-emerged. Recently (2007), APA President Sharon Stephens Brehm appointed a task force to review re-orientation therapy. Initiated by Division 44 (The Society for the Psychological Study of

Lesbian, Gay and Bisexual Issues), the task force reflects virtually no diversity. Though a number of re-orientation therapists who were also APA members were nominated, all were rejected in favor of well-known gay activists including Judith M. Glassgold (past president of Division 44); Jack Drecsher, M. D. (gay activist psychiatrist who serves on the board of the Journal of Gay and Lesbian Psychotherapy); Lee Beckstead (a gay activist and former practicing Mormon); Beverly Green (founding editor of APA Division 44 series, Psychological Perspectives on Lesbian, Gay, and Bisexual Issues); Robin Lin Miller, who has written for gay publications; and Roger L. Worthington, who received the 2001 Catalyst Award from the Lesbian, Gay, Bisexual, Transexual (LGBT) Resource Center, University of Missouri, for "Speaking up and out and often regarding LGBT issues" (APA Press Release, May 21, 2007).

When questioned why rc-orientation therapists were not included among the Task Force members, Clinton Anderson, representing the APA, stated, "We cannot take into account what are fundamentally negative religious perceptions of homosexuality—they don't fit into our worldview" (Advocate, July 21, 2007). So it is not science but ideology that determines the composition of the Task Force, and the APA's worldview trumps other worldviews? This is the first admission that ideology (not science) guides APA in this endeavor and that religious worldviews are not welcomed.

With the APA's constant drumbeat to the tune of diversity, this task force is hardly an unbiased group. It remains to be seen whether the APA is poised to violate client autonomy and client self-determination, and to silence intellectual diversity by banning re-orientation therapy. Ironically, the final sentence at the bottom of the task force press announcement page includes the following: "APA works to advance psychology as a science, as a profession and as a means of promoting human welfare (APA Press Release, 2007)." This statement is starkly contrary to the activism clearing being demonstrated in this matter.

A continuation of the gay activism influencing APA was manifested in the resolutions approved by the APA Council of Representatives, July 2004 (p. 66). One resolution supported homosexual marriage. Spurred by a committee of activists, (Armand Cerbone, Beverly Green, Kristen Hancock, Lawrence Kurdek, Sharon Duchesneau, and Letitia Anne Peplau), the Council offered no scientific evidence to support the resolution. Rather, APA offered research demonstrating that loving relationships foster mental health, concluding that homosexual marriage was conducive to mental health and therefore is healthy (APA, July 28, 2004).

Dr. Nicholas A. Cummings, a former APA president, responded with the following line of reasoning:

> This scientific justification is so lame, the following could be concluded. I love my collie. Should, heaven forbid, I be widowed from my bride of 57 years, and since close relationships foster mental health, would I be justified in marrying my dog? And would PETA come to my aid calling for an enactment of laws legitimizing loving unions between people and their pets? All people, gay and straight, have the right of choice and freedom from discrimination, but must the gay lobby in the process walk us through the theatre of the absurd? (Cummings, 2005)

Similar tactics were used in justifying another resolution on adoption by homosexual couples. The dearth of research on homosexual couples and parenting, along with the absence of longitudinal data, allows no conclusions to be reached by anyone, including the APA. The research that is available suffers from serious limitations including small sample sizes, non-representative and self-selected samples, reliance on self-reporting subject-to-social-desirability biases. The extensive review conducted by Lerner and Nagai offered a detailed review and concluded,

> The claim has been made that homosexual parents raise children as effectively as married biological parents. A detailed analysis of the methodologies of the 49 studies, which are put forth to support this claim, shows that they suffer from severe methodological flaws. In addition to their methodological flaws none of the studies deals adequately with the problem of affirming the null hypothesis, of adequate sample size, and of spurious correlation (Lerner & Negai, 2000).

The APA Committee supported their resolution on homosexual parenting by citing the research of Golombok, Spencer, Rutter, as well as Golombok and Tasker (APA, 2004). Nowhere did they acknowledge the methodological flaws or the unreported differences. For example, Williams, in his re-analysis of the 1983 data of Golombok, Spencer, and Rutter, and the Golomobok and Tasker 1996 research found a significant number of children to either have considered engaging in a homosexual relationship, or already engaged in a homosexual relationship. There were also significant, but left unreported, differences in self-esteem between children of homosexual and heterosexual parents, as well as significant but unreported differences in social and emotional difficulties experienced by children of homosexual parents (Williams, 2000).

Even the meta-analysis conducted by Stacey and Biblarz (2001) was given only cursory attention. This meta-analysis repudiated over 20 years of research that said that there were no differences between children raised by homosexual and heterosexual parents. In contrast, Stacey and Biblarz found that lesbian mothers had a feminizing effect on their sons and a masculinizing effect on their daughters. They reported the following about the study:

> The adolescent and young adult girls raised by lesbian mothers appear to have been more sexually adventurous and less chaste...in other words, once again, children (especially girls) raised by lesbians appear to depart from traditional gender-based norms, while children raised by heterosexual mothers appear to conform to them (2001, p. 171).

Of particular concern was the Committee's reliance on the research of Charlotte Patterson, whose studies were questioned and subsequently excluded from a Florida Court. The Court concluded:

> Dr. Patterson's impartiality also came into question when prior to trial, she refused to turn over to her own attorneys copies of documentation utilized in her studies. This court ordered her to do so (both sides having stipulated to the Order), yet she unilaterally refused despite the continued efforts on the part of her attorneys to have her do so. Both sides stipu-

> lated that Dr. Patterson's conduct was a clear violation of this Court's order. Her attorneys requested that sanctions be limited to the exclusion of her personal studies at trial and this Court agreed to do so.
>
> Patterson testified as to her own lesbian status and the Respondent maintained that her research was possibly tainted by her alleged use of friends as subjects in her research. This potential was given more credence than it should have been by virtue of her unwillingness to provide the Respondent as well as the Petitioner, with the documents ordered to be produced (Petition v. Floyd & Joynson, 1997).

Not only are such limitations and biases downplayed and in many cases discarded by the APA, but the APA fails to consider the abundance of peer-reviewed, empirical studies which stress the role of gender complementarity in parenting for both male and female nurturance and role models for children (Byrd, 2004).

Neither resolution was based on scientific research. The Leona Tyler Principle would suggest that the APA remain silent, and not offer such opinions. Instead, the APA has elected to offer such resolutions which find no support in the research literature.

One could reasonably conclude that the APA does not value religious diversity as much as it values sexual orientation diversity. Neither does it value what science can and cannot say on such matters. The lack of scientific evidence on matters regarding homosexuality, homosexual marriage, and homosexual adoption create a situation where the APA should make no position statements and offer no resolutions. The APA's voicing opinions on matters for which it has no expertise does not preclude individual psychologists from taking positions or supporting efforts as individual citizens. However, when the APA offers activism masquerading as science, it further erodes the value of the science.

Conclusion

The APA's attacks on religion in general, and on Mormonism in particular, have been documented in this article. The sponsorship of the blatant bigotry of the APA-supported film at the 2004 Convention, the attempt to delete Footnote 4, resolutions claiming scientific evidence where there is little to none (or conflicting results) such as in controversial areas impacting religious tenets like those associated with abortion, the treatment of unwanted homosexual attractions, homosexual marriage, and homosexual parenting is tantamount to an attack on religious groups such as Mormons, whose doctrines support the traditional family. Issues such as abortion and homosexuality are ethical, moral, and political issues, not scientific issues. The APA's messages of diversity ring hollow unless they extend to include religious diversity.

The media continues to portray Mormons in negative ways. In 2000, the New York Times printed an article in support of an anti-Mormon book. The article was titled, "Theocracy in the Desert" (Eagan, January 9, 2000).The article drew parallels between Mormonism and fanatical religious groups (e.g. Al-Quaeda). Joseph Smith was compared to Jim Jones of the Jonestown massacre. Such mischaracterizations and gross inaccuracies may be considered freedom of the press but, when the largest doctoral level group of mental health professionals in the country joins such journalistic bigotry by declaring that the Mormon church is an organization without a heart, does brain washing and mind control, it gives psychologists permission to engage in open prejudice without impunity. Such mischaracterizations of Mormons are not atypical. To the contrary, a simple internet search reveals how commonplace such bigotry is. The findings from such an internet search clearly demonstrates that anti-Mormonism is an open, accepted prejudice. Does the APA not think that such sanctioned discrimination is not harmful? In fact, if colleagues made such statements about other faith traditions, most would immediately lose their jobs. Perhaps it is time for the APA to re-examine its commitment to social justice as well as its commitment to minority issues. With minimal effort by the APA and with a focus on education, prejudiced beliefs could easily be replaced by accurate, positive perceptions of the Mormons. In fact, if the APA simply exercised more care in its resolutions and position statements, particularly those statements for which the APA has no expertise, it would foster less discrimination toward people of faith. One could argue that the APA's positions on such non-scientific issues, issues that are more the domain of ethics and morality, actual fosters discrimination toward faith traditions, particularly those faith traditions that are conservative in nature.

It is time for the APA to revisit the Leona Tyler Principle and to refrain from position statements and resolutions for which it has no expertise. Perhaps it is time for the APA to support religious diversity training first among its own administration and then encourage training among psychologists who provide psychological care to religious individuals. Moreover, the APA needs to deal swiftly when presented with evidence of religious prejudice or discrimination. Waiting ten months for a tepid response to a clear case of religious bigotry is unacceptable.

The APA is ethically committed to base its resolutions and statements on science and to respect religious diversity. In the Preamble to APA's Code of Ethics, such obligations are clearly stated. Psychologists are "committed to increasing scientific ... knowledge of behavior and people's understanding of themselves ... and to use such knowledge to improve the conditions of individuals, organizations, and society." Further, the Code of Ethics emphasized psychology's commitment to social justice and respect for diversity. Referring again to the Code, psychologists should

> respect the dignity and worth of all people....Psychologist are aware of and respect cultural, individual....differences, including those based on age, gender, gender identity, race, ethnicity, culture, national origin, religion, sexual orientation, disability, language, and socioeconomic status and consider these factors when working with members of such groups. Psychologists try to eliminate the effect on their work of biases based on those factors (APA, 2002).

The APA's commitment to diversity, to respecting different worldviews, must include religious diversity. Polls have been remarkably consistent in concluding that 90% of Americans believe in God (Newport, 2007). Faith tradition is very much a part of American life and religious discrimination should not be tolerated, certainly not by the largest doctoral-level mental health organization in the United States. In the spirit of respect for religious diversity and social justice, the APA is in need of a house cleaning for its discrimination against faith traditions in general and Mormonism in particular.

Michael R. Ritter (2004), in his excellent unpublished paper, offers recommendations to the APA not only for this house cleaning but for proactive efforts to combat "Mormophobia" both within its own ranks and in society in general. They include the following action by the APA:

1. The APA should issue a formal resolution and policy statement recognizing the past and present discrimination toward Mormons, not only as a religious group but a minority religious group. The resolution should include a denouncement of all discrimination and perpetuation of Mormon stereotypes in the media (e.g., television, movies, newspapers, radio, books) and by so-called "countercult" groups. The APA should censure any individuals, groups, organizations, or corporations that discriminate against Mormons, including but not limited to, academic institutions.

2. The APA should allocate research funding and issue a call for papers to support the development of Mormon minority research. This might include support for the development of scales that measure false beliefs or stereotypes regarding Mormons. Researchers need to explore the negative impact that widespread discrimination has had on Mormon individuals, families, and congregations.

3. The APA should support research to determine the best approaches for decreasing Mormon stigmatization.

4. The APA should support outcome research that evaluates the efficacy of programs aimed to educate the public and to promote Mormon affirmative images. Pamphlets, newspaper articles, and videos could be created that promote affirmative and factual discussions of the Mormon Church and its members.

5. The APA should increase its contact with Mormons by includ-

ing them in existing program efforts to increase minority participation in the field. In this regard, the APA should expand their definition of ethnic minorities to include Mormons. Similarly, Mormons should be included in the Minority Undergraduate Students of Excellence Program (Rabasca, 2001). In this regard, the COA should insure that discrimination against Mormons does not occur in any of its accredited programs. When evidence of such is found in any accredited programs, appropriate action should be taken quickly.

6. The APA should promote and facilitate psychologists' acquisition of competencies, including relevant cultural knowledge, attitudes, and skills in providing psychological care to Mormon individuals and couples in counseling.

Operating in a multicultural society, it's time for the APA to develop within its own ranks a kind of cultural humility accompanied by the realization that diversity—real diversity—includes different worldviews, worldviews that differ starkly from the current narrow politicism under which the APA seems to be operating. The APA needs to divest itself of the influence of special interest groups who rely more on activism than science as they press their ideological agendas. The case for Mormonism could serve as an APA model for religious diversity. This might begin with counselor competency training that requires a basic understanding that Mormons operate from a different worldview than the majority of practicing psychologists who are substantially more liberal than the public community in which they serve (Redding, 2001, and Yarhouse & Burkell, 2002). Rosik (2003) explains that liberals are more likely to rely on a worldview based on the ethics of autonomy in their justification of social issues. The ethics of autonomy is generally concerned with harm and their moral domain is focused on issues that involve rights, welfare, and justice. Mormons and other moral conservatives tend to make judgments from within two evaluative frameworks: the ethics of community and the ethics of divinity (Haidt, 2001).

The ethics of community involves concern over social order and social roles (e.g., how things are "intended" to be; a universal order) and fears about potential social decay. The ethics of divinity focuses on concerns about purity, sacredness, and living a life commensurate with the eternal laws established by God (Rosik, 2003). While there are many clinical issues or disorders in which a secular therapist and a Mormon client would work well together (i.e., trauma, parenting, panic disorder, bipolar), there may be other issues in which they might disagree (abortion, homosexuality, divorce, marriage, feminism, "the good life"). Discrimination can arise when well-meaning liberal psychologists use the ethics of autonomy to evaluate the moral judgments made by religious minorities like Mormons, who are operating under a different worldview. For example, treating a Mormon male who is struggling with same-sex attraction with gay-affirmative therapy or encouraging an LDS man to divorce his spouse in pursuit of his or her own ambitions could be considered a violation of the APA Code of Ethics. The APA must take action to make certain that practitioners are not causing harm to Mormon clients by failing to respect religious diversity.

The APA should develop a religious advocacy group to spearhead these proposals into action. Currently, the APA public policy office Web site includes a long list of advocacy committees for various minority groups (aged, women, HIV/AIDS, gay, lesbian, and bisexual). Given the substantially lower proportion of religious individuals in the field, an advocacy group for religion is noticeably absent from the list. A Mormon advocacy group could emerge from such a group and take charge of current and future proposals.

Endnote

[1] This Web site is currently devoted to firefighters. A complete copy of the Web site is in the possession of the author.

References

Adams, C. S. (2004, September 13). Letter to Dr. Halpern, a copy of which is in the possession of the author.

Adler, N. E. (1989, March 16). *The medical and psychological impact of abortion on women.* Testimony on behalf of the American Psychological Association before the U. S. House of Representative, Committee on Government Operations, Subcommittee on Human Resources and Intergovernmental Relations. Washington, DC: APA Council of Representatives.

Advocate. (2007, July 12). American Psychological Association to review gay counseling practices. Retrieved from http://www.advocate.com/news_detail_ektid4711.asp

American Psychological Association. (2002). Ethical principles of psychologists and code of conduct: Preamble. Washington, D.C.: Retrieved from http://www.apa.org/ethics/code.2002.html#preamble

American Psychological Association. (2004, July 28). APA supports legalization of same-sex civil marriages and opposes discrimination against lesbian and gay parents. Retrieved from http://www.apa.org/releases/gaymarriage.html.

American Psychological Association. (2004, July 31). [Brochure about documentary *Get the fire* by N. Du Plessis.] APA Ad Hoc Committee on Film and Other Media, Hawaii National Convention.

American Psychological Association. (2005, August). 113th Annual Convention Program. [Brochure] Washington, DC.

American Psychological Association. (2007). APA appoints task force to review recent science on therapeutic responses to sexual orientation. APA Press Release. Retrieved from http://www.apa.org/releases/therarespt f07.html

Baumrind, D. (1994). The influence of parenting style on adolescent competence and substance use. *Journal of Adolescence, 11(11)*, 59-95.

Bayer, R. (1981). *Homosexuality and American psychiatry.* New Jersey: Princeton Press.

The Becket Fund (2001a). Retrieved from http://www.becketfund.org/litigate/APA.html.

The Becket Fund (2001b). Retrieved from http://www.becketfund.org/litigate/APApositionpaper.html.

The Becket Fund For Religious Liberty. (2005). *American Psychological Association leaves Footnote 4 alone.* Retrieved February 2, 2005 from http://www.becketfund.org/index.php/article/145.html

Benson, S. (2005). *Patriarchal panic: Sexual politics in the Mormon Church.* Speech made at APA, September 1, 1979, New York City. Retrieved from http://www.exmormon.org/mormn/mormon415.htm

Biller, H. B. (1993). *Fathers and families: paternal factors in child development.* West Point, CT: Auburn House

Blankenhorn, D. (1995). *Fatherless America: confronting our most urgent social problem.* New York: Basic Books.

Byrd, A. D. (2004). Gender complementarity and child-rearing: where tradition and science agree. Journal *of Law and Family Studies, 6 (2)*, 213-235.

Carpenter, B. (2007). Email Correspondence from the Clinical Director of BYU's Clinical Psychology Program.

Cummings, N.A. (2005, November). The painful education of a well-intentioned APA president. *NARTH Annual Conference Reports.* Marina Del Ray, CA. p.6

Davis, R.J. (1992). Antipolygamy legislation. *Encyclopedia of Mormonism* (Vol. 1). New York: MacMillan.

Eagan, T. (2000, January 9). Theocracy in the desert. *New York Times Book Review.*

Enstrom, J.E. (1989). Health practices and cancer mortality among active California Mormons. *Journal of the National Cancer Institute, 81*, 1807-1814.

The First Presidency. (1976, October 22). [Statement] Retrieved from http://www.lds.org/portal/site/LDSOrg/menuitem.b12f9d18fae655bb...

The First Presidency. (1991, November 14). *Standards of morality and fidelity.* [Statement]

The First Presidency. (1994, February 1). *Same gender marriages.*

[Statement]
The First Presidency and the Council of the Twelve Apostles of The Church of Jesus Christ of Latter-day Saints. (1995, September 23). *The family: A proclamation to the world.* Salt Lake City, UT.
Gallagher, M. (2001). *Religious liberty vs. orthodoxy: the case of footnote 4.* Keep Media. Retrieved from http://www.keepmedia.com/pubs/uExpress/2001/1 1/19/560284/print/
Groom, G.L. (2004, August 10). Copy of letter to Diane F. Halpern, in possession of the author
Haidt, J., & Hersh, M.A. (2001). Sexual morality: The cultures and emotions of conservatives and liberals. *Journal of Applied Social Psychology, 31,* 191-221.
Haldeman, D. C. (2000, August). *Gay rights, patients rights: The implementations of Sexual Orientation Conversion Therapy.* Paper presented at the meeting of the American Psychological Association, Washington, DC.
Haley, M. L. (2004, September 15). Letter to Dr. Groom, a copy of which is in the possession of the author.
Halpern, D. F. (2004, August 16). Letter to Dr. Groom, a copy of which is in the possession of the author.
Halpern, D. F. (2004, November 23). Letter to Drs. Groom and Adams from Dr. Halpern, a copy of which is in possession of the author.
Hansen, W.D. (2001). Letter sent to Susan Zlotlow at APA on September 6, 2001. Retrieved from http://www.ed.gov/policy/highered/guid/secletter/010906.html.
Hinkley, G. B. (2006). *Church responds to Nightline story on Mormons and homosexuality.* Retrieved from http://lds.org/ldsnewsroom/v/index/jsp?vgnextoid=d4ec39628b.
Kimball, S. W. (1978, September 30). *Official declaration.*
LDS Newsroom. (2007). *Political neutrality.* Retrieved from http://www.lds.org/ldsnewsroom/v/index.jsp?vgnextoid=6203d93c86.
Lerner, R., & Nagai, A. K. (2000, March). *Out of nothing comes nothing: homosexual and heterosexual marriage not shown to be equivalent for raising children.* Paper presented at the Revitalizing the Institution of Marriage for the 21st Century, Brigham Young University, Provo, UT.
Madsen, C. C. (1992). Woman suffrage. *Encyclopedia of Mormonism*

(Vol. 4). New York: MacMillan.
Moore, C. A. (2005, April 30). Psychology group calms Utahns over film on LDS. *Deseret Morning News.* Retrieved from deseret-news.com.
Morris, S. B. (2005, February 25). Posted on upaforum@lists.apa.org, a copy of which is in the possession of the author.
Nelson, R. M. (1999, May). Our sacred duty to honor women. *Ensign*, p.38.
Newport, F. (2007). Americans more likely to believe in God than the devil, heaven more than hell. *Gallup News Service.* Retrieved from http://www.galluppoll.com/content/?ci=27877
Oaks, D. H., & Wickman, L. B. (2006, August 14). *Same-gender attraction.* Retrieved from Newsroom@lds.org
O'Donohue, W., & Caselles, C. E. (2005). In R. H. Wright & N. A. Cummings (Eds.), *Destructive trends in mental health: The well-intentioned path to harm.* New York: Routledge.
O'Donohue, W. T., & Dyslin, C. (2005). In R. H. Wright & N. A. Cummings (Eds.), *Destructive trends in mental health: The well-intentioned path to harm.* New York: Routledge.
Perloff, R. (2002). In R. J. Sternberg (Ed.), *Psychologists defying the crowd.* Washington, DC: American Psychological Association. (pp. 183-184)
Petitioner v Floyd P. Johnson. (1997, June) *AMER,* p. 11.
Popenoe, D. (1996). *Life without father.* New York: Mark Kessler Books:
Pruett, K.D. (1993). The paternal presence. *Families and Society, 74,* 46-54.
Quackenbush, D. (2005, February 25). Posted on upaforum@lists.apa.org, a copy of which is in the possession of the author.
Rabasca, L. (2000). Attracting more minority students to psychology programs. *Monitor on Psychology, 31.* Retrieved from http://www.apa.org/monitor/mar00/muse.html
Ranks, D. (2005, February 25). Posted on upaforum@lists.apa.org, a copy of which is in the possession of the author.
Redding, R. E. (2001). Sociopolitical diversity in psychology: The case for pluralism, *American Psychologist, 56,* 205-215.
Reynolds, C. S. (2005, March 9). Posted on upaforum@lists.apa.org, a

copy of which is in the possession of the author.
Ritter, M.R. (2004). *Discrimination against Mormons: Magnitude, psychological impact, and proposal for action*. [Unpublished paper, quoted with permission.]
Rosik, C. H. (2003). Motivational, ethical, and epistemological foundations in the treatment of unwanted homoerotic attraction. *Journal of Marital and Family Therapy, 29*, 13-28.
Smith, B.B., & Thomas, S. W. (1992). Gospel principles and the roles of women. *Encyclopedia of Mormonism* (Vol.4). New York: MacMillan.
Smith, D. (2002, January). Accreditation committee decides to keep religious exemption. *Monitor on Psychology, 33(1)*. Retrieved from http://www.apa.org/monitor/jan02/exemption.html
Sommers, C.H. (2001). *The war against boys*. New York: Simon and Schuster.
Stacey, J., & Biblarz, T. J. (2001). Does sexual orientation of parents matter? *American Sociological Review, 66(2)*, 159-183.
Wallace, T. (2005, February 26). Posted on upaforum@lists.apa.org, a copy of which is in the possession of the author.
Watson, F.M. (2007, May). Statistical report, 2006. *Ensign*, p. 7.
Williams, R. N. (2000). A critique of the research on same-sex parenting. In D. C. Dollahite (Ed.), *Strengthening Our Families*, Salt Lake City, UT: Bookcraft, p. 352-355.
Wright, R. H., & Cummings, N. A. (Eds.). (2005). *Destructive trends in mental health*. New York: Routledge.
Yarhouse, M. A. & Burkett, L.A. (2002). An inclusive response to LGB and conservative religious persons: The case of same-sex attraction and behavior. *Professional Psychology Research and Practice, 33*, 235-241.

Chapter 9

Psychology's War on Islam: Who Is Rejecting Whom?

Nicholas A. Cummings, Ph.D., Sc.D.

One man was so mad at me that he ended his letter:
"Beware. You will never get out of this world alive"

—John Steinbeck.

This might have been a short chapter, as this author was not able to discern any war on Islam by psychology. Quite the contrary, psychology has shown inclusiveness of Muslims, has been openly sympathetic to the plight of the Palestinians, and one prominent psychologist staunchly supported the late Yasser Arafat as a great humanitarian (McCauley, 2007). On the other hand, some Muslims, particularly fundamentalists, distrust

American psychology, are wary of its emphasis on freedom of thought, are troubled by its avoidance of spirituality, and strongly reject its liberal attitude toward sexuality. As a consequence, Muslims are not consumers of psychotherapy, are more likely to seek religious guidance, and are in the process of defining an Islamic psychology that is vastly different. Nonetheless, in spite of there being no war on Islam by American psychology, there are a number of issues that impinge on the relationship between the two, and these will be addressed.

Inclusiveness by American psychology is certainly positive and commendable, but one can not help but be curious, that since so many of the Islamic practices and beliefs are in conflict with accepted psychological principles and in direct violation of the liberal proclamations of the American Psychological Association (APA), why organized psychology is so silent when it never seems to hesitate to critique other religions. Consider, for example, the lower status of women as one glaring example. When any semblance of religiously supported male dominance is present among certain Christian and Jewish sects, it is strongly decried by feminist psychologists as well as the profession generally. Yet psychology is strangely silent about such practices in the Muslim world. Why is Islam getting a pass from psychology?

It is very unlikely that the APA or the discipline of psychology feels intimidated by threats from Islamic extremists who are highly intolerant of any criticism. It is true that Danish cartoon depictions of Muhammad incited riots, and the writings of a prominent Danish journalist may have resulted in his death. A *fatwa* (in this case, a death sentence) was issued on Salmon Rushdie for his *Satanic Verses,* causing him to go into hiding for over a decade. There have been other examples less violent and less publicized, while still others, such as the revelations that Hitler's *Mein Kampf* continues to be a best seller in some Muslim countries, sparked vigorous protests and threats of violence. The denial of the existence of the holocaust remains a popular belief among a large portion of the Muslim world, and it does not evoke the outrage that such a belief receives when expressed by neo-Nazis or other Aryan groups (McCauley, 2007). Psychology's eagerness to give Islamists a pass does not seem motivated by fear.

It is more likely that psychology's tolerance for practices of Islam, which would be denounced in other religions, is driven largely by political correctness. The often used explanation is, "But that is cultural," demonstrating a curious intersection of political correctness with multiculturalism (Wright & Cummings, 2005). Egregious Western cultural practices, such as the German anti-Semitism under the Nazis, the prevalent bias against Gypsies in Eastern Europe, and the segregation of African Americans in the recent South, are rightly not accorded such an excuse even though one might say these, too, are "cultural."

No other explanation seems plausible when the slightest infringement of women's rights among any sector of American society provokes outrage among feminist psychologists, yet the same feminist psychologists are curiously silent regarding such egregious violations of women's freedom as the forced wearing of veils, a man's right to rape a woman who is not completely shrouded, female genital mutilation in childhood (especially in Egypt), and even honor killings (McCauley, 2007). This last practice refers to the obligation for a family to restore its honor by killing a female member who violated a series of sexual taboos that not only includes infidelity to one's husband, but also premarital sexual encounter or indiscretion. There is now a group of Muslim women who are rebelling against these practices, especially that of beatings for not complying with male dominance. Yet psychology has not risen to defend, encourage and support them. Rather, what prevails in the Muslim community, absent any such support from American psychology, is denunciations such as that of Said Mansour who stated publicly, "Either you are completely a Muslim or you are not. These women are not Muslims, they are democratized" (ABG Films, 2007). Even more startling is the deafening silence regarding the barbaric sectarian murders by Sunnis and Shi'ites of each other, as noted by three-time Pulitzer Prize winner and *New York Times* writer Thomas Friedman (Friedman, 2007).

Moderate, Fundamentalist and Extremist Defined

The overwhelming majority of Muslims, especially in the United States, are moderate. A fair number are fundamentalist, and only a few are extremists. Those who would say otherwise are unfair to a hard-working population that migrated to find a better life and are struggling to accommodate their faith into Western culture. They are not looking to establish an Islamic state in America. However, it only takes a few fanatics to form a terrorist cell and it is they who receive the most media attention.

Both the Qu'ran and the Christian Bible address such a wide spectrum of topics, often with one passage contradicting another, that opposing interpretations are frequent using ostensibly the same scriptures. Thus both the Bible and the Qu'ran have been invoked to promote pacifism or promote war. Not surprisingly, Protestant Christianity, which was founded as part of the religious reformation splitting from the Roman Catholic Church, is fractionated into scores of sects, some with only a shade of difference, but nonetheless crucial to the respective followers. For example, Baptists and Methodists both espouse baptism, but the Methodists accept "sprinkling" while only total immersion is acceptable to the Baptists. Furthermore, Americans have always disagreed passionately when science and religion come into conflict (Brookhiser, 2007). Controversies such as creationism versus evolution, pro-choice versus pro-life, and the existence of a hereafter have a long shelf-life because people care about them. So "neither religion nor science can expect a free pass in the court of public opinion or in the voting booth," (Brookhiser, 2007, p. 53). The difference between Islam and the West is that such controversies are free and open in a democracy, but limited in a theocracy. It is to be anticipated that moderate Islam would be more open to knowledge, debate and science than would be their fundamentalist counterparts.

The same continuum of moderate, fundamentalist and extremist can be applied to Christians on a variety of other social issues. *Vis-à-vis* abortion, for example, the Roman Catholic Church is strongly opposed to abortion, while the Greek Orthodox Church tacitly accepts a woman's right to choose. Yet both of these religions sprang from the same locale and in the first century A.D. Evangelical Christians tend strongly toward a fundamentalism that opposes not only abortion, but also gay marriage, evolution, equality of wives with their husbands, female clergy, and any restrictions on prayer in schools, while other Christian sects not only perform gay/lesbian marriages, they ordain openly gay pastors and even bishops. Moderate Christians, especially the more liberal sects, are sympathetic to a woman's right to terminate a pregnancy even though they may not be vocal about it. Fundamentalists are strongly pro-life and would roll back Roe v. Wade, through the ballot box or the courts, while an infinitesimal number are extremists, who believe that all abortion is infanticide, and can justify the bombing of abortion clinics and the killing of "murderous doctors."

Differences in Beliefs: Fundamentalist versus Moderate Muslims

It is true that various Christian sects can be fundamentalist on one issue and moderate on another, but our rule-of-thumb applies in its simplest form and can also describe a range of views in Islam.

Fundamentalist Muslim beliefs (Barrett, 2007 and Gregg, 2007):

- Islam literally means voluntary submission to Allah, originally the Moon God of the Arabian peninsula.
- No other religion is accepted by Allah (Qu'ran 2:256), and Muslims are forbidden to have Jewish or Christian friends, as these are declared to be infidels.
- Allegiance is to the five pillars of Islam and to Mecca, toward which he/she turns in congregational prayer five times a day. Muslims are required to make at least one pilgrimage to Mecca in their lifetime.
- They must submit to the mullahs, who are the interpreters of the Qu'ran and do not allow freedom of religion or expression in belief, worship, behavior and dress.
- Men are instructed to marry four women (obviously not enforced in the United States) and beat and scourge their wives when they disobey (Qu'ran 4:34).
- Politically as well as religiously, Muhammad and the Qu'ran do not allow government by consensus inasmuch as it may result in determinations contrary to *sharia* (Islamic law). A

theocracy is regarded as the ideal, so it is not surprising that almost every Muslim government is either dictatorial or autocratic.[1]

Although there is much overlap with the above, moderate Muslims differ in the following critical respects (Gregg, 2007):

- They oppose extremist Islamic organizations, whose followers are often called *Islamists*, such as al-Qaeda, Hamas, and Hezbollah.
- They link terrorism to the corruption of Islam
- They do not seek to establish an Islamic state in the West.
- They reject movements seeking to restore the so-called *global caliphate.*
- They fully embrace religious pluralism. They, therefore, may have Jewish and Christian friends, though inter-marriage remains rare.
- They appreciate the freedoms accorded by a democracy.
- They reject calls for the annihilation of Israel and Jihad against all infidels.

With these differing attitudes, acculturation is not only possible, but probable. Moderate Muslims are rightly troubled that most Americans are not aware of these differing attitudes, and resent being lumped into a fundamentalist stereotype.

Sunnis and Shi'ites: Why Do They Hate Each Other?

Islam's schism began in 632 A.D. when the Prophet Muhammad died without having named his successor. Some of the followers believed that the role of Caliph, or viceroy of Allah, should pass down through Muhammad's bloodline, beginning with his cousin and son-in-law, Ali ibn Abi Talib, known in history as Ali. The majority of followers, however, backed the Prophet's friend, Abu Bakr, and made him the second Caliph after the Prophet Muhammad. Ali was eventually named the fourth Caliph, but he was soon murdered in A.D. 661 by a heretic, throwing the entire succession once again into such dispute that it led to a formal split. This time the majority favored Yazid, the son of the Governor of Syria, while those soon to be known as Shi'at Ali (partisans of Ali) insisted on naming Ali's son Hussein. The split was so strong that the two sides met in a battlefield near modern Karbala, Iraq where Hussein was killed and beheaded. This spurred the Shi'ite movement to become more militant in its veneration of the martyred Hussein who stood up to injustice and oppression, and the annual mourning of Hussein is known as Ashura, the most spectacular of Shi'ite ceremonies where the extremely devout flagellate themselves with swords and whips (Ghosh, 2007).

Those loyal to the Mu'awiyah, Governor of Syria, along with his successor Caliphs, came to be known as Sunnis, meaning followers of the Sunnah (or Way) of the Prophet. Geographically today 90% of Islam is dominated by Sunnis, occupying Islamic North Africa, Saudi Arabia, Bahrain, Egypt, Jordan, Kuwait, Lebanon, Oman, Qatar, Syria, Turkey, Yemen, the U.A.E., most of Iraq, Afghanistan, Pakistan, and all the other "Stans." The Shi'ites comprise the majority of the population in Iran and southern Iraq, but they constitute sizeable minorities in other Islamic states, including Saudi Arabia, Lebanon, and Pakistan. Syria is somewhat of an anomaly, since it has a Sunni majority but is ruled by a small Shi'ite offshoot known as the Alawites. Historically the Sunnis maintained political power by excluding the Shi'ites from the military and government bureaucracies, and the rulers treated the Shi'ites as an underclass. They maintained power by a religious interpretation that branded the Shi'ites as heretics rather than genuine Muslims, thus justifying their oppression.

Relations between the two sects worsened during the 16th century, after the seat of Sunni power had moved to Istanbul. When the Turkish Sunni Ottomans fought a series of battles with the Shi'ite Safavids of Persia (now Iran), the Arabs were caught in between, and survived by adroitly playing first one side and then the other. The Ottomans eventually gained full control of that area and cemented the Sunni dominance that exists today. The animosities of that era, however, persist; to this day the Sunni Arabs pejoratively call the Shi'ites "Persians" or "Safavis" (Ghosh,

2007).

Following World War I the British handed Iraq over to the Sunni's even though, at the time, there was a Shi'ite majority. The Shi'ites enjoyed a couple of decades of respite from oppression, but with the Ayatullah Khomeni's revolution in Iran, Saddam Hussein instituted full scale repression of the Shi'ites in fear there would be a similar uprising in Iraq. With the first defeat of Saddam Hussein in Desert Storm in the 1990s there was a Shi'ite uprising that was quickly and brutally quelled when the Western forces under the first President Bush failed to come to their aid. It's no wonder, following the final defeat of Saddam Hussein in the West's second invasion (Operation Iraqi Freedom) under the second President Bush, the Shi'ites kept the Sunnis from assuming power again. Unfortunately, the toxicity of the current sectarian war in Iraq has obliterated all memories of any good will that may have existed.

How to Tell Sunnis from Shi'ites

The Sunnis and Shi'ites not only share allegiance to the same God, they have ethnicity, language, apparel and cuisine in common. The ways they may differ are subtle, varying from region to region, and making differentiation difficult, and mistakes frequent. Nonetheless, there are slight differences in the naming of children, exercise of faith, and home décor that Muslim's themselves use to identify to which sect a particular Muslim belongs (Ghosh, pp. 30-31).

Names

Most names are common to both sects, but Abu Bakr, Omar, and Uthman were early Caliphs hostile to Ali, and therefore today are almost always Sunni. Those named Abu Abdel-Hussein and Abdel-Zahra are most likely Shi'ite.

Prayer

Sunnis almost always pray with one arm folded over the other, just below the rib cage. Shi'ites prefer to keep their arms straight down at their sides. Devout Shi'ites touch their heads on a small clay tablet (*turba*, made in the holy city of Najaf), and in time this makes a small callous in the forehead. Islam requires congregational prayers five times a day, and Sunnis have five separate prayer times. Shi'ites have the option of praying three times and doubling up on two days. In calling the faithful to prayer, Sunni mosques invoke Allah and Prophet Muhammad, while Shi'ites also mention Ali. For Shi'ites prayer times are a few minutes behind the Sunnis. During the fasting month of Ramadan the two sects break their fast at slightly different times. The somber ceremony of Ashura with its self-flagellation is uniquely Shi'ite. Sunnis pay only one tithe (*zakat*), while Shi'ites pay two kinds of tithe: *kuhms*, which is a fifth of their income, and a smaller one, *zakat*.

Mosques

Sunni mosques tend to have domes and minarets, while Shi'ites often worship in community centers called Husseiniyas that combine religious and community activities, and may not have domes. Shi'ite mosques are usually adorned with traditional green and black flags and are decorated with portraits of Ali and occasionally also Hussein. Sunni mosques tend to be more austere. The Sunni clerics usually wear white headgear, while their Shi'ite counterparts are more colorful, wearing white, black or green headgear.

Homes

Shi'ite homes like to display portraits of Ali, and during important religious occasions will fly colorful flags of traditional black and green on their roofs. Sunnis regard portraiture of holy men as a form of idolatry, and prefer calligraphy of quotations from the Qu'ran. They, too, may fly flags from their roofs on important religious occasions, but they are invariably white.

Accents and Dialects

Since southern Iraq is overwhelmingly Shi'ite, in Baghdad anyone with a southern dialect is assumed to be Shi'ite. On the other hand, the patois of Anbar province identifies the speaker as Sunni.

Cars

Shi'ites carry their fondness of portraiture to their automobiles and hang pictures of Iman Ali in their rear windows, and an *alek*, a strip of green ribbon, from their rearview mirror. A give away is often the car's license plate, with Anbar plates assumed to be Sunni, while a Basra plate is seen as Shi'ite. Overt signs of sectarian faith can be fatal in today's violent Iraq, so these are tending to disappear in homes, cars and in naming of children. The safest auto license plate is from Baghdad so Iraqis try to finagle a way to register their cars there.

A Retrospective and a Comparison

Unquestionably the vast majority of Muslims, whether living in the Middle East or in Western countries, are far from being extremists, or what has been termed Islamist rather than Islamic. Those who would say otherwise are grossly in error, and may be reacting to the relative difficulty Muslim immigrants are experiencing in assimilating, far less in America than in other Western countries. Several of my Muslim friends confess that whenever they hear of a terrorist attack, whether in the United Kingdom, in Spain, Pakistan or Iraq, they silently pray, "I hope it never happens here." Yet it is curious that the Muslim community is amazingly silent, even when Al Jazeera shows beheadings of Americans on TV, radical mullahs call for outright jihad, extremist clerics cry "Death to all infidels" (ostensibly Christians and Jews), or when Iran's leader calls for the extermination of Israel. Some would say that they feel intimidated, that the wrath toward infidels will be visited upon them as retaliation for sympathy with the West. Undoubtedly fear can be a factor, but only a relatively minor one. A comparison might reveal other reasons.

Born in early 1920s, the author has lived all of his childhood and much of his adult life during the era of segregation in the South. Lynching was overlooked, the Ku Klux Klan (KKK) was rarely if ever brought to justice, the rape of black women was seldom prosecuted, and when it was, acquittal was common. The KKK was a small group of extremists, although its members often secretly had the direct participation or tacit approval of prominent leaders in the community. Overwhelmingly, Southerners were not extremists, but good, kind, hard-working and god-fearing citizens who were not given to violence and shuddered at the news of lynching, and the beating or raping of African Americans. Yet they were silent and stood by as the police enforced segregation of drinking fountains, buses, public toilets and generally all places where the public traveled, congregated, dined or was entertained. Their silence abetted the violence of the extremists, even though personally they would never condone such violence. There was a cultural head-in-the-sand attitude that finally began to abate about the time of the release of the landmark movie starring Gregory Peck, *To Kill a Mockingbird,* that helped awaken the nation. Note, however, this was in the early 1960s and about one hundred years after the Civil War.

Why did this seemingly good population in the South look the other way when the perhaps only 5% of them were the extremists who inflicted terror and violence on equally good African American fellow citizens? The answer, of course, lies in the fact that Southern whites of that era agreed with, and were committed to, segregation. They ultimately believed that the "Negro race" was inferior and had to be kept "in its place." Fundamentalist Christian doctrine played a prominent role, but this would not have been enough, as religious dogma is often re-interpreted to fit society's preconceptions. Social historians (Catton, 2004 and Miller, Stout & Wilson, 1998) attribute much of this bias to the South's loss of its status as the closest thing to aristocracy in America. The concept of Southern gentlemen and ladies, and their superiority over boorish Northerners, though largely a myth embodied in such popularizations as the film *Gone with the Wind*, was lost after the Civil War. In their post-war hard economic times Southern whites longed for the return to a prosperous economy fueled by slave labor. In spite of the success of the Civil Rights Movement, this bias did not begin to seriously abate until the nation's population began shifting from the North to the sunbelt well after World War II, resulting in the new economic prosperity that ameliorated the nostalgia to return to a past era.

The era from the 9th to the 13th centuries is known as Islam's magnificent Golden Age. It brought about major advances in mathematics, science and medicine, and kept knowledge alive while the Christian world was experiencing the Dark Ages. In spite of this glorious past, according to Pervez Amirali Hoodbhoy, chair of the department of physics at Quaid-i-Azam University in Islamabad, Pakistan, no major invention or discovery has emerged from the Muslim world for the past seven centuries. He refers to the present "marginalization of Muslims as a growing sense of injustice and victim hood" (11, p. 49) that may be silently harbored by the vast majority of moderate, non-violent Muslims throughout the world.

A Longing for the Past

According to Professor Hoodbhoy (2007), this attitude of victimhood widens the gulf between the Muslim and Western worlds and threatens a bloody clash of civilizations. In the least, the longing for the golden past is pervasive, and may be reflected in the silence among moderates in the face of growing acts of terrorism. He further laments that "as intolerance and militancy sweep across the Muslim world, personal and academic freedoms diminish with the rising pressure to conform" (Hoodbhoy, 2007, p. 57). In Pakistani and other Middle Eastern universities the veil is now ubiquitous, and he states it is the common observation of his colleagues that over time veiled female students "...have largely lapsed into becoming silent note-takers, are increasingly timid, and are less inclined to ask questions or take part in discussions" (Hoodbhoy, 2007, p.58). He decries this and other fundamentalist practices that portend a continued decline of knowledge and science in the Muslim world, and the perpetuation of a culture of longing for the past while resenting the marginalized present.

The pioneering sociologist Max Weber (Hoodbhoy, 2007) claims that currently Islam lacks an *idea system* critical for sustaining a scientific culture based on innovation, new experiences, quantification, and empirical verification. The result is fatalism and an orientation toward the past that makes progress difficult and even undesirable. Hoodbhoy would add that such scientific achievement:

> ...is not reconcilable with religious demands made on a fully observant Muslim's time, energy and mental concentration: The faithful must participate in five daily congregational prayers, endure a month of fasting that taxes the body, recite daily from the Qur'an, and more. Although such duties orient believers admirably well toward success in the life hereafter, they make worldly success less likely (Hoodbhoy, 2007, p. 63).

Democracy, a cornerstone of current Western civilization, is not only absent in the Islamic world, but may be contrary to the teachings of the Qu'ran. As was stated before, consensus in a democracy may reach conclusions differing from *sharia*, something forbidden by the Imans. It is not an accident, therefore, that almost every Muslim government is a theocracy confirming Allah's ultimate and complete wisdom to govern.

Muslims bristle with the kind of discussion found in this chapter, but enlightenment may come as it did to the Old South's intolerance only after there has been economic prosperity. Some Muslim countries may be experiencing varying stages of such economic prosperity—among them Qatar, the United Arab Emirates (UAE), Pakistan, Malaysia, Saudi Arabia, Iran, and Nigeria. Along with it has come increased funding of science and education, a loosening of fundamentalism, and an enlightened search for change. Unfortunately, it has also emboldened Islamists to increase the pressure to return to Islamic law. As one example, prosperity has pitted the populace of Iran against the mullahs, and although the totalitarian fundamentalist regime is still firmly in control, the eventual outcome is yet to be decided. Iranians experienced years of tolerance in which the rulers were mercurial, "cracking down on some social freedoms one season and tolerating the most outrageous pastimes the next" (Moaveni, 2007, p. 43). The affluent in Iran, and especially the younger generation, have adopted a number of Western ways in dress and entertainment, and with the growing antagonism between the United States and Iran, the rulers are increasingly uneasy, especially when recently a number of gasoline stations were set afire in protest. "The more threatened the hard-liners feel, the more paranoid they will become," observes Farideh Frahi, Iran expert and professor of political science at the University of Hawaii (Moaveni, 2007, p. 44).

Those of us who have been to Malaysia were startled to see the Muslim majority decorating their own Christmas trees along with the Christian minority. In visiting Dubai a tourist will see one of the most modern cities of the world. Here is a capitalistic center, perhaps one of the most vigorous anywhere, that is accomplishing economic miracles in spite of *sharia* which forbids interest-bearing transactions of any kind. Yet debt-financing is not only imperative in business, it is the very essence of capital leveraging. The booming Dubai economy is simply playing a semantic game as it substitutes religiously compatible words for that of "interest" (Moaveni, 2007, p. 122).

Religious fundamentalism of whatever persuasion is always bad news for science and progress: coupled with poverty and a continued nostalgia for the golden past, it can only perpetuate and even increase problems. But the converse is also true: prosperity, knowledge and science can launch enlightenment and tolerance.

The Inclusiveness by American Psychology

There has been an active inclusiveness and reaching out by the American Psychological Association to the Islamic community since 9/11. For example, the APA's Board of Professional Affairs, sponsored at its 2006 annual convention in New Orleans, a well attended and highly publicized panel of psychologists of Middle Eastern decent, "Reaching Out to Muslims and Arab Americans" (Winerman, 2006). Making the point that not all Muslims are Arab, and not all Arabs are Muslim, the panel of Ph.D.s from the universities of Yale, Iowa, and Windsor, and from services agencies in Detroit and Dearborn, stressed that "psychologists who want to help must concentrate on reaching out to the Muslim-American community" and "we need to step away from the idea that people will come to us" (Winerman, 2006, p. 55). The panel referred to the negative attitudes that many Muslims hold toward formal psychological services. These mitigate strongly against seeking services in spite of the tensions resulting from being caught in the crossfire of political tensions between the U.S. and the Arab world.

The panel listed a number of practical suggestions, among them to offer Arabic language translators, see the patient in the home if possible, provide same-sex therapists, refrain from asking about sex or alcohol use on the first session, seek help and advice from Islamic community leaders, and involve Muslim graduate students as familiar faces and as part of their training. Although these are important practical suggestions, remarkably absent was any discussion of cultural roadblocks to assimilation, reactions to the unceasing news about terrorist attacks and the possibility of more in the future, attitudes toward 9/11, fundamentalist versus secular clerics in their community, and the inevitable clash between the Muslim generation born in America with that of its parents—a clash that has occurred with every preceding wave of immigration. These are important psychological issues that extend beyond format and procedure, even if their discussion risks political incorrectness.

The Psychology of Islam

Most psychologists are unaware that there is a World Islamic Association of Mental Health; an International Association of Muslim Psychologists; the *Journal of Muslim Mental Health* edited by Mona Amer, Ph.D., a Fellow at the Yale University School of Medicine; and a growing array of articles and books describing the psychology of Islam and its differences with American psychology (Muslim Mental Health, Inc. website). Islam and humanistic psychology have partnered in a movement to affect prison reform, and to address the needs of the growing numbers of convicts in American prisons who convert to Islam (Jalali-Tehrani). The Australian Psychological Society has been perhaps even more inclusive than the APA in its promotion of the very active Islam and Psychology Interest Group chaired by Shehzi Yusaf, who quotes from the Prophet Muhammad, "Seek learning even as far as China" (Yusaf, 2007).

Islamic psychology has a number of differences with American psychology, among them America's socially liberal stances and lack of emphasis on spirituality. But its most serious contention regards the APA's acceptance of gay, lesbian and transgender life styles. There are scores of articles and books delineating the often indistinguishable views of the Qu'ran and Islamic psychology on homosexuality (www.fortunecity.com\meltingpot\jellyfish347\Isl). One is reminded of the writings of G. Stanley Hall and William James, the founders of American psychology, whose views in the latter part of the 19th century made psychology almost indistinguishable from the study of religion and spirituality (Benjamin, 1992). In its striving to achieve scientific status, American psychology has shed its ties to religion, but Islamic psychology very much reflects the Muslim faith.

Today Muslim psychology is a spiritual psychology, comprising the scholarly understanding of the process of spiritual purification called Tasawwuf, or Sufism (16). In the Wahhabi (or fundamentalist) view, the soul is inherently rebellious and bad, and in need of the mind's stern discipline to keep it on the right path. In the 1980s an Islamic science was posed as an alternative to Western science and the governments of Pakistan, Saudi Arabia and Egypt gave it much support, financial and governmental.

Muslim ideologues in the U.S., such as Ismail Faruqi and Syed Hossein Nasr, announced that a new science was about to be built on lofty moral principles such as *tawheed* (unity of God), *ibadah* (worship), *khilafah* (trusteeship), and rejection of *zulm* (tyranny), and that revelation rather than reason would be the ultimate guide to valid knowledge (Hoodbhoy, 2007, p. 62).

There were many elaborate and expensive Islamic science conferences around the world, which included psychologists, with such scientifically unlikely papers calculating the temperature of hell, or the composition of the heavenly *djinnis*, but no one produced a new machine, conducted a bona fide experiment, expanded our knowledge of mental illness, or even formulated a single testable hypothesis (Hoodbhoy, 2007).

Even what has been termed Islamic psychosomatic medicine seems primitive or obvious. For instance, in his widely read book *Islam and Psychosomatic Medicine* Mohammad Ahmad (Ahmad & Ahmad, 2003) gives five ways of avoiding stress: (a) a mid-day nap, (b) faith in the almighty creator and sustainer, because lack of faith in Allah leads to neurosis and psychosis, (c) faith in life hereafter and accepting the inevitable, (d) care of one's neighbors, and (e) appropriate posture in sleep. He recommends *salat*, a concentrating on Allah, as the means of relaxation, and he concludes from all of this that researchers have confirmed the superiority of Islamic practices. There is no end of examples of Islamic psychology mirroring the Qu'ran, reflecting a strong spiritual basis, and mirroring the religious emphasis of the founders of American psychology which the successors had to transcend to establish psychology as a science (Benjamin, 1992). Vestiges of this persist as one recent American psychiatrist, J. Martin Spiegelman (2007), describes the spiritual intersection of Islamic and Jungian psychologies.

With increasing numbers of Muslims entering graduate programs in psychology, it will be interesting to watch the development of Islamic psychology as these students graduate and assume significant and influential positions in the mental health systems of the United States, other Western countries, and the Middle East. In the meantime, American psychology would do well to address such vexing issues as what might prompt a moderate Muslim to become an extremist. This is not only imperative but well within the province of psychology, but it would require rising above the limitations imposed by political correctness.

Endnote

[1] A summary of the differences between moderate and fundamentalist Muslims can be found in the article "Defining 'Moderate' in the Muslim World," *NewsMax,* June 2007, p. 33.

References

ABG Films (2007, June 24). *Muslims against jihad*. Fox Cable Network.

Ahmad, M., & Ahmad, N. (2003). *Islam and psychosomatic medicine.* Retrieved from http://www.muslimmentalhealth.com/Association_Docs/edit.

Barrett, P. M. (2007). *The struggle for the soul of a religion.* New York: Farrar, Straus and Giroux.

Benjamin, L. (Ed.) (1992). The history of American psychology. *American Psychologist* (special issue), *47(2),* 144, 149, 158, 290-297

Brookhiser, R. (2007, August 6). Matters of morality: A history. *Time,* 52-53.

Catton, B. (2004). *The Civil War.* New York: Heritage Foundation Books.

Friedman, T.L. (2007, January 24). Muslim silence. Reprinted from the *New York Times* in its International Edition, *The Times Digest*, 7.

Ghosh, B. (2007, March 5). Why they hate each other. *Time,* 29-40.

Gregg, G. S. (2007). *The Middle East: A cultural psychology.* Oxford: Oxford University Press.

Hoodbhoy, P.A. (2007, August). Science and the Islamic world – The quest for rapprochement. *Physics Today,* 49-65.

Jalali-Tehrani, S.M. (2007). Psychology and Islam: Partners in prison reform. Retrieved from www.ahpweb.org/aboutahp/intlnetwork.html.

McCauley, C.R. (2007). *The psychology of terrorism.* Boston: Bryn Mawr.

Miller, R.H., Stout, H.S., & Wilson, C.R. (1998). *Religion and the American Civil War.* New York: Heritage Foundation Books.

Moaveni, A. (2007, September 10). Intimidation in Tehran. *Time,*

42-45.
Morais, R.C. (2007, July 23). Don't call it interest. *Forbes,* 122 and 133-134.
Muslim Mental Health, Inc. Retrieved from http:// www.muslimmentalhealth.com/Association_Docs/edit.
Spiegelman, J.M. (2007). *Sufism, Islam and Jungian psychology.* Reno, NV: Amazon Books.
Winerman, L. (2006, October). Reaching out to Muslim and Arab Americans. *Monitor On Psychology, 37(9),* 24-25.
Wright, R.H., & Cummings, N.A. (Eds.). (2005). *Destructive trends in mental Health: The well-intentioned path to harm.* New York: Routledge (Taylor and Francis).
Yusaf, S. (2007). *Islam and Psychology Interest Group of the Australian Psychological Society.*
Email: shehsiyusaf@optushome.com.au.

Chapter 10

Buddhism: It's Chic but They Could Have It Wrong

Akihiko Masuda, Ph.D.
and William T. O'Donohue, Ph.D.

While rejecting other spiritual traditions, the field of psychotherapy seems to have favorable attitudes toward Buddhism. Early psychologists were said to be profoundly influenced by Zen Buddhism (Fromm, 1998; Horney, 1998; Suzuki et al., 1960). Karen Horney integrated a Zen perspective into her theory of ego. Erich Fromm acknowledged the values of Zen teaching in overcoming sufferings derived from a narrowly identified self (e.g., narcissism).

Many other psychologists and researchers have also discussed Buddhism in various contexts. In regard to psychological wellbeing, Jung was concerned about a Buddhist concept/experience of emptiness and selflessness as a source of suppressing the healthy ego development (Jung, 1963). Buddhist accounts of psychopathology were introduced to Western professionals in the context of discussing Eastern psychotherapy (e.g., Doi, 1998; Iwai & Reynolds, 1970; Kora & Sato, 1958; Matsubara, 1973). Mikulas (1978) and de Silva (1984, 1985) addressed the similarities between Buddhism and behavior therapy in their shared focus on experiential learning and self-control and suggested the integrations of these two disciplines (e.g., Mikulas, 1978; Shapiro & Zifferblatt, 1976). Finally, a series of studies (e.g., Benson et al., 1975; Lehrer et al., 1999) have investigated the benefits of meditative practices, revealing that these methods, in fact, altered physiological and psychological responses in a positive manner. In sum, while there has been some criticism against Buddhism, Western psychologists generally have been interested in Buddhism in part because of its potential benefits for psychological wellbeing and the alleviation of psychological sufferings.

More recently, empirical clinical psychologists have paid greater attention to Buddhism than ever. This trend is called *mindfulness, acceptance-based* psychotherapy or a new wave of cognitive behavioral therapy (CBT). Examples include Acceptance and Commitment Therapy (ACT) (Hayes et al., 1999), Dialectical Behavior Therapy (DBT: Linehan, 1993), Integrative Behavioral Couple Therapy (IBCT) (Jacobson & Christensen, 1996), Mindfulness-Based Cognitive Therapy (MBCT) (Segal et al., 2002), and several others. Some of these therapies have explicitly acknowledged the influence of Buddhism on their philosophy and therapeutic methods (e.g., Linehan, 1993). Others have discussed their similarities with Buddhism (e.g., Hayes, 2002). These psychotherapies apply mindfulness, acceptance, and nonjudgmental techniques to psychological distress, rather than exclusively relying on deliberate change and disputation strategies (e.g., Hayes et al., 1994; Hayes et al., 2004).

Buddhism cautions us not to practice Buddhism for a wrong purpose, however (e.g., Omori, 2001). Buddhism says that it is detrimental if Buddhism teaching is introduced to psychotherapy superficially, especially when the premise of psychotherapy remains intact (Magid, 2002; Suzuki et al., 1960). The goals of psychotherapy often differ from the heart of Buddhism. The heart of Buddhism is to transcend or to live fully in a given moment (e.g., Omori, 2001; Tsushimoto, 1999). As mentioned later in this chapter, Western psychotherapy could be extremely vulnerable to the removal from vital here-and-now experience (e.g., the domination of over-intellectualization). This problem predominantly results from dualistic and essential perspective practiced in the present society as well as in contemporary psychotherapy. Zen Buddhism often discusses the importance of intuition and transcendence (Sayama, 1986) over intellectualization. This seems paralleled with Buddhism's concerns about contemporary psychotherapy (e.g., emphasis on narrowly defined "mind" over experience and reality).

Buddhist's Concerns about Contemporary Psychotherapy

Buddhism is concerned about contemporary psychotherapy, especially its approach to so-called *human psychopathology* or *psychological symptoms*. Due to economic forces, Western psychotherapy has become more and more symptom-focused (Magid, 2002). We tend to view symptoms as something abnormal, wrong, and unacceptable. As a result, the goal becomes the complete elimination of symptoms. One crucial fact, which is often ignored, is the inevitability of psychological struggles, including the experience of particular psychological symptoms, in life (Szasz, 1960). Buddhism says that our resistance and struggle against this very nature could be extremely detrimental (e.g., Hagen, 1997).

Additionally, when symptom-reduction is of great focus, the individual who experiences symptomatic events is often ignored in therapy. Suppose a client who experiences a panic attack is treated by a therapist specialized for anxiety disorders. After several sessions, the person's panic attack is reduced, but he or she is still experiencing strong dissatisfaction in life. Is this a treatment success? Who is the client, the psychological symptoms or the person who happens to experience these difficult events?

Related to the issue of symptom reduction, the attachment to the idea of a *quick fix* seen in contemporary psychotherapy seems problematic. In many ways, this is our cultural practice. In research, psychotherapy is often evaluated in terms of how quickly it reduces psychological problems. It is important to say that there is nothing wrong with quick fix if it is satisfactory to the client; and we are not advocating that psychotherapy should always be long-term. Instead, we are highlighting the fact that there are things in life (e.g., resilience, discipline) that require time and are manifested through continuous practice and effort. Things that psychotherapy and Buddhism can jointly foster.

Another related issue is contemporary psychotherapy's attitudes toward psychological discomfort, stress, and hardship. Similar to our attitudes toward so-called psychological symptoms, psychological professionals appear to negatively view these experiences, as if they are all toxic to psychological wellbeing or personal growth. In many contexts, it is important to comfort clients in therapy session. However, it is important to emphasize that our job as psychological professionals is not simply to comfort clients for the sake of comfort. Rather, our job is to facilitate our clients' everyday functioning.

Self-Esteem and Me-Me-Me Society

According to Buddhism, the experience of psychological hardships, failure, and disappointment is an inevitable aspect of our life (Hagen, 1997). It empowers clients when they face and go through stressful events, rather than avoiding them. Although the confrontation with challenges and hardships may produce extreme degrees of pain and discomfort initially, it gives clients opportunities for growth.

This topic may be related to our emphasis on *self-esteem*. Self-esteem is considered a major psychological factor associated with psychological wellbeing. A common definition of self-esteem is the perceived sense of self-worth and confidence. From a Buddhist perspective, contemporary psychotherapy could be iatrogenic in its attempts at promoting and protecting client's narrowly defined self or self-esteem. Therapists often suggest their clients to be self-confident by stressing how special they are. Buddhism acknowledges the uniqueness of the individual, but it does say that we do not have to use this aspect as an individual source of pride.

Excessive attachment to self-esteem turns into self-absorption. What could be more problematic is that clients' perceived self-worth could become relatively independent from their actions, the consequences of their actions, or relationships with others and their environment. In problematic cases, the promotion of self-esteem results in the promotion of a *me-me-me person* characterized by the abandonment of responsibility. Additionally, because narrowly defined self-esteem is emphasized extensively in the contemporary society as a key to psychological wellbeing, any factors that could shake the sense of self-esteem are considered problematic or something to be avoided (e.g., constructive criticism, discipline, and hardships).

Paradox of a Feel Good Society

According to Buddhism, psychotherapy may not treat the core of human suffering manifested as many different forms. As discussed more in this chapter, the philosophy of contemporary psychotherapy is now more on the basis of principle of feeling good. Simply put, psychological health is about feeling good and psychopathology is about feeling bad. Buddhism says that happiness is not about feelings—especially not of feeling good. Buddhism, especially Zen, suggests that happiness and psychological wellbeing are embodied in transcending joys and sorrows in our lives.

According to Buddhism, we humans experience sufferings due to the lack of understanding reality (e.g., Sayama, 1986). The lack of grasping reality results from the domination of our mind that is dualistic and essential in nature. The mind in this sense is separated from the body or a perceived entity identified as self that is distinguished from the world and others. Zen says that this perceived sense of the self and the world are all illusions.

Mind-Body Dichotomy

Finally, Western psychotherapy tends to place emphasis on the mind over the body (e.g., Freud's classical psychodynamic theory of personality). While our mind (e.g., a whole process of logical thinking, problem-solving, rationality, self-knowledge, etc.) is useful in some life contexts, it could also be extremely detrimental in other contexts. The pursuit of happiness and the elimination of psychological problems, which is the formula of logical thinking and rationalization is, according to Buddhism, the source of human suffering. Buddhism says that such desires become dominant because of excessive intellectualization that prevents the individual from being sensitive or open to here-and-now experience. Unlike western psychotherapy, Buddhism, particularly Zen, places more emphasis on the body and actual experience rather than intellectual understandings in life.

The Buddhist Perspective on Human Psychological Suffering

While psychotherapy is generally helpful in bringing clients psychological health, Buddhism is concerned about the potential paradox of psychotherapy and mindfulness-based and Buddhism psychotherapy. This is because the fundamental premises of Buddhist could be quite different from those of contemporary psychotherapy. The standpoint of Buddhism is nicely delineated in the Four Noble Truths. The Four Noble Truths (as cited in Hagen, 1997) state that:

1. All life is inevitably sorrowful.
2. Sorrow is due to the attachment to self-absorbed and egocentric desire.
3. Sorrow can only be stopped by the detachment from desire.
4. This can only be done by a course of careful conduct.

These four statements seem radically different from the Western understandings of how our life should be and how our problems are developed and maintained. We all desire something all the time. For example, the pursuit of happiness and elimination of suffering and discomfort (e.g., self-defensive desires) have been culturally supported notions in our society for many years. However, Buddhism states that these desires themselves are major problems. Buddha's story of the eighty-fourth problem delineates this paradox (as cited in Bayda, 2002). In this story, a farmer went to tell Buddha about various problems in his life. After he was finished, he then asked Buddha to help him fix these problems.

The desire for a pain-free life is rooted in the fundamental premise of psychological health shared by the majority of clients as well as psychological professionals. In fact, these desires are at the core of the medical model. However, if our actions as psychological professionals, which are regulated by this desire, leads to unintended effects, we must seek an alternative path.

Experience over Intellectualization

Before we discuss the Four Noble Truths in detail, it seems appropriate to look more deeply at the issue of mind vs. body from a Buddhist perspective. Western society tends to draw a clear line between mind and body and seemingly stresses the mind (e.g., rational and logical thinking, moral reasoning) over the body. On the other hand, Buddhism treats them as one in principle. Buddhism, especially Zen, states that there is no such distinction as mind vs. body and that everything is a unified and interrelated whole (emptiness). According to Buddhism, our beliefs of a mind-body distinction or a self different from others and the world are arbitrary and illusory.

Metaphorically, Zen states that the mind is not in the head, but below the belly button and that life is in every single breath (Tsushimoto, 1999). Dogen, the originator of Soto Zen in Japan, emphasized Zazen (a Zen meditation practice) without purpose ("the purpose of Zazen is to zazen"). This could be understood as Buddhism's greater emphasis on learning from actual experience rather than from intellectualization. Given the importance of experience over intellectualization, experiencing the Four Noble Truths fully is crucial to truly knowing the Four Noble Truths. Buddhism tells us to know the reality by fully experiencing and tasting it. Knowing the Four Noble Truths intellectually is different from experiencing or embodying the wisdom of Four Noble Truths.

First Noble Truth

The statement that life is suffering ("All life is inevitably sorrowful") is one of the most striking and controversial messages from Buddhist teaching. Buddha said "Birth is suffering; death is suffering; sorrow, and lamentation, pain, grief, and despair are suffering; association with the unloved or unpleasant condition is suffering, separation from the beloved or pleasant condition is suffering; not to get what one wants is suffering." (Nikaya, 1997, pp. 17-18). According to Buddhism, life is hard because nothing is essential or permanent, and everything is constantly changing. Although Buddhism does not claim that our life is solely suffering, the perpetual inevitability of suffering is a strong theme.

With respect to psychological suffering, a recent epidemiological survey appears to concur with the First Noble Truth, addressing that over 25% of us experience diagnosable psychiatric disorders each year (Kessler, Chiu, et al., 2005), and that the lifetime prevalence of psychological disorder is nearly 50% (Kessler, Berglund, et al., 2005). There are many ways to interpret these data, particularly because the cutoffs between diagnostic significance and subclinical problems are somewhat arbitrary. However, at least from a statistical point of view, psychological struggle may *not be abnormal*, and perhaps it is quite *natural, inevitable, and familiar to us*.

A very important point here is how we see and live in this reality. For example, as a response to the First Noble Truth, a client may say with frustration, "So, do I just have to suck it up and accept it?" In fact, this is a common reaction to the First Noble Truth. This is not what the First Noble Truth is saying, however. Rather, it says that it is quite liberating if we see and live along with the inevitability of sweetness and sourness of life. In many ways, we do not need to fight our psychological pains or to react to them as if they are our enemies.

Additionally, it is important to note that Buddhism does not minimize the fact that these experiences are often extremely painful. Instead, it says that there is nothing right or wrong with these experiences. The First Noble Truth says to us, "if suffering is a natural part of our life, how do we live our life right here and right now?" This constructive message from the First Noble Truth is profound and yet often ignored by contemporary psychotherapy.

In sum, the First Noble Truth challenges contemporary psychotherapy in many ways. As mentioned before, psychotherapy often attempts to ease or eliminate the client's pain. Often times nonjudgmental techniques are used simply for comforting the client ("It's OK to feel sad..." "Wow, it must be very hard for you"). However, merely providing comfort does not foster the client's personal growth and the development of resilience, which are long-term benefits to the client. While their peaceful sides are often emphasized in media, Zen and Buddhism practice is usually hard, uncomfortable, and sometimes painful, requiring patience and resilience. We do not advocate that all clients and professionals should practice a tough Zen meditation (e.g., Zazen). Rather we are saying that Buddhism seems to have more balance in providing opportunities in both comforting clients and providing opportunities for personal growth. If the First Noble Truth is the case, what would we (psychological professionals) say to clients about their struggles in daily livings?

Second Noble Truth

The Second Noble Truth states that our suffering comes from us, especially from our *mishandling* of self-absorbed desires (e.g., Hagen, 1997; Tsushimoto, 1999). In short, self-absorbed desire is our 84th problem. We often believe that the fulfillment of our desire to completely eliminate suffering is the way of being happy. However, according to Buddhism, our desires to eliminate all problems and pursue what is missing in our life are paradoxical, causing endless suffering unique to human beings. The paradox here is that, even if we obtain things that we long for, we tend to then want something else. This irony can be seen in many of our clients as well as us as therapists. For example, a client who is diagnosed with an eating disorder often says that the more she tries to get rid of the sense of self-hatred (by losing weight), the more she hates herself.

Buddhism does not see all human desires as problems. It treats only desires rooted in a narrowly identified self as very sticky (Magid, 2002). It is also important to state that the Second Noble Truth is not of a blame game (e.g., "our suffering comes from us, so it's our fault."). In many ways, we cannot stop having ego-related desires. The Second Noble Truth may say to us that, if our suffering comes from us, it is possible that we are capable of doing something for it.

Recent psychological research has also shown the futility of pursuing self-absorbed desire. Gilbert and his colleagues (Gilbert & Ebert, 2002; Gilbert et al., 1998), for example, stated that we have a tendency to overestimate our emotional reaction to future events that we desire to achieve. We are likely to think that the achievement of material wealth and personal status lead us to greater happiness. However, people who had made such achievements are no happier than those who had not, and the happiness due to the achievement tends to fade as time goes by (Gilbert et al., 1998). Furthermore, such a biased prediction about desired change can hinder people from optimizing their happiness and wellbeing (Gilbert & Ebert, 2002). In practice, clients are saying, "If I can fix this (e.g., anxiety, the sense of inferiority, etc), I can be happy" and therapists are trying to fix these problems. However, if the Second Noble Truth is the case, elimination attempts may entangle clients and therapists more and more (Morita, 1998).

Furthermore, Buddhism states that the core problem is not desire itself, but the *attachment* to desire. Tsushimoto (1999), a student of Zen, stated that thoughts and emotions become desires only when a person excessively attaches to them. Stated another way, desire is a matter of a person's relationship with these events. A story of a farmer whose horse ran away may capture this point.

That evening the neighbors gathered to commiserate with him since this was such bad luck. He said, "May be." The next day the horse returned, but brought with it six wild horses, and the neighbors came exclaiming at his good fortune. He said, "May be." And then, the following day, his son tried to saddle and ride one of the wild horses, was thrown, and broke his leg. Again the neighbors came to offer their sympathy for the misfortune. He said, "May be." The day after that, conscription officers came to the village to seize young men for the army, but because of the broken leg the farmer's son was rejected. When the neighbors came to say how fortunately everything had turned out, he said, "May be" (Watt, 1975, p. 31).

All things or moments of experiences are aspects of a constantly changing and interdependent whole (Suzuki, 1997). The resistance to letting things come and go as they are (i.e., attachment) is the problem.

When we are attached to self-defensive desire, we try to fix our psychological struggles. For example, people with depression try to replace the feeling of depression with the sense of confidence or happiness. Those who have anxiety concerns attempt to eliminate the feelings of anxiety and fear. As contemporary psychology also suggests (e.g., Morita, 1998; Hayes et al., 1999), the problem here is that our psychological problems are difficult, if not impossible, to fix. Our intentional attempt to control events is unworkable and often extremely paradoxical and detrimental. What is even more problematic is that our attempts to fix things often prevent us from living fully, with purpose and personal values.

Origin of Human Suffering

Zen states that problems of human sufferings (e.g., attachment to self-absorbed desires, attempts at eliminating psychological suffering completely) come from the lack of grasping reality. We tend to believe that the world consists of infinite independent entities. Zen says that such an idea is an illusion. D. T. Suzuki (1997) stated that the world is a whole, including self, and that it is our mind that creates a dualistic and categorical view. This is the filter through which we interact with the world. According to Suzuki, the arbitrary dualistic perspective (e.g., self vs. others, self vs. world, mind vs. body, good vs. bad, therapist vs. client, us vs. them, etc.) inevitably creates psychological conflicts (e.g., comparison, evaluation, and reason-giving) among things, removing us from the raw, here-and-now experience (e.g., embodiment of transcendent and vital living).

A recent scientific investigation of human cognition and language has supported Zen's account of the paradoxical effects of mental activities (e.g., language, cognition; Hayes et al., 2001). For example, a client may say to the therapist, "I was happy before, but I'm so depressed now. I don't want to feel this way anymore." We can see a complex categorical (e.g., "I", "happiness vs. depression"), comparative (temporal comparison, such as happy then vs. depressed now), and evaluative (e.g., "happiness is good, and depression is bad," "I was good, and I am bad") web in the statement of the client. This kind of emotionally-loaded mental event can take place anytime against our will, especially when we do not want to have it. This line of research investigation has also suggested that the domination of mental activities removes individuals from here-and-now experience. With respect to the paradoxical effect of narrowly defined mind, Sayama (1986), a student of Zen and a psychotherapist, stated as followed:

> Dualism, however, is an ontological error with widespread consequences. It has led us to believe in a universe consisting of independently existing, mechanistically interacting elementary particles. It has led us to identify the self with an ego in a dying body alienated from the rest of life. It is leading to a world lacking in higher principles and meaning, with people ironically coping with existential anxiety by enhancing egocentric interests at the expense of the more fulfilling common good (p.1).

Third and Fourth Noble Truths

The Third Noble Truth is about the ending of sorrow. From a Zen Buddhist perspective, the Third Noble Truth is to put an end to mental traps, such as dualism (e.g., mental categorization), essentialism (e.g., illusion that things are stable and permanent), and even any notion of enlightenment (Magid, 2002). Breaking through dualism is to see and experience the world as it is and to let oneself merge into the whole. This is to transcend. When the impact of mental categorization is undermined, we are not influenced so much by such distinctions as me and not-me, good and bad, or joy and suffering. We experience our mind, but the mind is no longer separated from the body. The mind is merged into the body, becoming one, and a whole personal experience is centered in the body. What is left is a boundless whole (e.g., Hagen, 1997; Suzuki, 1997). This is also to fully live in the stream of change in any given moment. The web of interdependency among events is experienced. Undermined is the literal impact of the belief that events posses an inherent, permanent, and fixed being of an autonomous nature (i.e., essentialism). Because a narrower view of self becomes weakened, attachment to self-absorbed desires is undermined. At the same time, more clarified personal values naturally emerge. This is the experience of what Buddhism calls *emptiness*.

While advocating the transcendence of dualism (e.g., mental activities), Buddhism does not suggest abandoning our mental process. While not necessarily against the use of words (e.g., thinking, evaluating, etc), Buddhism is simply well aware of the fact that words are liable to become detached from reality and turn into merely conceptual understanding that could cause suffering. As mentioned above, our mental processes, including our desire, are inevitable and somewhat uncontrollable, and no action or set of actions is capable of draining them away.

Buddhism simply teaches us to engage in our mind without being caught by its literal trap—to transcend categorization and judgment and fully expose our entire self (mind and body) to the very moment. The process of breaking through the dualism is described in the following Buddhism teaching.

> First, a person sees a mountain as a mountain.
> Second, the person does not see it as a mountain.
> Finally, the person sees it as a mountain.

The first stage describes seeing the world through categorical perspective, intruded by preconception and evaluation. The second stage delineates the process of undermining the literal impact of language, negating linguistic practice (which is impossible to do, however). The final stage describes a person who experiences the world as it is with the use of language, but not affected by the literal impact of his mind. In other words, the mind is experienced as one with the body as a whole. Additionally, in this experiential point, a person sees the self as himself or herself. However the self is one blended into the whole. Our world becomes our self. Zen, therefore, does not negate the importance of self. Zen simply rejects the narrower view of self as an isolated being.

Another misunderstanding is that practicing Buddhism will eliminate our suffering completely and lead us to the stage of enlightenment (e.g., a pain-free and somewhat euphoric experience). According to Zen Buddhism, however, such a desire is the result of dualism (e.g., strong desire of self-protection) and detachment from life. The goal of Buddhism, if we must state it explicitly, is to live or function fully here and now. Letting go of dualistic and essentialist perspective does not eliminate our suffering completely. Rather, it allows us to live more freely in this world without wasting our time and energy in pursuing the desire for a problem-free life. Magid (2002), a student of Zen Buddhism and a psychoanalyst, stated it this way:

> What would *consistently* functioning from oneness look like? One characteristic of a life lived from a thoroughly nondualistic perspective is that *we no longer have any problems*. That is, we no longer divide our life into the good parts and the problematic parts; there is simply life, one moment after another. Problems don't disappear *from* our life, they disappear *into* our life (p. 51).

Mindfulness Meditation: Centering the Body

The Fourth Noble Truth addresses careful conduct as the embodiment of living fully and transcending ego-centric illusion (e.g., dualism and essentialism). Throughout the growing popularity of Buddhism in recent years, many of psychological professionals and clients have knowledge about the Four Noble Truths. We have seen individuals who use the Four Noble Truths as a recipe for happiness (or enlightenment), and fail to be happy. In this case, people merely understood the Four Noble Truths intellectually, and transcendence of self and desire is not yet embodied. Individuals are not fully experiencing them.

Zazen, a practice of centering the body, allows a student to develop and promote living fully, shifting our focus from intellectualization to actual experience. In other words, Zazen practice creates a context in which the person builds skills of undermining or transcending literal/mental traps. It allows the person to co-exist with struggles and joys. It allows the person to see what it is like to experience and appreciate moment-by-moment experience fully, with his or her entire body. It allows the person to be who he or she is. It allows the person to be one with the universe in the flux of change (transcendent life).

Focus on Life

Buddhism and Zen often advocate a simple and ordinary life, rather than the pursuit of happiness or success. Additionally, while psychotherapy more or less places its focus solely on the mind (psychological health), Buddhist teachings cover every facet of our living (e.g., eating, working, relating to others, etc.). In other words, while psychotherapy tends to extract clients' psychological/ behavioral concerns from their life contexts and treat them, Buddhism teaching is about living life.

The teachings of Zen and Buddhism can be applied to every aspect of our living (e.g., way of greeting, way of eating, way of meditating, way of walking, etc.). Many Westerners are intimidated by this seemingly ritualistic and structured life because it threatens their sense of freedom. While this daily practice appears to some to be a kind of pathological perfectionism, this is really done because Buddhism and Zen emphasize living life in every single moment.

Living fully is to be fully in the present moment. There is not much place for thinking about accomplishment because being in the moment in what is important. As mentioned earlier, being in the moment is not about experiencing particular feelings (e.g., joy, sorrow, tranquility, etc.). Students of Buddhism and Zen do not practice being in the moment to achieve something (e.g., the state of enlightenment). This position of Buddhism and Zen is radically different from symptom-based contemporary psychotherapy.

Buddhism and Psychotherapy

One important thing to acknowledge is that although we primarily discuss a Buddhist account of human conditioning and psychological suffering, this perspective is not unique to Buddhism or Eastern perspectives. Historically, we acknowledge, allow, and even appreciate the changing and interrelated nature of living (e.g., Tsushimoto, 1999; Suzuki, 1997; Magid, 2002). However, as our society evolves and continues to seek ultimate contentment, our primary focus has become the achievement of pain-free and pleasure filled life (e.g., fear about the destruction of the self). An example is the rat race of desire that has contaminated our lives. Mass media inflames desires by inducing the idea of perfection (e.g., body shape, relationships, and lifestyle) by either implicitly or explicitly advocating, "You cannot be happy or worthwhile if you do not have such and such." A salient example is the desire for and pursuit of a perfect physical appearance that induces so many adolescents and adults in our society.

Likewise, our primary goals in psychotherapy appear to have shifted to the achievement of contentment and the elimination of pain and discomfort (i.e., 84th problem). We no longer normalize the inevitability of psychological suffering. We do not accept or allow ourselves to experience psychological struggles or disappointment. In assessment and diagnosis, a mental disorder is defined based on the presence of particular sets of "negatively evaluated" bodily sensations, feelings, thoughts, and overt behaviors (e.g., racing heart, fear, suicidal ideation, lower self-esteem, and so on). In practice, we strive to eliminate symptoms as completely as possible. In research settings, we deliberately attempt to develop, refine, and disseminate therapeutic techniques for this purpose in a way that is superior to existing technologies. New treatments are published continuously and yet psychological professionals have not eliminated psychological suffering completely. This reality, again, may suggest the need of a fundamentally different perspective of psychological health in psychotherapy.

Cautions in Applying Buddhist Practice to Psychotherapy

As mentioned above, there are criticisms of control-based psychological interventions (Weisz, Rothbaum, & Blackburn, 1984) and a number of therapies that now incorporate methods, such as mindfulness, acceptance, and validation (e.g., Hayes, Follette, & Linehan, 2004). While found to be effective for various psychological problems, these therapies can be the victim of the fundamental perspectives of dualism and essentialism, however. The shortcoming is that Zen-like practices can be detrimental if they are used to eliminate psychological suffering (Magid, 2002; Suzuki, 1997). In psychotherapy, Zen-like meditation is sometimes used to increase the feeling of relaxation in the service of fixing psychological problems. If a therapy becomes successful, clients may temporally alleviate the feeling of anxiety or depression because the issues targeted in therapy are resolved. However, if they do not learn how to live along with the inevitability of suffering, the paradoxical effects are likely to occur. As soon as they resolve a given issue in therapy, they are subject to other struggles needing to be resolved. In other words, clients are still vulnerable to sufferings from the 84th problem. Their desire to resolve new issues can easily bring them back to the similar psychological suffering that might require more psychotherapy. Given this paradox, Suzuki (1997) stated that what is crucial in Zen or other mindfulness exercises is to fully taste and accept the impermanent nature of our life by breaking through dualism and essentialism.

From our standpoint, the reality of our living is a life delineated by the Four Noble Truths. As Szasz (1960) addressed, there will always be problems in living and that individuals cannot be distinguished by whether or not they have problems. This notion is fundamental in our experience, but typically rejected and unnoticed. The meta-message here is that we all are constantly exposed to the fear of suffering as the story of 84th problem delineates. In general, traditional psychotherapy, however, appears to deal with only acute instances of psychological suffering, not the fundamental fear of suffering that continuously brings individuals into struggles. Magid (2002) stated that: "To covey the radical force of this definition to American ears, I have sometimes said that the common goal of Zen and psychoanalytic practice is *putting an end to the pursuit of happiness"* (p. 82).

In this, Magid did not negate the importance of happiness in life. Rather, he cast the paradox of our excessive attachment to happiness and narrow view of self by ignoring the very nature of human life. The deliberate pursuit of happiness—including the attachment to the desire of enlightenment—generate suffering, not happiness. Zen, on the other hand, seems to acknowledge and treats this meta-level message effectively.

Buddhism's Concerns About Traditional Cognitive Behavior Therapy

Cognitive behavioral therapy (CBT) is a current treatment of choice for many forms of psychological disorders. Despite its effectiveness, Buddhism is concerned about its premise and approach to psychological suffering and psychological heath. CBT seems to place greater emphasis on the *intellectual* aspect of human activities. CBT follows the principle of dualism and treats cognitions or other personal experiences as either good or bad, rational or irrational. Clients are then trained to be right, logical, and rational. True to its dualistic nature, CBT then treats cognitions or schemata as the core of human suffering and attempts to eliminate and fix them, in form and frequency, if they are evaluated negatively.

In therapy, they are identified and somewhat directly challenged. Clients learn to detect irrational cognitions and dispute them, to notice cognitive errors and logically correct them, to extract core beliefs and conduct behavioral experiments to evaluate their validity. Likewise, from a CBT perspective, what Zen and Buddhism call the 84th problem might be directly challenged and disputed (e.g., "You should not feel that way. Accept the problem").

What is overlooked by CBT is that dualism (e.g., the evaluative aspect of being "right" and "logical") can be the source of suffering that might bring clients back to other sufferings. CBT can be problematic because it does not treat the meta-desire of a pain free life.

Additionally, while CBT focuses more on the elimination of problems, Buddhism is a constructional approach that assists us in living fully in the present moment. Zen Buddhism does so by focusing more on our direct experience than on our intellectual understanding (Welwood, 1983). In Zen, students learn to live fully in the constantly changing and interdependent world, while simply acknowledging or transcending the suffering due to attachment to the dualistic and essential view. This is a stance of nonjudgmental awareness. The problem of our mind is addressed and transcended in Zen Buddhism, not because some thoughts are negative or irrational, but because they prevent us from raw experiences and living fully with true purpose.

Finally, it is important to note that Buddhism does not attempt to eliminate or fix negatively evaluated thoughts and feelings. From a nondualistic perspective, there are no such distinctions as right or wrong, or rational or irrational; and no events need to be rejected or disputed. Rather, Buddhism teaches us to rearrange our relations with these events (i.e., the function of these events) experientially by simply letting them go as just momentary phenomena, so that they no longer regulate the actions that lead us to additional suffering.

Buddhism's Concerns About Mindfulness- and Acceptance-based Psychotherapy

Mindfulness- and acceptance-based psychotherapy is an emerging force in contemporary psychotherapy. The movement distinguishes itself from traditional therapeutic approaches by incorporating acceptance, mindfulness, nonjudgment, and decentering perspectives into therapy, particularly in the areas of private experiences (e.g., cognition, emotion, and physiological responses). However, from a Buddhist perspective, there are several notable slippery slopes in this approach. In many ways, problems of mindfulness- and acceptance-based psychotherapy are tricky, because they appear to be concurring with Buddhism teaching and practice. The following are several pitfalls that are likely to be seen in mindfulness- and acceptance-based psychotherapy.

Something new is good. Many psychologists are now interested in mindfulness- and acceptance-based psychotherapy simply because it is new to them. For many of us, newness is usually understood and evaluated topographically. For example, because of its unique technique, the Eye Movement Desensitization and Reprocessing (EMDR) once became very popular in the field of psychotherapy. However, it was later suggested that the EMDR is another form of exposure intervention. Mindfulness- and acceptance-based psychotherapy seems to share the feature of topographical uniqueness. For example, it is, in a way, unique to ring a meditation bell at the beginning of therapy session to start with mindfulness exercise (although it is not sure if it has the same impact on Eastern clients). It looks extremely provocative to say "accept pain" instead of "control pain." "I'm not judging you" seems to fit really well to our shallow value of political correctness. What happened to EMDR may happen to the contemporary mindfulness movement, if the richness of Buddhism that is behind mindfulness techniques continues to be overlooked.

Topographical assimilation, but not enough time. Dogen, the originator of Soto Zen, taught his students to fix the outside first in order to fix inside the self (Soto-Shu Shumucho, 1989). From this perspective, introducing mindfulness practices topographically to clients is a reasonable first step. However, what is overlooked is the inevitability of life-long practice. Mindfulness and meditation practice may help clients learn to live fully, but like many other important skills in life, they take time. It is still unclear if mindfulness psychotherapy allows client to have a context to learn to be fully mindful. Just like a little knowledge of psychology is harmful to client, a little practice of mindfulness could be detrimental.

Additionally, the way of living fully conflicts with the notion of *quick fix*. The premise of quick fix is outcome-oriented: its premise is that once treated, the problem is gone. This may not be the case, if Buddhism teaching is true. Additionally, the way of living fully is an ongoing process, rather than an outcome. What is important here is our awareness and appreciation of the inevitability of psychological struggles. It seems more helpful if clients learn to live with resilience in the flux of change, instead of trying to achieve a certain state of being (e.g., happiness).

Strong judgment called nonjudgment. It is quite ironic that, if a therapist does not transcend the conditions of dualism and essentialism, advocating a nonjudgmental stance becomes quite judgmental. Sometimes, therapists verbally suggest clients to be nonjudgmental as if being judgmental is *bad* (being nonjudgmental is *good*) and clients *should not* be judgmental. In other contexts, therapists may say to clients, "I'm not judging you... but..." These are very sticky issues.

A fundamental fact is that we cannot help having judgmental thoughts toward everything, because this is the very nature of our mind (e.g., categorization, comparison, evaluation, etc.). What is possible, however, is to transcend them. For contemporary psychologists, instead of trying to follow a nonjudgmental stance deliberately and strictly, simply willing to see what is in front of our eyes mindfully and living fully, without being caught up by judgmental thoughts seems so much more balanced.

Mindfulness for what? Again, as mentioned above, mindfulness is often introduced to clients primarily as an alternative way of dealing with their difficult thoughts and feelings. This could also be a case in mindfulness-based psychotherapies. Although mindfulness practice, in fact, could reduce daily struggles or induce the sense of relaxation (e.g., Benson et al., 1975; Segal et al., 2002), this perspective of mindfulness seems very limited.

Again, a major concern regarding mindfulness-based psychotherapy is that the First Noble Truth and the 84th problem are often overlooked. With respect to the First Noble Truth and 84th Problem, mindfulness is to live fully in the sweetness and sourness of life as a whole, while not being caught up by the desire to remove entire problems in an individual's experience. Experiencing and appreciating the First Noble Truth seems inevitable to transcend the dualistic and essential trap of the human mind. Otherwise, it brings clients back to other unneeded suffering. It appears that this very issue is sometimes overlooked in mindfulness-based interventions.

Additionally, for the present authors, mindfulness is living fully (Omori, 2001). Instead of narrowly focusing on symptoms reduction, the focus on the constructive side of a client living should be placed more in mindfulness-based psychotherapies. Morita therapy (Morita, 1998), an Eastern psychotherapy, concurs with this position and places a greater emphasis upon the client's constructive living. Acceptance and Commitment Therapy (ACT, Hayes et al., 1999) also emphasizes the importance of mindfulness and value-directed living as a whole in a given moment (Wilson & Murrell, 2004).

Self as the flux of change. Early psychologists, such as Karen Horney and Erich Fromm, acknowledged the values of Buddhism in relation to human suffering derived from our sense of self. As Magid (2002) suggested, Western culture tends to facilitate and maintain the strong sense of self as an essential and distinct being that is separated from others and the world. The contemporary mindfulness movement tries to tackle self-related sufferings, but it seems fall short.

In some mindfulness-based therapies, clients are often taught to distinguish themselves from their own psychological experiences (e.g., thoughts, emotions, memories, physiological reactions, etc.) by simply observing and noticing them nonjudgmentally. They are also taught to identify personal values and act along with them. What seems to be overlooked here in the treatment of self is the development and identification of self in context (i.e., the flux of change). Buddhism addresses interrelatedness as a core principle of living (Hagen, 1997). This is not a simple acknowledgement that one is related to or influenced by others or the world outside one's skin. Rather, the interrelatedness, from a Buddhist perspective, is to identify the self with others and the world as a whole. From this experiential standpoint, true compassion and empathy seem to emerge. Unless clients and therapists build this experience of the self, value-directed living and acceptance could fall into the web of detrimental self-defense.

Conclusion

From a Buddhist perspective, a major goal of psychotherapy is to help clients live fully while gradually undermining the impact of their fundamental desire (e.g., the desire for a pain-free life) on their everyday function. Therefore, the elimination of psychological struggles is not the goal. In the present paper, we have discussed that the problem of our meta-desire to eliminate all problems (e.g., 84th problem) arises from the very nature of the mental process (e.g., linguistic practice) that regulates our problematic behaviors. We have also stated that this meta-desire needs to be addressed and transcended in psychotherapy in order to assist clients in reclaiming their lives.

Taking these into account, Sayama (1986) suggested that psychotherapists also fully taste sweetness and sourness in life—the continuous stream of change—as they are. As psychological professionals, we are prone to use therapeutic techniques to prevent us from experiencing our own psychological sufferings and struggles. However, seeing and fully experiencing life as it is may be a first step to an alternative approach to client problems with true empathy and compassion. Buddhism and Zen say that if one is wise (living along with the stream of change in life), it does not matter which way one takes. It is always the right path. It does not matter which therapeutic orientation one is following. It is always the way.

References

Bayda, E. (2002). *Being Zen: Bringing mediation to life.* Boston, MA: Shambhala.

Benson, H., Alexander, S., & Feldman, C. L. (1975). Decreased premature ventricular contractions through use of the relaxation response in patients with stable ischemic heart disease. *Lancet, 2,* 380-382.

de Silva, P. (1984). Buddhism and behaviour modification. *Behavior Research and Therapy, 22,* 661-678.

de Silva, P. (1985). Early Buddhist and modern behavioral strategies for the control of unwanted intrusive cognitions. *Psycho-*

logical Record, 35, 427-443.
Doi, T. (1998). Morita therapy and psychoanalysis. In A. Molino (Eds.), *The couch and the tree: Dialogues in psychoanalysis and Buddhism* (pp. 86-95). New York: North Point Press. (Original work published 1962).
Fromm, E. (1998). From psychoanalysis and Zen Buddhism. In A. Molino (Eds.), *The couch and the tree: Dialogues in psychoanalysis and Buddhism* (pp. 65-71). New York: North Point Press. (Original work published 1960).
Gilbert, D. T., & Ebert, J. E. (2002). Decision and revisions: The affective forecasting of changeable outcomes. *Journal of Personality and Social Psychology, 82,* 503-514.
Gilbert, D. T., Pinel, E. C., Wilson, T. D., Blumberg, S. J., & Wheatley, T. P. (1998). Immune neglect: A source of durability bias in affective forecasting. *Journal of Personality and Social Psychology, 75,* 617-63 8.
Hagen, S. (1997). *Buddhism: Plain and simple.* Boston: Tuttle Publishing.
Hayes, S. C. (2002). Buddhism and Acceptance and Commitment Therapy. *Cognitive and Behavioral Practice, 9,* 58-66.
Hayes, S. C., Barnes-Holmes, D., & Roche, B. (Eds.). (2001). *Relational Frame Theory: A post-Skinnerian account of human language and cognition.* New York: Plenum Press.
Hayes, S. C., Follette, V. M., & Linehan, M. M. (Eds.). (2004). *Mindfulness and acceptance: Expanding the cognitive-behavioral tradition.* New York: Guilford.
Hayes, S. C., Jacobson, N. S., Follette, V. M., & Dougher, M. J. (Eds.). (1994). *Acceptance and change: Content and context in psychotherapy.* Reno, NV: Context Press.
Hayes, S. C. Strosahl, K. D., & Wilson, K. G. (1999). *Acceptance and Commitment Therapy: An experiential approach to behavior change.* New York: Guilford Press.
Horney, K. (1998). From free associations and the use of the couch. In A. Molino (Eds.), *The couch and the tree: Dialogues in psychoanalysis and Buddhism* (pp. 35-3 6). New York: North Point Press. (Original work published 1952).
Iwai, H., & Reynolds, D. K. (1970). Morita psychotherapy: The views from the West. *American Journal of Psychiatry, 126,*

1031-1036.

Jacobson, N. S., & Christensen, A. (1996). *Integrative couple therapy: Promoting acceptance and change.* New York, NY: Norton.

Kabat-Zinn, J. (1990). *Full catastrophe living: Using the wisdom of your body and mind to face stress, pain, and illness.* New York: Dell Publishing.

Kessler, R. C., Berglund, P., Demler, O., Jin, R., & Walters, E. E. (2005). Lifetime prevalence and age-of-onset distributions of DSM-IV disorders in national comorbidity survey replication. *Archives of General Psychiatry, 62,* 593-602.

Kessler, R. C., Chiu, W. T., Demler, O., & Walters, E. E. (2005). Prevalence, severity, and comorbidity of 12-month DSM-IV disorders in the national comorbidity survey replication. *Archives of General Psychiatry, 62,* 617-627.

Kora, T., & Sato, K. (1958). Morita Therapy: A psychotherapy in the way of Zen. *Psychologia, 1,* 219-225.

Lehrer, P., Sasaki, Y., & Saito, Y. (1999). Zazen and cardiac variability. *Psychosomatic Medicine, 61,* 812-821.

Leone G. (1995). Zen meditation: A psychoanalytic conceptualization. *The Journal of Transpersonal Psychology, 27,* 87-94.

Linehan, M. M. (1993). *Cognitive-behavioral treatment of borderline personality disorder.* New York: Guilford.

Magid, B. (2002). *Ordinary mind: Exploring the common ground of Zen and psychotherapy.* Boston, MA: Wisdom Publication.

Matsubara, T. (1973). Japanese psychotherapy (Morita Therapy) and its relationship to Zen Buddhism. *National Association of Private Psychiatric Hospitals Journal. 5,* 9-14.

Mikulas, W. L. (1978). Four noble truths of Buddhism related to behavior therapy. *Psychological Record, 28,* 59-67.

Morita, S. (1998). *Morita Therapy and the true nature of anxiety-based disorders (shinkeishitsu).* Albany, NY: State University of New York Press.

Nikaya, S. (1997). In R. Dhamma, *The first discourse of the Buddha.* Boston: Wisdom Publications.

Omori, S. (2001). *An introduction to Zen training.* Boston: Tuttle Publishing.

Robins, C. J. (2002). Zen principles and mindfulness practice in Dialectical Behavior Therapy. *Cognitive and Behavioral Prac-*

tice, 9, 50-57.

Roemer, L. & Orsillo, S. M. (2002). Expanding our conceptualization of and treatment for generalized anxiety disorder: Integrating mindfulness/acceptance-based approaches with existing cognitive-behavioral models. *Clinical Psychology: Science & Practice, 9,* 54-68.

Sayama, M. K. (1986). *Samadhi: Self development in Zen, swordmanship, and psychotherapy.* Albany, NY: State University of New York Press.

Segal, Z. V., Williams, J. M. G., & Teasdale, J. D. (2002). *Mindfulness-based cognitive therapy for depression: A new approach to preventing relapse.* New York: Guilford.

Shapiro, D. H., & Zifferblatt, S. M. (1976). Zen mediation and behavioral self-control: Similarities, differences and clinical applications. *American Psychologist, 31,* 518-532.

Soto-Shu Shumucho (1989). *Shobogenzo-zuimonki.* Tokyo, Japan: Soto-Shu Shumucho.

Suzuki, D. T. (1997). *Touyouteki na mikata* [Eastern way of thinking]. Tokyo: Iwanami Shoten.

Suzuki, D. T., Fromm, E., De Martino, R. (1960). *Zen Buddhism & psychoanalysis.* New York: Harper & Brothers.

Szasz, T. (1960). The myth of mental illness. *American Psychologist, 15,* 113-118.

Tsushimoto, S. (1999). *Zazen: Ima, koko, jibun wo ikiru.* [Zazen: Living here and now]. Tokyo, Japan: Shunjusha.

Watt, A. (1975). *Tao: The watercourse way.* New York: Pantheon.

Weisz, J. R., Rothbaum, F. M., & Blackburn, T. C. (1984). Standing out and standing in: The psychology of control in America and Japan. *American Psychologist, 39,* 95 5-969.

Welwood, J. (1983). On psychotherapy and meditation. In J. Welwood (Eds.), *Awakening the heart: East/West approaches to psychotherapy and the healing relationship* (pp. 43-54). Boston: Shambhala.

Wilson, K. G., & Murrell, A. R. (2004). Values work in Acceptance and Commitment Therapy: Setting a course of behavioral treatment. In S. C. Hayes, V. M. Follette, & M. M. Linehan (Eds.), *Mindfulness and acceptance: Expanding the cognitive-behavioral tradition* (pp. 120-15 1). New York: Guilford.

An End to the Hostilities?

Chapter 11

Reformed Theology is a Resource in Conflicts between Psychology and Religious Faith

Arthur C. Houts, Ph.D.

Introduction

In the broad Western cultural context of conflicts between science and religion, psychology has a twofold reason to have an inferiority complex. On the one hand, the mental health field continues to feature debates about what constitutes science and what should be banished as "pseudoscience" (Lilienfeld, Lynn, & Lohr, 2003). One does not have to be a psychoanalyst to suspect that there is something larger afoot with all this wrangling over fundamentals and with the one-upmanship game to claim legitimacy under the flag of science. Physicists and chemists rarely have such arguments at such a basic level of science versus non science. On the other hand, mental health practitioners have reason to wonder if they are in fact winning the competitive struggle with religion that marked the beginnings of psychotherapy. In "The Question on Lay Analysis," Freud defended the view (and also his psychologist colleague, Theodor Reik) that medical training was not required for competence in psychoanalysis. He also noted that the psychoanalyst was less like a medical doctor and more like a secular pastoral worker (*Seelsorger*) (Freud, (1927/1959)). The vision of the mental health professional as a secular priest who cures the soul with science rather than religion remains alive within certain enclaves (Woolfolk, 1998), but at least within the broader U.S. culture, it would appear that enthusiasm for religious life is once again making a come back. If it can be said that there is a war between psychology and religion, the roots of the conflict are most likely in a larger conflict between a certain scientific world view and a theological outlook associated with various Christian fundamentalisms.

The conflict between scientific world views and Christian fundamentalisms is especially heated because both sides hold steadfastly to their own brand of superiority and rigidity. Proponents of science from the psychology side are typically dismissive of religious ideas and display the grossest possible ignorance of intellectually respectable theological thought and literature (Vitz, 1977). Proponents of fundamentalism from the religious side are often suspicious that psychologists are promoting an atheist agenda—as they often are (Ellis, 1980)—and fundamentalists show little appreciation for methods of scientific evaluation. For somewhat different reasons, scientism and fundamentalism are equally objectionable. In this chapter, I argue that theological thinking and literature from within the Reformed Protestant (RP) tradition offer important intellectual resources for critiquing both scientism and fundamentalism.

In over 25 years of training doctoral students in clinical psychology, I have been surprised at how intellectually empty the training models have been when it comes to interchange between Christian faith and the science of psychology. In my limited experience (at the University of Memphis), most students came to graduate school with a youthful and enthusiastic rejection of religious traditions, and found support from fellow students and from faculty. Being located at "the buckle of the Bible belt," we also had a minority of students who came to graduate school with very strong family ties to Christian fundamentalism of one sort or another. These latter students often had great difficulty reconciling their religious upbringing with what they were learning about science and human behavior. Some "converted" to atheism and joined the mainstream of academic psychology. Others managed the intellectual contradictions by various forms of intellectual segregation and compartmentalization. I am writing this chapter for both groups of students, in the hopes that they and future students entering the field can get a glimpse of yet another way to grapple with the conflicts and contradictory notions that our current cultural climate readily offers up as a Hobson's choice between two intellectually bankrupt outlooks. Our so called Culture War should be renamed because both sides sorely lack culture altogether.

This chapter is comprised of five parts. First, I place the conflict between science and theology within a broader historical frame of reference by locating the conflict within the larger antinomy of Western culture, the opposition and difference between Athens and Jerusalem. This is the enduring tension between the rationalist Western philosophical tradition of Greece and Rome as expressed in the founding philosophical cannon of the West, in contrast to the historical and experiential Hebrew and Christian tradition expressed in the mainstream Protestant Bible (Anderson, Metzger, & Murphy, 1991). Second, I stake out the basic tenets of what I am calling scientism. Third, I do the same for what I think are the immediately relevant basic tenets of Christian fundamentalism. Fourth, I outline and briefly summarize what I call the RP tradition as it pertains to issues of science and theology, comparing and contrasting scientism and fundamentalism with the RP tradition. This involves showing what is philosophically weak and limited about thoroughgoing rationalism and what is theologically weak and limited about Christian fundamentalism. Finally, I will use the doctrine of creation as a case illustration to show how the RP tradition deals with issues of the so called conflict between evolution and intelligent design. In this latter illustration, I am less concerned with the details of debates between traditional biologists and the intelligent design advocates and more concerned to show that the doctrine of creation is a theological doctrine intended to be understood theologically. As a theological proposition, the doctrine of creation can be quite compatible with modern scientific understandings of biology and physics and may be socially useful for those concerned with the ecological stability of the planet earth.

Two self reflections are important at the outset. First, my view of what constitutes the RP tradition is idiosyncratic and limited. I have a rather peculiar view of that tradition that strongly favors European theology over anything that could be regarded as "home grown" American theology. In this chapter, the fourth section spells out some of the basic ideas in this context. It is also the case that many of those and related ideas are presented implicitly in the sections on scientism and fundamentalism, respectively. Hopefully, the way of thinking I call the RP tradition and some of the key resources for further reading cited will have become clear to the reader by the end.

Second, I am a believing Christian and have been for as long as I can remember. I can recite, and more importantly mean, every word of the Apostles Creed. However, it would take me many chapters and months of conversation to explain myself to either a fundamentalist or a scientifically literate atheist. For me, a prerequisite for any such conversation is that my interlocutor makes a serious effort to understand major theologians in the RP tradition and also philosophy and social studies of science. Much of what currently passes in our culture as the dialogue between science and religion is ill prepared on both sides. The scientists who make pronouncements on religious ideas barely understand the limits of their own discipline and typically show even less knowledge of intellectually respectable theology. The same can be said in parallel for the few intellectual sympathizers of the religious right. Science is very difficult to understand and takes years of education and training. Why would anyone think that understanding God would be any easier?

On the Conflict between Athens and Jerusalem

Within western culture, the major sources of concepts for making sense out of life reside in two broad traditions that are themselves often in conflict regarding basic conceptual outlooks and available tools for understanding the world and the self. Any cursory summary such as is offered here is necessarily superficial given that entire lives and even generations have been spent struggling with these antinomies. Nevertheless in this context even a superficial map is useful for the purpose of comparing, and especially for contrasting, some basic concepts issuing metaphorically from Athens and Jerusalem (Shestov, 1966). My emphasis is on the differences rather than the similarities because those differences were part of what animated the RP tradition, in protest to the previously dominant Roman Catholic synthesis exemplified in St. Thomas Aquinas.

A general mapping of the key differences is illustrated in Table 1. What this table shows are polar oppositions in categories or modes of thinking. Immersed as we are in both cultures, it is difficult to grasp the polar opposites at their extremes and any such exercise of emphasizing the polar extremes is bound to meet with problems because we will have a difficult time finding examples of the pure extreme of either pole. What we can discern are relative emphases where, at any given point in time and for any given historical example, we can say that a particular case leans more to one side or the other. In what follows, the polar extremes are deliberately exaggerated in order to highlight differences, conflicts, and oppositions. Examples are chosen accordingly.

Detachment / Objectivity/ Universal versus Involvement / Subjectivity / Particular

This polar-opposite pair denotes a relative emphasis on the abstract versus the concrete in terms of the object of thought and knowledge. To say that human thought tends to emphasize the universal, echoes the Platonic vision of the pure forms of thought that make contact with another world-beyond the world of ordinary sense experience. The goal of inquiry is to take a disinterested, detached, and objective stance so that one can discern what is universally true, what would be acknowledged as compellingly true by any rational person. This is the world of pure thought and of the timeless forms. One might even think of this as a "spiritual" world or a metaphysical world behind the experienced world. What is real is what is eternal and true for all time beyond the material

Table 1
Basic Conceptual Differences Between Thought Categories of Athens and Jerusalem

Athenian Pole	Jerusalem Pole
Detachment / Objectivity/ Universal	Involvement / Subjectivity / Particular
Chronos	Kairos
Being	Becoming
Logic / Reason	Decision /Emotion / Will
Necessary / Inevitable	Contingent

Note: *These are deliberately presented in extreme forms in order to highlight the contrast between the basic thought styles and categories available from the two main sources of Western culture.*

body and accessible to the soul (mind) as always true. In somewhat more modern terms, this is illustrated by the Cartesian longing for the world of clear and distinct ideas that may be contacted by rational intuition. It is a world of philosophical abstraction and ideals not subject to the vagaries of human experience and history. It is a world that goes on and on forever in timeless being.

In contemporary terms, we see intimations of this universal emphasis in mathematical physics where there is a dream of some grand unifying theory that provides a rationally coherent account for everything in the material universe (Randall, 2005). In cognitive science this emphasis is illustrated by the dream of universal principles of how the brain works across cultures and time, in the search for the basic modules of cognition. With this emphasis we search for what is true across particulars, what is repeatable over time, and what is unchanging with respect to historical epoch and cultural milieu. In terms of ethics, this emphasis on the universal seeks ethical principles that reason discerns and that are universally applicable.

At the other end of the universal-versus-particular-pole lies the individual instance. In focusing on this way of thinking, the individual person and what goes on in the emotionally laden and embodied musings of the heart are the focus of concern and the model for how to think. The Hebraic and early Christian texts of the Bible are filled with examples of stories about individuals. Teaching is conducted by concrete example rather than abstract principle (even though this too occurs, especially as the texts themselves came to be influence by Hellenistic and Roman thought). God speaks to Abraham and to Job in all of their particularity, and from these particular stories about individuals, religious institutions later constructed principles, rules, and more abstracted generalities of theology and ethics. In the sayings of Jesus, we often find teaching in the form of parables, which are specific stories presented as pictures and intended to call the hearers to immediate action in the context of the presentation and the life situation of Jesus (Jeremias, 1963).

Some of the clearest exposition of this relative emphasis on the particular, as contrasted with the universal, can be found in Kierkegaard whose works have done much to clarify the differences between Biblical and Greek thought. Kierkegaard often juxtaposes the emphasis on the individual as opposed to the abstract "mankind" and the preeminence of the subjective over the objective (Kierkegaard, Lowrie, & Nelson, 1962). In this way of thinking, thought moves from some defining, overwhelming and revealing experience (the exodus from Egypt, the resurrection of Jesus) outward instead of moving from some postulates of reason and on to rational arguments. Truth is obtained, not from detachment, but from engagement and commitment to some particular tradition encountered in powerful experiences. The ultimate authority is God and not reason. In Greek thought, even the gods are bound by reason. The gods love an action because it is good, according to Socrates' dialogue with Euthyphro (Plato, Hamilton, & Cairns, 1961). By way of contrast in Hebraic thought, God and not reason is the ultimate determiner of what is good. An action is good because the gods (God) loves it. Abraham is blessed because he agrees to carry out God's command to murder his only son, an act that is clearly unethical by standards of reason (Kierkegaard, 1954).

In this Biblical way of life, the purpose of living is to be engaged rather than detached. The "real" world is to be found in commitment, engagement, and emotionally charged faithfulness to something not seen with the light of reason, but only encountered when reason, logic, and those ways of comportment fail and breakdown in self contradiction and limit.

Chronos Versus Kairos

Greek and Hebrew conceptions of time are strikingly different, but we have lost sight of those differences, primarily because our own way of thinking about time is so thoroughly imbued with the Greek conceptions. This lack of insight has led to countless misunderstandings of the Biblical texts. What is even more confusing is that over the centuries of compilation of the Biblical texts, those texts themselves have represented a melding of both Greek and Hebrew thinking about time. Sorting out the critical differences between these two very different notions of time is crucial to making sense of the theological thought that is based on Biblical texts.

A place to start is with two different Greek words, *chronos* and *kairos*. Chronos is the word from which we get such expressions as chronology and chronological time. This term is found throughout ancient Greek literature, much of which has no connection to the Biblical texts. In those "purely Greek" contexts, the meaning of *chronos* is close to what we understand by ordinary time with the tripartite division along a line of past, present, and future. In Greek thought, time is best understood in spatial metaphors of movement through space and extension across space; hence the metaphor of the line even though the line is sometimes pictured as a circle (Boman, 1960). Time is also marked by the movement and positions of the heavenly bodies in space. In this way of thinking, time is objectified and is something more abstract and separated from the human actor. Cullmann (1964) described the Greek conception of time as follows:

> For the Greeks, the idea that redemption is to take place through divine action in the course of events in time is impossible. Redemption in Hellenism can consist only in the fact that we are transferred from existence in this world, an existence bound to the circular course of time, into that Beyond which is removed from time and already and always available. The Greek conception of blessedness is thus spatial; it is determined by the contrast between this world and the timeless Be-

yond; it is not a time conception determined by the opposition between Now and Then (Cullmann, 1964, p.52).

Time is both conceived and perceived as an external dimension that can be objectified. Oddly enough, what many Christians describe as "heaven" turns out to be the paradise of Greek philosophy rather than any Biblically based depiction of a future time.

The use of the term *kairos* to denote time in New Testament writings provides something of a contrast to Greek thought about time. In ordinary Greek literature, *kairos* could be translated as a season or opportune time for some activity. In first century Christian theology, kairos took on the meaning of critical time, time of crisis, turning point, and time of great significance filled with meaning. The concept of kairos suggests that there is more to events than a mere marking along some extended spatial line of chronology. Certain times are more important than other times, and time is marked and measured in terms of these special events or occurrences. In this way, ordinary time takes on extraordinary meaning and significance.

This notion of a concrete time having special significance in what may be otherwise viewed as just another passing date is different from the Greek devaluation of time. Within Greek thought, the temporal is devalued relative to the universal and the eternal. In Greek thought, the goal of reflection is to escape time by discerning the more abstract patterns of events that signify contact with universal truth which is eternal and beyond mere concrete events. In contrast, within Judeo Christian thought, certain points in time bring about brand new things that have never been before, and what is significant is not what is repeated but what breaks into time for the first time and changes the relationship between God and humans (the covenant with Moses, the resurrection of Jesus).

Yet another difference is the engaged perspective of the Biblical tradition as contrasted with the detached perspective of the Greeks. Boman has noted that in Hebrew thought, the great distinction is whether or not an action is completed or not yet completed as opposed to the threefold division of past, present, and future. Moreover, the point of view about time is the speaker's point of view, not a detached spatial representation.

> While we, by means of our three tenses, move the actions about in space, while we cling to their falling upon a line, for the Semite it is the judgment of the speaker that is the fixed point to which the actions are oriented. In this case, two psychological possibilities exist: the actions could be considered concluded or still in process of development. For us, actions are oriented objectively, impersonally, and spatially; the Hebrews think subjectively, personally, and temporally (Boman, 1960, p.145). . . .
>
> From the psychological viewpoint it is absurd to say that we have the future before us and the past behind us, as though the future were visible to us and the past occluded. . . . What our forebears have accomplished lies before us as their completed works. . . . The present and the future are, on the contrary still in process of coming and becoming (Boman, 1960, p.150).

It is also noteworthy that both Hebraic and early Christian thought contained a notion of *contemporaneity* whereby we can be still experiencing something that occurred many years ago and that is still not concluded.

Finally, it is important to note that most of our thinking about eternity is Platonic rather than Biblical in that the eternal and the infinite are conceived spatially as "the world beyond" or "the next world" or "the other world." Interestingly enough, there is not an equivalent in Hebrew thought where notions of eternity are temporal and refer to the things of this life rather than some other place. The Hebrew concept is better translated as boundless time, and this could as well be boundless in both forward and backward senses. Again time is boundless from the standpoint of the speaker, not from the standpoint of some detached astronomical conception of time. As elaborated further below, the perspective on time found in the Bible is very much existential because time is measured from the standpoint of what is significant and personally meaningful to the individual.

Being versus Becoming

In focusing on a more objective and detached approach to life and the world, Greek thought emphasized being from the standpoint of reason and logic while Biblical thought was relatively more personal, subjective and focused on becoming. Those relative emphases became clearer with the development of existential philosophy in the early 20th century. But it is very important to note that Biblical thought preceded existential philosophy by centuries, and it is no coincidence that the first vestiges of what became existential philosophy appeared among Christian thinkers such as Pascal, Kierkegaard, and Dostoevsky. Some might argue that 19th and 20th century existential philosophy was imposed on New Testament texts and represents yet another misunderstanding from philosophical imposition (as Augustine with Plato and Thomas Aquinas with Aristotle), but it seems more likely that the development of existential thought and analysis of human ways of being opened a window into ways of thinking already present in early Christianity (Macquarrie, 1965).

Much of the difference between being and becoming has been played out in the various conceptions of God throughout the history of western theological thinking. As Christian thought became more and more entwined with Greek thought, the God of the early Christians, who was clearly also thought to be the God of the Hebrew tradition, became more and more the abstract object of reason and contemplation taken over from Plato and Aristotle. One of the consequences of the Protestant Reformation was to reject not only Roman Catholic authority, but also the Aristotelian thought of Thomistic theology. Rather than the Supreme Being or First Cause of Greek thought who is the object of contemplation, the RP tradition features more the personal God of the Hebrew tradition who is the object of the individual's "ultimate concern" that occasions a life changing decision. The life story of the believer and the path of becoming a disciple are more important than the products of reasoned thought and contemplation. The Greek notion of sharing in the being of the creator is deemphasized for the life long task of becoming a disciple who has a personal relationship with a God revealed in the form of a person.

Logic and Reason versus Decision/Will and Emotion

From the standpoint of the RP tradition, an argument for God is like a bake sale for Bill Gates. This is a succinct way of highlighting the stark difference between the Biblical and the Greek traditions regarding the place of rationality and logic, where in the latter tradition logic is the supreme arbiter of what is rational and what is not. From the culture of Athens, we have inherited the traditions of critical reflection and the use of rational argument to settle points of disagreement. From the dialogues of Socrates to the *Principia Mathematica* of Russell and Whitehead (Whitehead & Russell, 1910), rationality and its bedrock, logic, have been the central force of western philosophy as well as a chief ingredient in synthesizing theological expositions. In contrast to this rational emphasis on reasoned argument and the well crafted treatise, the Biblical traditions featured illustrative stories, recitation of great moments for decision and action, poetry, riddles, grand fantastic visions, and prophecy. At various times in the history of western culture, the conflict between these two very different modes of thought and expression has erupted in solitary thinkers and even in the culture at large.

Martin Luther and the advent of the RP tradition illustrate the conflict between a dominant rationalist tradition from Athens and the eruption of a contrary tradition from Jerusalem. Luther is often quoted for having said, "Reason is the Devil's whore." To our contemporary sensibilities, especially in the academic culture of psychology, where science is defended at the barricades against post modernism and other bugaboos, such a statement sounds particularly offensive if not downright crazy. However, as with Biblical and other far removed texts, historical context matters for understanding such a statement. Luther was reacting to the corruption of the Roman Catholic Church of the time and to the stifling mode of rationalist thought institutionalized in the dominant Aristotelian inspired theology of Aquinas. In their introduction to a translation of Luther's *The Bondage of the Will* (1957), a very impassioned yet quite logical refutation of Erasmus' claims for free will, Packer and Johnston provided a summary of the context as follows.

> Again, his unflagging polemic against the abuse of reason has often been construed as an assault on the very idea of rational

> coherence in theology, whereas in fact it is aimed only at the ideal of rational autonomy and self-sufficiency in theology—the ideal of philosophers and Scholastic theologians, to find out and know God by the use of their own unaided reason. It was in her capacity as the prompter and agent of "natural" theology that Mistress Reason was in Luther's eyes the Devil's whore; for natural theology is, he held, blasphemous in principle, and bankrupt in practice. It is a blasphemous in principle, because it seeks to snatch from God a knowledge of Himself which is not His gift, but man's achievement—a triumph of human brain-power; thus it would feed man's pride, and exalt him above his Creator, as one who could know God at pleasure, whether or not God willed to be known by him. Thus natural theology appears as one more attempt on man's part to implement the programme which he espoused in his original sin—to deny his creaturehood, and deify himself, and deal with God henceforth on an independent footing. But natural theology is bankrupt in practice; for it never brings its devotees to God; instead it leaves them stranded in a quaking morass of insubstantial speculation (p. 45-46).

Luther was not anti-rationalist or anti-intellectual and his pejorative statements about reason occurred alongside other statements extolling the virtues of reason for affairs of law and even theological argument. What he did clearly espouse was that reason has limited usefulness, especially in matters of faith. The Lutheran doctrine of salvation by grace alone, the heart of the RP tradition in Christianity, means that reason cannot possibly grasp the conditions of faith and salvation because reason will be confounded and always construe salvation as a matter of obeying the law and doing good works. The good news of the gospel is folly to the Greeks (a Pauline expression) precisely because it makes no rational sense. Grasping that good news requires the suspension of reason. The decisive moment of accepting the forgiveness of sins is only possible if reason is set aside and one is confronted with the absolute impossibility of doing anything to save oneself. In that sense even the "decision" to accept the forgiveness of sins is possible only because God provides not only the forgiveness but the conditions for the decisive moment. In that sense, it is incorrect to speak about a decision in the ordinary sense of cogitation. The "decision" is rather a decisive moment, a crisis in the believer's life where reason breaks apart against the walls of its own limitations, and this is an experience that can only be had when reason is suspended. In the moment one either accepts the gift or turns away. Luther clearly recognized that even after such an experience, reason had its place and useful purposes even in theological discourse and scriptural interpretation (Gerrish, 1967). The difference between before and after is that after the experience, reason would forever be limited and never again the sole arbiter of those things that matter most in the believer's relationship with a living God. From this point on, reason would be a servant to faith and never again its master.

There are numerous other examples of similar eruptions of the "irrationality" of the Biblical traditions, sometimes in protest to rationalist traditions and sometimes in efforts to synthesize the two or to at least bring them into some type of peaceful coexistence. As already noted, Kierkegaard is a prime example of one who tried to map out the limits of Socratic thought, which he took to be the pinnacle of life lived rationally, and to show what would be required to go beyond Socrates by using the Platonic/Hegelian categories to articulate how the New Testament thought of Paul moves from mere subjectivity (hedonism), through critical rational reflection (philosophy), and then beyond to a higher form of subjectivity (faith). Nietzsche, who overtly rejected the Judeo-Christian tradition, nevertheless showed striking parallels to Luther in his attacks on rational philosophy and the search for another way of life and thought (Shestov, 1966).

Necessary / Inevitable versus Contingent

In many respects, the great beauty of the Athenian tradition's reliance on logic is that conclusions based on logical argument are compelling if one accepts the starting point and places supreme value on rationality. This compelling force of logical argument is what is meant by the concept that conclusions and knowledge claims are necessary, i.e. they must be believed and endorsed or else you have to throw out the rational rules. A leading logic text asserts that, "It is the logician's business to serve the reasonable," which, of course, presumes that "the reasonable" (as a concept or a set of people) is not itself controversial (Kalish, Montague, Mar, & Fogelin, 1980, p. 1).

Within the Biblical traditions of thought, rationality holds less of a privileged place, and this reaches a pinnacle in the New Testament writings of Paul who states expressly that the gospel is folly to the Greeks. Necessity is the way of the law, but Paul, the former Pharisaic "lawyer," equates the way of the law with death and lack of freedom. Again, various theologians from the RP tradition have picked up on this theme and noted that, within the New Testament writings, there is an implied critique of the rationalist traditions of Greek thought. For Luther, to hold reason as the supreme value was a terrible mistake that signaled enslavement and fallenness rather than freedom. Similarly, Kierkegaard much admired Socrates as the supreme rationalist but placed Abraham above Socrates precisely because Abraham was willing to follow the irrationally unethical command to murder his only son, Isaac. In a rational and logical world, some things are not possible (e.g., the law of noncontradiction), but in a world of faith, all things are possible.

The Challenge of Western Thought

The great challenge of western culture is to work out a way of life and thought that navigates a path through two contradictory traditions. Our culture comprises two fundamentally different and often opposed sources of ideas. The task is to work out some type of coherent approach to life when the options are detached objectivity versus passionate commitment, timeless immortality versus critical historical decision, endless being versus passing away and rebirth, critical rational analysis versus emotionally laden decision, and compelling predictable necessity versus contingent unpredictable freedom. Some indication of these tensions is evident in the ways of thought that we engage day to day. We believe truth is objective and yet we admire those who are committed enough to die for the truth. We value rational models of ethics where there is universal assent and conformity to what every man would conclude, yet we still admire the individual hero who goes against the crowd because of firmly held personal belief in different values. American culture of the 1960s offered the "contemplative" option to tune in and drop out or the engaged and committed option to change the world and make it different by being part of social action. On the one hand, a fertilized human blastocyst can be a growth device for harvesting stem cells, and on the other hand, it might be a nascent human life deserving the protections of law afforded human persons.

Various attempts at some synthesis between the two traditions have been made in the past. For example efforts were made to put the content of Christian revelation into Greek categories as when St. Augustine synthesized Plato and the gospel and when St. Thomas systematized Aristotle with the Bible. Such approaches at reconciliation between the two cultures of Athens and Jerusalem most often resulted in a way of life where contemplation became more important than action. By the time of Descartes, God had become so philosophically abstract that God had nothing to do with embodiment. With Descartes, the Christian experience had been lost. With Hegel's grand synthesis, the God of the Bible was transformed into reason itself and all vestiges of highly individual and personal relationships with God were stripped away.

Pascal was among the first to challenge this Hellenizing influence of the Athenian tradition over the Jerusalem tradition among philosophers, and pointed out that the God of philosophers is not the God of Abraham, Isaac, and Jacob. Pascal noted, instead, that the God of the Biblical tradition was a God who is hidden and also personal. The God of the philosophers was undermining Christianity, and properly understood, the God of the Bible undermined rationality and human self sufficiency.

Scientism and fundamentalism represent extreme adaptations of the options available in western culture. Those two extremes are the focus of the next two sections of this chapter. Following those two sections, further elaboration of the RP tradition as it is conceived here is presented.

Scientism

Scientism is an ideology or belief system that is at once pro-scientific and also typically anti-religious. Ironically, as a set of beliefs for organizing activities of its adherents, scientism functions much the same as religion for its believers. For example, certain texts are considered privileged, communications are constrained by elite groups, meetings are held to celebrate certain accomplishments, outsiders are not welcomed, and those who fail to follow the rules are punished. In one of the funnier recent contributions to sociological analysis of science, Fuller has recently applied the sociological categories that Weber developed for analysis of religions to science. He has noted that modern science, especially big science with society funding, exemplifies these religious categories: mystery (esoteric knowledge), soteriology (a promise of salvation), saintliness (a special class of dedicated heroes), magical causation (increasing numbers of scientists will increase human welfare), and theodicy (science has long term redeeming value) (Fuller, 1997).

What I am calling scientism may be slightly different from how that term has been used in the past to label "the opposition" in various debates between scientists and humanists in the social sciences and even more recently in debates between scientists and post modernists in the so called science wars. Those debates are certainly relevant in a broader context, but I am more focused on the manifestation of scientism in psychology, and especially in the coincidence of this particular brand of scientism as opposition to religious belief. As noted in the introduction to this chapter, psychology has a long history of conflict with, and opposition to, religious traditions. Freud certainly saw psychoanalysis as some type of "pastoral" counseling, but a type specifically cleansed of the illusion of religion (Bakan, 1958). A very strong theme of John B. Watson's popular writings about behaviorism was the advocacy of materialism and the belief that religion and the social institutions religion promoted stood in the way of engineering a better social order (Buckley, 1989). As in many academic fields for the past century, some of the elite contributors to psychology have been advocates for atheism who regarded religious belief as at least mistaken if not actively harmful (Ellis, 1980; Skinner, 1953; Skinner & Epstein, 1980). A recent survey of clinician members of APA reproduced the general findings of several comparable surveys from the closing decades of the 20th century. Psychologists are much less likely to endorse theistic beliefs and to participate in religious activities than the general population, and a majority of psychologists are either atheistic or at least agnostic (Delaney, Miller, & Bisono, 2007).

For purposes of this discussion, Table 2 shows a core set of beliefs that make up scientism.

Table 2
Core Beliefs of Scientism

Reason (logic) is the ultimate commitment and final arbiter
Atheism is the rational stance with respect to religion
Religion is cognitive error
Religion is superstition and an unscientific approach to nature
Elite scientists are atheists
Metaphysical materialism
Science as salvation
Unity of science

Reason as Ultimate Commitment and Value

As can be seen, and consistent with the Athenian perspective, reason is taken to be the highest possible value and foremost commitment of the believer. In this set of beliefs, reason is typically contrasted with faith, and faith is rejected as unreasonable or not warranted. It is interesting that the scientistic outlook is similar to the RP tradition in drawing out the sharp contrast between reason and faith. But, unlike the RP tradition that concludes that there is something higher than reason (e.g. faith), the scientistic outlook rejects faith altogether precisely because reason is not regarded as limiting, and further, to permit the suspension of reason for any reason is not tolerable. Once reason is enshrined as the ultimate arbiter of all things, it is perfectly reasonable to reach a consistent conclusion that atheism is the most reasonable conclusion with regard to religious matters. Rationalists who hold to some type of *fallibilism* (Albert, 1985) might opt for agnosticism, but agnosticism itself is far from a positive endorsement of faith.

Atheism

What typically goes along with atheism in this view is also the contention that religious belief is some type of cognitive error or mistake. It has always been something of an embarrassment for confident rationalists that so many people could be so mistaken for so long. One reaction to that embarrassment has been various attempts to develop arguments for natural religion and religion within the limits of reason alone (Collins, 1967). Another reaction has been to explain how so many people could be fooled for so long. The latest version of this type of reaction has been offered by anthropologist Scott Atran, who appeals to evolutionary psychology to claim that religious beliefs are so pervasive because they are side effects or accidental consequences of brain modules that evolved because those modules had survival advantages (Atran & Norenzayan, 2004). The modules he identifies are causal agency detection (some dangerous agent is making the rustling sound in the woods), superior memory for counterintuitive events (miracles), and metarepresentation of counterintuitive worlds (heaven and the underworld). He further "explains" the persistence of religious belief as a type of coping strategy for moral uncertainty and existential anxiety. To his credit, Atran is more empirically minded and "scientific" than many of his contemporary, and more vociferous and pedantic promoters of atheism (Dawkins, 2008; Dennett, 2006; Harris, 2005; Hitchens, 2007), but he shares the same starting place. From the RP tradition perspective, it is of course obvious that faith is (rationally speaking) crazy, and that is precisely why the gospel is "folly to the Greeks." To set out on a path to "explain" faith rationally is every bit as absurd as faith itself.

Another corollary of the atheistic stance of scientism is the age-old claim that religious belief is not only irrational from a logical point of view, but it is also developmentally primitive, childish, or even retarded. The intellectual arrogance of this view presumes that modern scientific understanding of nature is evidence of some type of maturation process or progress in the metaphorical evolution of culture or even the human brain. The histories of Western science and culture have typically been written from this point of view. According to this type of analysis, just as earlier cultures apparently got so much wrong about causal relationships between material events, their lack of correct physics led them to false beliefs not only about the world but also to the invention and persistence of religious beliefs. Religious beliefs have also been associated with more child-like or immature thinking. These types of claims are evident in some of the recent uses of evolutionary psychology to explain religion, studies where younger children and scientifically uneducated adults typically show more teleological and purposive interpretations in experiments that present events with ambiguous causes (Kelemen, 2004).

In psychology as in many other academic disciplines, elite scientists are often atheists and some are very outspoken about this. The highly visible and the outspoken can dominate the field and set expectations for what it means to be successful. Any former Ph.D. student in clinical psychology who attended one of the elite programs can readily attest to the need for caution in discussing or revealing religious beliefs. Such things are typically not talked about, and students learn quickly enough not to challenge faculty pronouncements about the virtues of life based on science and free from the mistakes of religion. The belief that real scientists are atheists is very likely not true, based on surveys of scientists conducted in roughly parallel form across much of the 20th century. Those results have shown that about 40% of scientists consistently endorsed beliefs in an active God who could be influenced and in an afterlife (Larson & Witham, 1999). Equally clear is a conclusion that 95% of elite scientists (Members of the National Academy of Science) reject such beliefs.

Metaphysical Materialism

This is a familiar core belief of the unity of the physical world in that the entire universe is composed of the same core elemental "stuff" or substance. The idea is that ultimate reality is material in nature, and there is an explicit denial of any dualism or non-material reality. In many versions of this concept, material substance is all that there is and humans have access to the possibility of complete understanding of this "all that there is." In other versions of this concept, material substance is all that there is, but humans may not yet or may not ever have access to the complete picture of the "all that there is." As they appear within the scientism that is the focus of this particular exposition, these concepts serve the function to deny non-material (soul, spirit) dualisms and to deny the possibility that there is anything knowable beyond the natural world, typically defined in terms of physics. This type of metaphysical materialism is specifically opposed to the concepts of supernatural and to God as some type of force, entity, subject or object that acts outside of the laws of physics or somehow contravenes the laws of physics.

Philosophers have spent centuries debating various versions of metaphysical materialism and there have been numerous attempts to reconcile what appear to be contradictory claims of Christian theology with rational materialism. It is important to note that much of this stark contrast between the material and the non-material (spiritual, mystical, etc.) is rooted not in Christianity but in Greek thought. One of the first heresies that early Christians opposed was the Gnostic tradition, which was very much a striking dualism between the physical and the non-physical. The problem of dualism, and of what became the mind/body type of dualism was actually opposed by early Christian theologians such as Paul (Bultmann, 1951). Among the grandest confusions of contemporary U. S. culture is the notion that Christianity requires some type of belief in a spiritual world or parallel universe of non-material reality when in fact, this very idea of substance dualism is straight out of Hellenistic thought and inimical to Biblical thought. From the perspective of the RP tradition, Christian thought opposes New Age and other forms of spiritualism not just because they are focused on the wrong god, but more importantly because they deny the body and seek to escape the body.

Both scientistic atheists and fundamentalist believers have misread Paul's fundamental concepts and categories for what it means to be human. This basic mistake has led to more misplaced criticism of Christian faith, and erroneous defenses of the faith, than any other mistake. Both scientistic critics and fundamentalist defenders are caught in Hellenistic categories of dualism and fail to see that New Testament thought, as exemplified by Paul, rejects mind/body, spirit/material, supernatural/natural categories of dualism. Modern atheists reject the Christian tradition because they think it requires them to posit some other parallel world they cannot see or contact; fundamentalists reject science because they think that it requires them to deny their soul or spirit. Irony of ironies, the atheist is actually taking a position consistent with the New Testament, and the fundamentalist is siding with the Greek dualists. From the RP tradition perspective, the two parties are on the exact opposite side of where they think they are.

Science as Salvation

The belief that science, and technology as the product of science, can lead to a better life is a fundamental belief of Western culture marking the advent of modernism and the pinnacle of the Enlightenment's rise of modern science (Stahl, 2002). This belief animates the advocacy for science in psychology and is reflected in the various calls for more research, for greater emphasis on scientific methods, and for empirically supported psychological treatments. Culturally speaking, especially in the academic culture of mainstream psychology, it is regarded as heresy to question this faith in science. To be sure, there are many signs of anti-scientific movements in professional psychology programs that offer advanced degrees for would-be practitioners where program requirements carry minimal instruction in scientific methods. However, much of that anti-scientific momentum is unrelated to religious concerns and is more often associated with efforts to keep alive various now-questioned traditions such as psychoanalytic and humanistic therapies from whose point of view the now-dominant cognitive and behavioral therapies are too limiting and stifling, both intellectually and economically.

Outside of psychology, the clash between those who believe in science as salvation and those who hold Christian fundamentalist views is more apparent and stark. Controversies about the teaching of intelligent design and about stem cell research are examples of the more direct clash. The scientistic faith in science over religion has been stated very explicitly by E. O. Wilson in his Pulitzer Prize winning book *On Human Nature*.

> So let me give again the reasons why I consider the scientific ethos superior to religion: its repeated triumphs in explaining

> and controlling the physical world; its self-correcting nature open to all competent to devise and conduct tests; its readiness to examine all subjects sacred and profane; and now the possibility of explaining traditional religion by the mechanistic models of evolutionary biology. The last achievement will be crucial. If religion, including dogmatic secular ideologies, can be systematically analyzed as a product of the brain's evolution, its power as an external source of morality will be gone forever (Wilson, 1978, p. 201).

In such a view, science, conceived as some unitary body of knowledge and method, could become the new "religion" because it promises to free humans once and for all from the false knowledge claims of traditional religion, and even explain why the deception occurred in the first place. That is a promise not only to save humanity from ignorance, but also a promise to provide humanity with the means for saving itself from whatever catastrophe might arise. Ironically and nearly thirty years later, Wilson has recently called upon fundamentalists and creationists to join him in another Promethean venture to save the planet by working to preserve biological diversity, which is being threatened by global warming (Wilson, 2006).

Unity of Science

A key component of the cluster of beliefs that comprise scientism, as used here, is the claim that there is some basic unity to all of the sciences. In other words, despite the fact that there are various disciplines (particle physics, astronomy, microbiology, evolution) each with their own idiosyncratic methods, that call themselves sciences, all share some common ground which distinguishes them from other branches of human activity called by a host of other names (arts, literature, philosophy). With the collapse of the grand Thomistic system of the Middle Ages and the appearance of the Protestant schism in Christianity, as well as the opposition of empirical science to Aristotelian philosophy of nature, started a general reorganization of knowledge that culminated in the science versus humanities "(Two Culture") split noted by C. P. Snow in the 1950s (Snow, 1959). The roots of the unity of science theme go back at least to the 17th century with the emergence of Enlightenment philosophy, but for our purposes in explicating the unity of science theme within scientism, we can look more recently to the rise of the unity of science movement within philosophy, specifically to the dawn of the philosophy of science in the 1920s Vienna and Berlin circles that became logical positivism.

A major theme of 20th century positivist philosophy of science and its offshoots was to show how the various sciences could be viewed as following similar methods and evidencing a hierarchical and reductionist structure with physics as the bedrock foundation. The positivist program for philosophy and science was widely adopted within psychology when the European founders of positivism escaped Nazi Europe and came to the United States. A running joke among psychology students in the 1970s was that logical positivism had died in Europe in the 1930s and been re-born in the United States in the 1940s. That is certainly an overgeneralization, and incorrect in many respects regarding the details (Smith, 1986), but much of what shows up in psychology as scientism typically assumes the unity of science theme of the positivists. Most of current mainstream academic clinical psychology from within the now dominant cognitive and behavioral perspective rests on positivist type assumptions and methods, and this can be readily evoked in discussions where the scientific standing of clinical psychology is threatened by introduction of less than well-researched procedures such as power therapies and other esoteric procedures that claim to be efficacious (Lilienfeld et al., 2003).

As a set of core beliefs about the nature of the world and about what constitutes bona fide knowledge, scientism has been used to characterize religious belief as intellectually lacking and childishly superstitious. In that respect, the garden variety atheists who have emerged in popular culture and in much of psychology have found an easy target in refuting Christian fundamentalists.

Christian Fundamentalism

To judge from the current U. S. political influence of "the religious right," one might get the impression that the U. S. has always been a highly religious country and that the so called separation of church and state is some type of myth. In fact, it is more accurate to say that the U.S. has a history of cyclical periods of religious enthusiasm followed by periods of relative calm. The periods of enthusiasm or "awakenings" have happened before and been eclipsed as well. Consider the following estimate of fundamentalism from Shipley's 1927 book entitled *The War on Modern Science: A Short History of Fundamentalist Attacks on Evolution and Modernism*: "If the self-styled fundamentalists gain their objective of a political takeover, much of the best that has been gained in American culture will be suppressed or banned, and we will be headed backward toward the pall of the Dark Age" (quoted in Marsden, 2006, p. 189).

The founding fathers (and mothers) were far less inclined to mix religion with politics than are politicians today, and that was probably consistent with their constituencies during and after the Revolutionary War (Meacham, 2006). At the start of the 19th century, for example, less than 10% of the U.S. population were members of churches. What has been termed the second great awakening began in the early decades of the 19th century, and by the start of the Civil War, church enrollment and membership in various religious groups called societies had mushroomed (Walker & Handy, 1970). Many of the people who made up these societies and Bible study groups were outside the mainstream churches, but as they expanded, they were eventually joined by groups from within the mainstream churches that broke away over various doctrinal and social/cultural disagreements.

The varieties of fundamentalism common in the U.S. today are traceable to the 1840s with the expansion of various local revivalist movements. It is important to note that these new variations of Protestantism were not necessarily consistent with the broader RP tradition associated with the Reformation in Europe, but were instead more distinctly local and American. Noll (2002) summarized the point as follows: "It is not an exaggeration to claim that this 19th-Century Protestant evangelicalism differed from the religion of the Protestant Reformation as much as 16th-Century Reformation Protestantism differed from the Roman Catholic theology from which it emerged" (Noll, 2002, p.3). In many respects, the rise of the distinctly American brand of fundamentalism was associated with the rejection of Darwinian ideas of evolution, and with rejection of the advance of historical critical studies of the Biblical texts at the end of the 19th century. If we see a certain line of continuity from the Reformation to the rise of modern science, and through the Enlightenment to the appearance of Darwinian concepts and modern Biblical scholarship, then American fundamentalism looks like a fairly typical backward movement intended to "circle the wagons" and shut down the intellectual advances of Western culture. In many respects that is exactly what fundamentalism was and still is. Even though American fundamentalism developed to include certain Protestant sects, the overall outlook of fundamentalism is anathema to the broad RP tradition.

The most immediate precursor to the current "religious right" was the coalition of independent Bible conferences and disaffected mainstream Protestants that emerged in the 1920s, who first self identified as fundamentalists (Marsden, 2006). They were decidedly anti-modern, and opposed both Darwinism and the historical critical study of the Bible that had developed mainly in Europe with archeological and philological studies of the Biblical texts in the latter half of the 19th century. Interestingly, they were champions of Baconian inductive methods and common sense philosophy in opposition to what they perceived to be theory-laden and hypothesis (presupposition) driven theology of the historical critical method. They believed that their approach to interpretation was the "true" scientific approach and that every word of the Bible was true because it came directly from God. They even used metaphors of dictation and photography to describe the transmission of the words from God to the text. Most of these groups were preoccupied with the second coming of Jesus and the 'correct" reading of Biblical prophecy. The early fundamentalists were dominated by dispensationalists, who devised from selected Biblical texts the view that all of history could be divided into 7 periods or dispensations. This scheme had its own internal logic and facilitated their doctrines of literal truth and inerrancy of scripture because it rendered logical what might otherwise be regarded as contradictory information from different parts of the Bible. Marsden described the thinking as follows:

> They were absolutely convinced that all they were doing was taking the hard facts of Scripture, carefully arranging and classifying them, and thus discovering the clear patterns which Scripture revealed. . . . "Inerrancy," which was to become a code word for much of the fundamentalist movement, had a scientific quality that was related to the view of truth as directly apprehended facts. . . . Thus, the millenarian's view of Scripture was, in effect, modeled after the Newtonian view of the physical universe. Created by God, it was a perfect self-contained unity governed by exact laws which could be discovered by careful analysis and classification. . . . When Scripture was looked upon as the compellingly perfect design of God, every detail was significant. Hence, even though the Bible was not intended to teach science, God had guided even the poetic language so as to anticipate scientific discoveries (Marsden, 2006, p. 56-57).

Excepting certain assumptions about the reality of the supernatural and the text as the literal writing of God himself, early 20th century fundamentalists were following a rational and empirical program of thought worthy of admiration by the staunchest of logical positivists. This early 20th century version of fundamentalism ran aground on popular culture standards with the embarrassing incident of the Scopes "monkey trial" and the ensuring derision in the popular press. They did not, however, go away—as we now know at the dawn of the 21st century where the fundamentalist/ evangelical coalition is a formidable constituency in U.S. culture and politics.

Table 3 shows some of the basic beliefs of fundamentalism. These tenets of fundamentalism are briefly explained, and some of the differences between these beliefs and the contrasting approach of the RP tradition are discussed.

The Bible is Literally True

This familiar slogan is central to Christian fundamentalism of the American variety, and it is the source of many of the conflicts between fundamentalism and science. Within certain sects, this idea is referred to as the doctrine of inerrancy to indicate that "The

Table 3

Basic Beliefs of Christian Fundamentalism

The Bible is literally true

The individual believer is able to grasp Biblical truth unaided by education

Anti-modern:

- Opposed to historical critical method
- Opposed to Darwinian evolution

Antiliberal:

- Opposed to progressive liberal political reform
- Anticommunist and foreign policy involvement
- Antipsychology regarding sexual freedom and homosexuality

Bible" is the word of God, and by definition, God cannot make any mistakes. The assumptions of fundamentalism show three important missteps: (1) ignoring problems with asserting the unity of "The Bible", (2) indeterminacy of translation, and (3) the hermeneutic problem of the author and the reader.

It is important to unpack the phrases in this slogan in order to see just how problematic they are. A first thing to notice is "The Bible" is used as if there were one set of texts upon which everyone agreed, regarding not only their Old Testament Hebrew and New Testament Greek content, but also their respective English translations. Historical critical study of the Biblical texts has made it very clear that these texts are compilations of multiple texts from many sources, including textual material that was likely preserved from oral tradition when there were no texts whatsoever. In actual practice for most fundamentalist practitioners, "The Bible" refers to the King James Version (KJV) of 1611, which was based on Hebrew and Greek texts that have themselves been updated and informed by more modern Biblical scholarship and relevant new discoveries of ancient texts previously not available, such as the Dead Sea Scrolls. Even though the KJV has had a profound influence on English language and literature, there is no good reason to privilege this translation over others that may have a closer and more informed relationship to original language texts. The very idea of "The Bible" is highly confused because there are in fact many fragments of manuscripts that came to be canonized by the Roman Catholic Church, and there are moreover, many different English translations (not to mention other language translations). Pretending that "The Bible" was dictated by God and then handed down like stone tablets in one unified text is simply fantasy and altogether false. Such an assumption is the first of several missteps in the chain of assumptions that make up fundamentalism.

A second misstep occurs with the use of the phrase "literally true." An obvious problem with this assertion is the problem of translation. As anyone knows who has studied other languages, there is no literal translation; only approximations to literal translation. For example, the *koine* Greek of the New Testament is far more grammatically simple than the *attic* Greek of Athenian literature and philosophy, but it still retains the complexity of the Greek verb which has tenses not found in English. This turns out to be theologically significant because it permits a type of expression for some event to have happened in the past and yet can still be actively occurring. There is really no true equivalent of the aorist tense in English, and failing to know that can lead to misunderstanding of basic New Testament assertions about eschatology and the general eschatological perspective of Pauline theology, for example. Furthermore as the multitude of English translations shows, the matter of translation alone renders any claim of a single "literal" meaning of English-language Bibles impossible.

A third misstep in fundamentalist assumptions occurs with failure to consider the historical setting of Biblical texts, specifically the intention of the human compilers of the texts. Even if one assumes (quite preposterously) that the text that has been canonized by the church was in fact dictation from God, it still had to get on the page by human mediation. Failing to consider the historical setting of the compiler can lead to all manner of erroneous conclusions because we are today many centuries removed from the historical situation. Making this mistake, and assuming that the text is talking about our concerns straightforwardly, leads fundamentalists to assume that the Bible can be treated as making claims about cosmology, geology, and physics when, in fact, nothing of the sort is the case. Since Clarence Darrow cross examined William Jennings Bryan at the Scopes monkey trial, making fun of and ridiculing believers who used the Bible as a textbook of geology and paleontology has been a favorite pastime of rebellious teenagers and village atheists. Not only do fundamentalists assume that it is possible to ignore the influence of the all too human text compiler, they also ignore the interpretive filter of the hearer or reader. This is achieved by positing a kind of immaculate perception on the part of the hearer.

The individual believer is able to grasp Biblical truth unaided by education.

A final misstep in the claim that the Biblical text is without error is an appeal by fundamentalists to empower the hearer or reader of the text with the needed equipment to hear and read the text correctly. Admittedly, this may have been influenced by Luther's notion of the "priesthood of all believers," but in the hands of American fundamentalism it is unlikely that this use of Luther is consistent with Luther's broader thought. Just as it was assumed that there was no influence on the transmission of the text passing through the human compiler of God's dictation, so too the reader of the text is assumed to be able to receive the meaning of the text without regard to whatever the reader's cultural and historical situation might be. Fundamentalists of the early 20th century who talked about this typically appealed to Scottish common sense philosophy which had a period of enthusiastic support in American philosophy especially at Princeton seminary at the turn of the 20th century. Marsden summarize this view as follows:

> Common sense philosophy, in contrast to most philosophy since Descartes and Locke, held that the immediate objects of our

> perceptions were not *ideas* of the external work, but (as the *Princeton Review* put it) "we are directly conscious of the external objects themselves." The same principle applied to memory. . . .
>
> This view that the past could be known directly through reliable testimony meant that Scripture was not regarded as representing the *points of view* of its authors respecting the past, but it was rather an infallible representation of the past itself. . . .
>
> The whole Princeton view of truth was based on the assumption that truth is known by apprehending directly what is "out there" in the external world, not a function of human mental activity. The mind discovers objective truth which is much the same for all people of all ages (Marsden, 2006, p. 113-114).

Such claims of common sense philosophy are just what they appear to be and were designed to address in their first iteration by Thomas Reid in the 18th century (Reid, Beanblossom, & Lehrer, 1983). They are psychological claims that are empirically tractable and ones that we can generally regard as false.

Anti-modern

The anti-modernism of American fundamentalism took the form of being opposed to both historical critical methods of Biblical study and to Darwinian evolution. Much of those positions remain true today. The opposition to historical critical methods of Biblical study was primarily a rejection of such methods because they threatened the doctrine of the inerrancy of the Bible. It was regarded as blasphemous to subject the sacred texts to the same methods of study used for other ancient texts, and this was regarded as especially threatening because it might lead the faithful to have a crisis in their faith if such study showed that some words of the Bible might not be true.

Anti-Darwinism was focused mainly on the preservation of a literal interpretation of the book of Genesis where the two Biblical accounts of creation were presented. The idea that humans may have come from a natural process and not from the handiwork of a supernatural being was again regarded as blasphemous. The recent resurgence of efforts to introduce so called intelligent design into public school classrooms and the growth of home schooling among fundamentalist Christians attests to the fact that, although modernism won a battle in the popular culture wars in the 1925 monkey trial, the war has continued and is by no means over (Numbers, 2006). Because I take up the issues about intelligent design and Biblical interpretation to show how the RP tradition resolves these issues at the end of this chapter, nothing further is needed at this point.

Antiliberal

Fundamentalism has always been a conservative enterprise in that its followers tended to want to preserve a theological status quo in opposition to what was perceived by them to be a general loosening of standards for the mission of the church and the living of a moral life. Against those liberals who endorsed the sprit of the times with the Progressive Era at the turn of the 20th century, the fundamentalists opposed church involvement in social programs and preferred to maintain the mission of the church to be the salvation of individual souls. Personal salvation was of paramount importance and remained so even though there was a brief period following World War I when fundamentalist Christians did engage a wider social involvement to save Christian civilization from the evils of modernism, secularism, and bolshevism. Also, in keeping with its roots in common sense philosophy, where even the uneducated can readily arrive at the conclusions of "rational man," fundamentalist ideas were also associated with political populism and agrarian reform. William Jennings Bryan appealed to sentiments of anti-big government authority and anti-establishment church authority to champion the sanctity of the "little man." Bryan was promoting the idea that simple people, without riches and the education that those riches could buy, could nevertheless understand both the Bible and science. Ordinary people did not have to rely on the authority of the mainline churches with their elite clergy or the prestigious universities with their elite professors.

In the post World War II period, fundamentalists were active in various anti-communist movements though they did not penetrate mainstream politics until the Reagan administration where they achieved some significant cultural prominence. Just as liberal church elites had partnered with the more liberal elements of the

Democratic Party during the Roosevelt years (Sifton, 2003), so too did fundamentalists and other conservative Christian groups partner with the Reagan-era Republican Party. More recently, the second Bush administration used fundamentalist groups to champion various social and foreign policy issues, from stem cell research and abortion to the "war on terror." American politicians of all persuasions have found it useful to have spokespersons of Christianity on their side to stir godly enthusiasm and garner votes.

The melding of fundamentalism with conservative political causes has occasionally brought psychology into conflict with conservative ideology, especially in relationship to issues of sexual behavior and sexual orientation. Such controversy erupted from the floor of Congress when the American Psychological Association (APA) published a review of the effects of child sexual abuse that concluded that the extant evidence regarding its harmful effects was less convincingly as bad as Republican politicians and members of the religious right believed them to be. The APA was threatened with congressional action that might drastically cut funding for social and behavioral sciences and even acted in ways that subverted its own peer review process when another psychologist sought to expose the donnybrook affair of compromise of publication standards (Lilienfeld, 2002a, 2002b). Conservatism about sexual mores, homosexuality, and same sex marriage has been championed by fundamentalist leaders and politicians who seek their support.

Reformed Protestant Tradition

As indicated briefly in the discussions of scientism and fundamentalism, what is meant by the RP tradition in this chapter is something related to the Protestant Reformation in Europe, but it is important to add that the RP tradition to which I refer extends well beyond that era and can be seen as a stream of influence in western culture from the 18th century into the present. This RP tradition of thought is strikingly different from American fundamentalism. Although the early years of American religious life had a narrow window of time in which the predominantly Protestant colonists followed theological thought consistent with the European

Reformation (Noll, 2002), that European tradition was largely lost by the middle of the 19th century. The dominance of fundamentalism and a unique American brand of evangelicalism followed. To be sure, there are remnants of the RP tradition I am referring to in the mainline Protestant churches and seminaries in the U.S. today, but among religious educators they are far outnumbered by those of a more conservative persuasion. The number of free standing evangelical seminaries has expanded significantly in the past 25 years. The former mainline seminaries continue to exist, but the demand for their graduates has declined as membership in the mainline Protestant churches has also declined.

The line of thought I am referring to as the RP tradition goes from the 16th century European Protestant Reformation with Luther and extends through Pascal and Kierkegaard into early 20th century German neo-orthodox theology (Barth & Hoskyns, 1933) and on through Bonhoeffer's call for a religionless Christianity (Bethge, 1970; Bonhoeffer, 1954). Some of the basic ideas of this RP tradition are presented in Table 4.

Table 4

Basic Ideas of the RP Tradition

- The Bible is the sole authority for the believer
  - Church tradition is not equal to the Bible
  - Rejection of papal authority
- Priesthood of all believers
  - Multiple interpretations of scripture
  - Democratization of epistemological authority
- Historical-critical study of the Bible is welcomed and needed for interpretation
- Modern empirical science is a welcomed side effect of the RP tradition
  - Reformation as seed bed for science
  - "Secularization" can be a positive development of faith

Bible as Sole Authority

The idea that the Bible is the sole authority for Christian faith came straight from Luther in his opposition to the authority of the Roman Catholic Church. In the Catholic tradition, church doctrine as it had accumulated over time through the institution of the church and the various writings of the bishops and the popes, had taken on authority within the church such that those writings could be of equal authority to the Bible. In many respects, the Protestant Reformation was all about rejecting the authority of the Catholic Church and the entire apparatus of authority erected around church doctrine, church offices and administrative functions. In rejecting the standing of the Pope as the last word on matters of faith, and rejecting the offices of the Catholic institutions, the RP tradition asserted that the only authority in matters of faith was the Bible itself. It was on the grounds of reasserting what was in the Bible itself that Luther and many others claimed that the Bible contradicted the teachings and practices of the Roman Catholic Church. Luther was himself an Augustinian monk and capable scholar who later translated the Bible into German so that it would be available to ordinary people to read in their own language without having to master Latin.

Again, it is very important to emphasize that this idea that the Bible alone is the authority for making judgments about faith is not the same as the American fundamentalist claim that the Bible is literally true and can be used to make judgments about cosmology and physics. Further, whereas it is true that the Protestant Reformation indeed coincided with some broad sweeping political and economic reforms that broke down old structures of power and authority and replaced those with more democratic or even populist structures, it is not the case that these changes entailed a rejection of the need for scholarship, study and education to understand the Bible. In other words, the European Protestant Reformation cannot be equated with the uniquely American fundamentalist movement in terms of its endorsement of the authority of common sense inspiration and the promotion of a literal interpretation of the Bible. In fact, the RP tradition continued to promote scholarship, science, and critical examination of various interpretations of the Bible. The anti-intellectual stance of American fundamentalism is altogether inconsistent with the RP tradition.

Priesthood of All Believers

The concept of the priesthood of all believers was part of the RP tradition's rejection of Roman Catholic authority as represented in the offices of the priesthood as a special caste within the social order. By asserting that each individual Christian was his or her own priest, the RP tradition not only undermined the authority of the priestly class and the Roman Catholic institutions, this relocation of the authority for faith in the Bible and in the believing individual had the effect of promoting multiple interpretations of the Bible and democratizing epistemological authority. The Roman Catholic Church no longer controlled what the Bible meant, and priests were no longer the only ones with knowledge about matters of faith.

By asserting that the individual Christian and his or her encounter with the Bible was the basis for making judgments about faith, this double relocation of authority meant that proper interpretation of the scriptures no longer resided solely in Rome. The RP tradition opened the door to multiple interpretations of scripture by decentralizing the whole matter of scriptural interpretation. The translation of the Bible from original languages into local languages and the gradual replacement of the Latin Bible carried the process further so that, by the 19th Century, the RP tradition was the main impetus for the development of historical critical study of the Bible.

Historical Critical Study of the Bible

In contrast to fundamentalist rejection of a historical critical examination of the Bible, the RP tradition has taken the view that historical critical study is not only desirable but needs to be promoted. The 19th century archeological and philological studies of the Bible were inspired by the doctrines of the authority of the scripture and of the believer. It is as if the RP response to these doctrines was: If the Bible is the sole authority for faith, then let's use every means available to us to find out everything we can about the text and what it says. Similarly, if every believer is his or her own priest, then let's do everything we can to educate the clergy with the best tools we have so that they can, in turn, go out and educate the laity. As can be seen in both Europe and the U. S. the Protestant churches were among the strongest supporters of education and the advancement of science and scientific institutions. From the 19th century well into the 20th century, the RP tradition was a driving force for both secular and religious education.

Modern Science is an Outgrowth of the RP Tradition

One of the side effects of the Protestant Reformation was that, with the displacement of the religious authority of the Roman Catholic Church in matters of theology, some discrediting of the then dominant Aristotelian authority in matters of nature also occurred. The great medieval synthesis of Aristotle and the Bible fell. Whether or not modern science would have emerged without the Reformation, we can never know, but there is little doubt that the Reformation certainly did not stand in the way of modern science and may have in fact been helpful, if not in fact germinal (Butterfield, 1957; Deason, 1986; Merton, 1970). The displacement of Aristotelian physics by modern empirically based concepts took many years, and the gradual shift to the Copernican cosmology did not occur quickly, but the seeds of doubt planted by the impact of the decentralizing of authority in the Reformation helped to grow a different physics and cosmology. In his doctoral dissertation of 1939 and echoing Weber's claims about the influence of Protestantism (Weber, 1958), Merton claimed that the habits of mind and culture found in 17th century English Puritanism accounted for his finding that many more of the new class of scientists came from Puritan stock than from other groups (Merton, 1970). Merton's claims have been variously misinterpreted and disputed, but there seems to be little doubt that the Protestant aim to show the wisdom of God's hand in nature was certainly one of many other propelling social influences in the vocational calling of young English students to a life in the new field of science.

With the growth of modern science from the 17th century and well into the present, there has also occurred an increasing secularization of Western culture. Many have viewed this secularization as undesirable and the lamentable consequence of the growth of modern science, as scientific knowledge replaced religious (especially fundamentalist) faith. The fundamentalists' circling of the wagons to oppose scientific advance because they viewed the expansion of science as discrediting their faith and the "truth" of the Bible is actually not at all consistent with the RP tradition. It will certainly come as a shock to many, even to some non-fundamentalist Christians, but a case can be made that the RP tradition itself promotes this increasing secularization. In other words, the RP tradition as here presented is consistent with a secularizing movement within Christianity itself. After all, it should be remembered that much of what appears in the New Testament, both in the sayings of Jesus and in the theology of Paul, was directed to the reformation and even outright rejection of the dominant religious tradition of the day, Pharisaical Judaism. Christianity as presented in the New Testament is a rather radical affair and calls into question not only the civil authority of the day but also, and especially, the theological and religious authority of the day (Myers, 1988).

One of the most striking examples of this embrace of secularization from within Christian theology comes from Bonhoeffer's letters from his prison cell composed nine months before his Nazi captors murdered him in April, 1945. Bonhoeffer had begun thinking about the displacement of the various versions of God that survived in Western thought through the Enlightenment, and he began to see that this God of reason was not the God of the Bible and the New Testament in particular. Rather than circle the wagons and retreat from the increasingly secularized world without this God of reason, Bonhoeffer sought a way to affirm the God of the Bible and still to affirm as well the passing of the God of the Enlightenment, what he referred to as the God hypothesis. Rather than speak of secularization with its negative connotations, Bonhoeffer cast the developments positively in terms of "the world come of age" (Bethge, 1970). The following is from a letter dated July 16, 1944 to his friend and fellow pastor, Eberhard Bethge.

> There is no longer any need for God as a working hypothesis, whether in morals, politics or science. Nor is there any need for such a God in religion or philosophy (Feuerbach). In the name of intellectual honesty these working hypotheses should be dropped or dispensed with as far as possible. A scientist or a physician who seeks to provide edification is a hybrid.
>
> At this point nervous souls start asking what room there is left for God now. And being ignorant of the answer they write off the whole development which has brought them to this pass. As I said in an earlier letter, various emergency exits have been devised to deal with this situation. . . . There isn't any such way, at

> any rate not at the cost of deliberately abandoning our intellectual sincerity. The only way is that of Matthew 18.3, i.e. through repentance, through *ultimate* honesty. And the only way to be honest is to recognize that we have to live in the world *etsi deus non daretur* [as if God were not there]. And this is just what we do see – before God! So our coming of age forces us to a true recognition of our situation *vis a vis* God. God is teaching us that we must live as men who can get along very well without him. The God who is with us is the God who forsakes us (Mark 15.34 [At three o'clock Jesus cried out with a loud voice, "Eloi, Eloi, lema sabachthani?" which means, "My God, my God, why have you forsaken me?"]). The God who makes us live in this world without him as a working hypothesis is the God before whom we are ever standing. Before God and with him we live without God. God allows himself to be edged out of the world and on to the cross. God is weak and powerless in the world, and that is exactly the way, the only way, in which he can be with us and help us. Matthew 8.17 [This was to fulfill what had been spoken through the prophet Isaiah, "He took our infirmities and bore our diseases."] makes it crystal clear that it is not by his omnipotence that Christ helps us, but by his weakness and suffering (Bonhoeffer, 1954, p. 163-164).

Though he did not live to finish the work, Bonhoeffer envisioned the possibility that western culture could come to terms with the God of the New Testament in a fresh way that might free theological thinking from the heavy overlay of rationalist influence and rediscover the meaning of Biblical Christianity.

> This is the decisive difference between Christianity and all religions. Man's religiosity makes him look in his distress to the power of God in the world; he uses God as a *Deus ex Machina.* The Bible however directs him to the powerlessness of the suffering of God; only a suffering God can help. To this extent we may say that the process we have described by which the world came of age was an abandonment of a false conception of God, and a clearing of the decks for the God of the Bible, who conquers power and space in the world by his weakness. This must be the

starting point for our 'worldly' interpretation (Bonhoeffer, 1954, p. 164).

To live as a Christian in a world come of age, God can no longer be used as a crutch or a rescuer from on high as in Greek drama where the god out of the machine comes and saves the day. Instead, to become a Christian in a world come of age is to take seriously the folly and the scandal of the cross where God shows himself to be powerless, defeated and driven from the world, yet still for us and still coming after us.

The RP tradition offers a way to deal with the intellectual contradictions between the traditions of Athens and the traditions of Jerusalem. One does not have to choose either the confining option of scientism or the intellectually bankrupt option of fundamentalism. A further illustration of the fruitfulness of this RP tradition can be seen in the manner in which it deals with issues of evolution and intelligent design.

Evolution and Intelligent Design Within the Reformed Protestant Tradition

Issues raised in the current controversy about the so called conflict between Christian versus scientific accounts of the origins of the universe and of human life are actually quite non-controversial from the standpoint of the RP tradition. As with most other Christian traditions, the founding documents for a doctrine of creation are the first two chapters of the book of Genesis. However, in stark contrast to fundamentalist interpretations, these founding documents are in no way taken to be literally true in the ways that fundamentalism intends literal truth. The RP tradition poses significant objections to fundamentalist interpretation of the two separate creation stories found in Genesis.

Two Biblical Accounts of Creation

A first objection is that there is no literal truth to the Biblical texts. We are now well over two thousand years removed from the origins of these texts. The texts themselves are editorial compilations from different periods in the history of Israel and, as such, reflect the issues and concerns of those who compiled them (Eissfeldt, 1965). In the first two chapters of Genesis, there are two quite different accounts of creation, so the fundamentalist is presented with an immediate problem. Which story is correct? Did God create humans before (2nd story) or after (1st story) plants and other vegetation? Did the male come first and then the female (2nd story) or were both created at the same time (1st story)?

There is no stepping outside the hermeneutical circle (Gadamer, 1975). Every understanding of the Biblical texts is an interpretive act, including those understandings rendered from within fundamentalist perspectives. As previously noted, the interpretive acts of fundamentalism rest upon a number of irrational assumptions. For example, if every word of the Bible is correct as it stands (and in the King James translation at that!), the so called inerrancy doctrine, then the fundamentalist eventually has to throw out logic and reason at every turn including the two sets of Biblical texts on creation. Never mind any presumed contradictions between the texts and modern scientific accounts of origins. The Biblical texts themselves present ample irreconcilable differences and contradictions between each other. Fundamentalism presumes we can read an English translation of a compiled set of Hebrew texts patched together by at least two quite complex editorial processes, themselves separated by several hundred years from each other, and further separated from us by over 2000 years, and then discern the meaning of the words with little more than an eighth grade education. This is preposterous and the height of conceit.

Fundamentalists and scientists are both in error when these interpreters make the common assumption that the Biblical creation stories can be taken as answers to the questions that we might raise regarding origins of the universe and the origins of human life. To pose our modern scientific questions regarding the physical explanation for the origins of matter or the biochemical explanation for the origins of life is something that we do now and not something that compilers of the Biblical texts did then. To pose these questions of the Biblical texts is to misuse the texts and to fail utterly to understand their theological use and intent. It is noteworthy that the question about the physical origins of the universe was not that important to Aristotle and hence to the theologians of the middle ages (Funkenstein, 1986, p. 324-325). More prominent then was the notion that the order of the world was set and remained the same forever as it had always been. Physical theorizing did not concern itself with the beginning of the universe because, consistent with Greek cosmology, the universe was presumed to have always been here and would continue to be forever. In some respects, fundamentalism as it appears today is itself a type of misguided reaction to modern scientific interests in questions about the origins of the universe and of human life. Fundamentalism and scientism are on the same page when it comes to their approach to the Biblical texts that are the foundation for a theological doctrine of creation. Both fundamentalism and scientism approach the texts seeking cause and effect types of answers, and both miss entirely a theological interpretation of the texts.

The creation stories were not intended to be used to provide a kind of "rational" accounting or causal explanation for the facts of the universe and the fact of human life. Doing that kind of interpretive act is to attribute to the Biblical text compilers a problem focus they never had. To ridicule the stories as naïve from a modern scientific point of view (scientism) is just as silly as to pretend that the stories were some alternative accounting of the sort that modern science offers (fundamentalism). The texts were not assembled to answer these questions of ours. Moreover, the texts have been used for other purposes for centuries in both Jewish and Christian theological traditions. Using the texts in the ways of both fundamentalism and scientism is like using the Sears catalogue to classify mental disorders. It is a misuse of the texts and a category mistake (Ryle, 1949) of the highest order (e.g. "What kind of movies does your toothache watch?"). Our questions are not the questions the story compilers addressed, nor are our questions the theological questions the texts still address.

Instead of addressing our questions of astronomy, geophysics, and biology, the Biblical texts of Genesis were compiled to address theological questions and concerns. That is also how the texts are used and interpreted within the RP tradition. The evidence for this focus of the texts comes from historical, critical study of the texts. The Biblical texts are focused on showing the hearers why the Hebrew God is both the true God and the unitary one God who deserves reverence and worship as against all other gods. This is *the* God who is so important and so powerful that this God created all that is before us. This is the God from whence everything issues, and this act of creation is an act of God's free will (Bonhoeffer, 1959). The world—and we humans—might never have been here at all but for the act of this God who comes to us and comes looking for us. The central aim of the texts is to declare the sovereignty of God over all things. The creation stories are assembled in light of the exodus experience from Egypt and are assimilated into the historical type of thinking characteristic of the Hebrew tradition and subsequently carried further by the Christian tradition. The founding event and defining encounter with God in the Hebrew traditions is the exodus from Egypt, and the analogous founding event in Christian traditions is the death and resurrection of Jesus as the Christ. I will say more about this below, but the point is that thought is organized more along the lines of the temporal dimension than along the lines of the material dimension. Creation is part of history and specifically the history of God acting repeatedly to seek out humans. The overarching story is about the faithfulness of this particular god to a particular group and then to all of humanity.

In addition to stating the importance and power of God, there is an emphasis on order and the place of humans within a certain order. The first creation story proceeds in some ordering of the process by which various parts of creation came to be (Pannenberg & Peters, 1993). The order is more liturgical than it is natural, or biological and cosmological. The order is to remind worshipers of their place relative to the preeminent place of God.

The account of creation found in the first chapter of Genesis (Gen I. 1-II, 4a) is actually the most recent and was likely compiled during the period of exile after the fall of Jerusalem (circa 587 BCE). This account of creation belongs to the Priestly (P) tradition of writings that were collected over generations from both oral and written traditions and used primarily in worship and teaching (Metzger, Coogan, & Oxford University Press., 1993). The linguistic forms reflect the rhythm of worship, and the refrains built into the passages are consistent with Temple practices. The three-tiered cosmology reflected in the text is the cosmology of heaven, earth, and waters under the earth, the very same cosmology of the surrounding Babylonian culture. Elements of this first creation story were no doubt quite ancient and show signs of oral tradition going back to the first half of the third millennium BCE (Rad, 1962). Of course they had the cosmology wrong, but that is of no concern because the text is not a book on physics or cosmology, and we would correctly never dream that we should first consult the Bible to determine the coordinates for a modern satellite launch. The point of the text is theological, not scientific. The text uses the "science" of its time to make a theological claim (Rad, 1962).

What does it mean today that the point of the text is theological? The point of the first creation story is to impress upon the hearers and reciters that the God of Israel is the one true god above all other gods because this God is transcendent, all powerful, and completely free to make the world, or not (Eichrodt, 1961). Anderson (1957) has summarized the theme of the Priestly (P) story as follows.

> The issue lies properly speaking, beyond the domain of science and is independent of any cosmology, whether ancient or modern. The purpose of the chapter is to declare that everything is dependent for its existence and meaning upon the sovereign God. Unlike ancient polytheistic myths, which depicted the birth of the gods out of the intermingling waters of chaos, P affirms the holy transcendence of the Creator. The heavens declare his glory, but he is not a part or a process of his creation. Nothing is independent, self-created, self-sustaining, but all things are dependent upon the sovereign will of God. If it were not for his power, which holds creation in existence, the world would revert to primeval and meaningless chaos (Anderson, 1957, pp. 385-386).

This is a text that makes a claim about God and uses the fact of the world to do so. It is not so much a text about the world as it is a text about the nature of God as understood from the cumulative traditions of Israel. It is not addressed to the concerns of science either modern or ancient. Rather, it is addressed to one of Wittgenstein's imponderable questions: Why is there something and not nothing (Monk, 1990)? Theological thinking is all about imponderables. It is thinking that occurs at the boundaries of thought and language. One might say this is nonsense, but then within the RP tradition, the central manifestation of God is "non sense" or the absolute paradox (Kierkegaard, 1962; Kierkegaard, Swenson, Lowrie, & American-Scandinavian Foundation., 1941). As echoed throughout Pauline theology, the idea that God took on human form is folly to the Greeks who valued reason above all, and the picture of a crucified God is offensive to the Jews who expected a triumphant messiah.

The second creation story (Gen II. 4b–25) is strikingly different from the first in both tone and content. In some respects, the only thing the two versions of creation have in common is some accounting of the creation of humans. The second story is most likely older with respect of compilation and tradition of origin (10th century BCE) (Bright, 1959). This second story comes from a different strand of writings referred to as the Jahweh (J) source. The focus of this story is on the relationship of God and humans, and the scope is very personal and confined in time and space to a small oasis in a vast surrounding of dry land. The grand vision of the P story is missing in the J story, which is much simpler, with immediate rivers and trees and animals. The scope of the J story is the immediate surroundings; the tone of the story is about the involvement of God with the first man and woman. Elements of the story were clearly borrowed from mythological accounts of the surrounding cultures (Vriezen, 1967). In this version of creation, God is portrayed as having a close personal relationship to his creatures and even speaks directly to them. In this respect, the story reflects the covenant relationship of the God who was first recognized by Israel in the exodus from Egypt, and that historical connection is now read backwards all the way to the beginning of human life where creation is part of the same history (Eichrodt, 1961). The concern is not to give a causal account of the origins of human life, but rather to connect up those origins (whatever the causal account) with the God of Israel first encountered in the community experience of the exodus from Egypt. The theological point is that humans belong to God, and God comes searching for and seeking them out. Also, humans are created and therefore subordinate. Humans are not the creators but are instead the created. The same type of backward movement from a later event to the origins of life itself occurs within the Christian traditions where the origins of life are linked to the birth, death and resurrection of Christ. As with the exodus, once there is an encounter with the risen Christ, all previous events get interpreted backward in light of that encounter.

From an RP perspective, the theological doctrine of creation is a separate matter from the scientific analysis of how the universe came to be within physics and how humans came about within biological processes. Claims that God created the world and also human beings are not claims of scientific knowledge: they are rather claims of religious faith. These claims assert the sovereignty of God over all of life and even over the physical universe. If the best explanation we can offer is some version of the big bang theory for the origin of the physical world, then that is the best we can do for now, and there is no reason to set that claim over against the theological claim that God is first in importance even before the physical world. The "knowledge" that God is first and the focus of ultimate concern (Tillich, 1958, 1967) is existential and issues from the experience of an encounter with God (in the exodus and/or in the cross). The religious person encounters the living God as real and then looks back to see that the world and life issue from God. That is a different type of thinking and a different type of experience than the thinking and experience of scientific analysis. The fact that it is a different type of thinking does not mean that it is of lesser value. It is no more remarkable than the fact that an astrophysicist can suspend formal scientific training and look into the night sky and see the heavens as a curved and vaulted dome hanging over the earth (Heelan, 1983). Analytic and calculative thinking is performed for certain purposes with desired results and other types of thinking for other purposes with different types of results (Heidegger, 1968, 1969). As a manifestation of Western culture, the RP tradition straddles the fence between Athens and Jerusalem but does so with a strong tilt toward Jerusalem. In rejecting the authority of the Roman Catholic Church, the RP tradition opened not only a door to modern, as opposed to Aristotelian science (Butterfield, 1957; Merton, 1970), but also a door to reinterpretation of Greek culture different from the scholastic tradition.

Theological Reasons to Reject Intelligent Design

Within the RP tradition, the doctrine of creation is a theological interpretation of the aforementioned two texts from Genesis. In terms of the recent versions of creationism that travel under the banner of intelligent design, the doctrine of creation within the RP tradition has much to say that is mostly critical. This includes rejection of arguments from perceived "design" in nature and by abduction back to God as well as arguments from natural religion such as those recently proposed by cognitive anthropology and evolutionary psychology.

A great deal of ink and hot air has been expended on the so called intelligent design debates. What is most remarkable about much of this exchange is just how unintelligent it is with respect to theology. From the standpoint of RP tradition, there is no need to appeal to some intelligent designer because the doctrine of creation is about the sovereignty of God and not some alternative to the best scientific explanations for the origins of the universe and of human life. The doctrine of creation has no need to invent a story about the signs of intelligence in the universe because God is revealed, not through nature and its many wonders, but instead through the death and resurrection of Jesus Christ which is sufficient and is the basis for the encounter with God. The god of the deist (Einstein, Paley, and Jefferson), the god of the pantheist, and the god(s) of the Greeks are, none of them, the God of RP tradition. Although it makes perfect sense that the blending of the cultures of Athens and Jerusalem in the context of the Enlightenment would lead to explorations in natural theology even within the RP tradition, the strand of RP tradition that I am emphasizing is one that rejects locating the divine in the natural and rejects naturalistic means and strivings to reach up to or out to God. Instead, this strand emphasizes that God comes to humans and no human capacity for reason is the means to engineer such an encounter (Barth, Bromiley, & Torrance, 2004). God is the wholly other (Otto, 1958) who chooses to reveal himself, and no amount of application of human capacities can bring that about or make that happen. God is outside of nature as the one who created nature out of nothing (Bonhoeffer, 1959). Theological thinking from the RP tradition of this strand has no need of naturalistic accounts of religious faith other than as interesting exercises of intellectual argumentation. The very idea that one could come to Christian faith "by reason alone" is rejected from the outset.

Appeals to design as evidence for God or as reasons to believe are missing the point from the RP tradition. As such, their flaws are more interesting than their strengths. For example, most arguments for seeing design in nature are based on faulty analogical reasoning. The classic example is Paley's analogy of God as watchmaker (Paley, 1831). As Hume noted well before Paley's argument, the problem is that whereas we can and do know the means by which the watch was made, we have no evidence that the causal mechanistic process by which the universe was "made" is of a like kind (Hume, 1965). Collins (1967) summarized the Humean objection as follows.

> In the design argument, it is not simply a case of arguing from like effects to like causes in some degree. The real task is to show that the natural world *must be construed as a crafted effect at all*, in the sense of being the outcome of a making process somewhat similar to the process of making on the part of the intelligent human maker. The very aboriginality and uniqueness of the cosmogonic making process prevents it from belonging in a wider class of makings which men can experience, and hence prevent the design analogy from having that experiential basis required for a sound analogical argument in everyday life and scientific inquiry (Collins, 1967, p. 56, italics added).

With the aid of high energy physics and advanced technologies such a super colliders, humans may be able to have some experience by analogy and that experience has pointed increasingly to stochastic processes and not toward some design, intelligent or otherwise. The same appears to be true in the case of human origins, where Darwinian processes of random genetic variation and natural selection are sufficient and not in need of some hidden hand doing the "designing." In the history of recent human thought, every attempt to make this case (ironically to the god of the Greeks) with some reference to intelligent design, as the basis for creationism, has been profoundly refuted by the available evidence

(Kitcher, 1982, 2007). The creationist strategy has been to presume there was a crafter and then search selectively for evidence to support some version of that presumption and also to identify so called hard cases that appear to defy random variation and selection as the mechanism of species differentiation. By any rational standards, it simply has not worked. The doctrine of creation is not about science and matters of fact; it is instead about theology and matters of faith. In that sense it is important to understand and to reiterate the historicizing process of theological thinking which locates the significance of creation in a certain way of thinking about time.

Creation as History and the Place of Humans in Theological Time

As we have already noted, the Biblical conception of time is different from the Greek conception of time. In Greek cosmology, time is cyclical and the world does not have a beginning; it simply is and always has been. In contrast, the Judeo-Christian tradition has more of a linear conception of time where there is some notion of beginning and end. Human time (chronos) happens between the beginning and the end, and humans only have some vague intimation of the beginning and the end through religious faith and revelation.

The significance of creation is not the agency of God as a first cause but is rather the starting point for the beginning of time and history, which is still in process of playing out. In that theological sense, it really does not matter what story we tell about the physics or the material constitution of the universe. From a theological point of view, what matters is that humans have a significance that comes from and belongs to their relationship to God. That relationship is one of creature belonging to creator. What is more, the creature is made responsible for the care of the creation. In that sense, there may indeed be some rapprochement between theologically literate Christians and atheist biologists such as Wilson (2006) who are concerned for the preservation of biological diversity on the earth.

Concluding Remarks

American culture has stayed far from its European heritage, and this has been particularly stark in the sphere of religious life among Christians. The rise of Christian fundamentalism in the U.S. has obscured the rich heritage of the RP tradition and has made it unnecessarily difficult for people to be at once scientifically sophisticated and religiously committed. There is a way out of this dilemma, and the way is to reject fundamentalism.

If fundamentalism is strikingly wrong headed, scientism is equally half hearted. We can no more throw out the Jerusalem side of our culture than the fundamentalist can throw out the Athens side. The task before us has been, and remains, the task of getting head and heart together without losing either one.

References

Albert, H. (1985). *Treatise on critical reason.* Princeton, NJ: Princeton University Press.

Anderson, B. W. (1957). *Understanding the Old Testament.* Englewood Cliffs, NJ: Prentice-Hall.

Anderson, B. W., Metzger, B. M., & Murphy, R. E. (1991). The new Oxford annotated Bible with the Apocryphal/Deuterocanonical books. New York: Oxford University Press.

Atran, S., & Norenzayan, A. (2004). Religion's evolutionary landscape: Counterintuition, commitment, compassion, communion. *Behavioral and Brain Sciences,* 27(6), 7 13-730; discussion 730-770.

Bakan, D. (1958). *Sigmund Freud and the Jewish mystical tradition.* Princeton, NJ: Van Nostrand.

Barth, K., Bromiley, G. W., & Torrance, T. F. (2004). *Church dogmatics* (1st pbk. ed.). London; New York: T. & T. Clark International.

Barth, K., & Hoskyns, E. C. (1933). *The Epistle to the Romans.* London: Oxford University Press, H. Milford.

Bethge, E. (1970). Dietrich Bonhoefer (3. durchges. ed.). München: Kaiser.

Boman, T. (1960). *Hebrew thought compared with Greek.* Philadelphia: Westminster Press.

Bonhoeffer, D. (1954). *Prisoner for God: Letters and papers from prison.* New York: Macmillan.

Bonhoeffer, D. (1959). *Creation and fall: a theological interpretation of Genesis 1-3.* New York: Macmillan.

Bright, J. (1959). *A history of Israel.* Philadelphia: Westminster Press.

Buckley, K. W. (1989). *Mechanical man: John Broadus Watson and the beginnings of behaviorism.* New York: Guilford Press.

Bultmann, R. K. (1951). *Theology of the New Testament.* New York: Scribner.

Butterfield, H. (1957). *The origins of modern science: 1300-1800* (Rev. ed.). New York: Macmillan.

Collins, J. (1967). *The emergence of philosophy of religion.* New Haven: Yale University Press.

Cullmann, O. (1964). *Christ and time: the primitive Christian conception of time and history* (Rev. ed.). Philadelphia: Westminster Press.

Dawkins, R. (2008). *The God delusion* (1st Mariner Books ed.). Boston: Houghton Mifflin Co.

Deason, G. B. (1986). Reformation theology and the mechanistic conception of nature. In D. C. Lindberg & R. L. Numbers (Eds.), *God and nature: historical essays on the encounter between Christianity and science* (pp. 167-191). Berkeley: University of California Press.

Delaney, H. D., Miller, W. R., & Bisono, A. M. (2007). Religiosity and spirituality among psychologists: A survey of clinician members of the American Psychological Association. *Professional Psychology: Research and Practice,* 38(5), 538-546.

Dennett, D. C. (2006). *Breaking the spell: religion as a natural phenomenon.* New York: Viking.

Eichrodt, W. (1961). Theology of the Old Testament. Philadelphia: Westminster Press.

Eissfeldt, O. (1965). *The Old Testament;* an introduction, including the Apocrypha and Pseudepigrapha, and also the works of similar type from Qumran: the history of the formation of the Old Testament. New York: Harper and Row.

Ellis, A. (1980). Psychotherapy and atheistic values: A response to A. E. Bergin's "Psychotherapy and religious values." *Journal of Consulting and Clinical Psychology,* 48(5), 635-639.

Freud, S. ((1927/1959)). Postscript to a discussion on lay analysis. In J. Strachey (Ed.), *Sigmund Freud: Collected papers* (First American ed., Vol. 5, pp. 205-214). New York: Basic Books.

Fuller, S. (1997). *Science.* Minneapolis: University of Minnesota Press.

Funkenstein, A. (1986). *Theology and the scientific imagination from the Middle Ages to the seventeenth century.* Princeton, NJ: Princeton University Press.

Gadamer, H. G. (1975). *Truth and method.* New York: Seabury Press.

Gerrish, B. A. (1967). Martin Luther. In P. Edwards (Ed.), *The Encyclopedia of philosophy* (Vol. 5, pp. 109-113). New York: Macmillan.

Harris, S. (2005). *The end of faith: religion, terror, and the future of reason* (1st Norton pbk. ed.). New York: W.W. Norton & Co.

Heelan, P. A. (1983). *Space-perception and the philosophy of science.* Berkeley: University of California Press.

Heidegger, M. (1968). *What is called thinking?* (1st ed.). New York: Harper & Row.

Heidegger, M. (1969). *Discourse on thinking. A translation of gelassenheit.* New York: Harper & Row.

Hitchens, C. (2007). *God is not great: how religion poisons everything* (1st ed.). New York: Twelve.

Hume, D. (1965). *Dialogues concerning natural religion.* New York: Hafner Publishing Company. (Original work published 1779.)

Jeremias, J. (1963). *The parables of Jesus* (Rev. ed.). New York: Scribner.

Kalish, D., Montague, R., Mar, G., & Fogelin, R. J. (1980). *Logic: techniques of formal reasoning* (2d ed.). New York: Harcourt Brace Jovanovich.

Kelemen, D. (2004). Are children "intuitive theists"? Reasoning about purpose and design in nature. *Psychological Science,* 15(5), 295-301.

Kierkegaard, S. (1954). *Fear and trembling, and the sickness unto death.* Garden City, NY: Doubleday.

Kierkegaard, S. (1962). *Philosophical fragments* (2d ed.). Princeton, NJ: Princeton University Press.

Kierkegaard, S., Lowrie, W., & Nelson, B. (1962). *The point of view for my work as an author: A report to history and related writings.* New York: Harper.

Kierkegaard, S., Swenson, D. F., Lowrie, W., & American-Scandinavian Foundation. (1941). *Kierkegaard's concluding unsci-*

entific postscript. Princeton: Princeton University Press, for American Scandinavian Foundation.

Kitcher, P. (1982). *Abusing science: the case against creationism.* Cambridge, MA: MIT Press.

Kitcher, P. (2007). *Living with Darwin: evolution, design, and the future of faith.* Oxford; New York: Oxford University Press.

Larson, E. J., & Witham, L. (1999). Scientists and religion in America. *Scientific American*, 281(3), 88-93.

Lilienfeld, S. O. (2002a). A funny thing happened on the way to my American Psychologist publication. *American Psychologist*, 57(3), 225-227.

Lilienfeld, S. O. (2002b). When worlds collide: Social science, politics, and the Rind et al. child sexual abuse meta-analysis. *American Psychologist,* 57(3), 176-188.

Lilienfeld, S. O., Lynn, S. J., & Lohr, J. M. (2003). *Science and pseudoscience in clinical psychology.* New York: Guilford Press.

Luther, M. (1957). *Martin Luther on the bondage of the will.* A new translation of De servo arbitrio (1525) Martin Luther's reply to Erasmus of Rotterdam. (J. I. Packer & O. R. Johnston, Trans.) Westwood, NJ: Revell.

Macquarrie, J. (1965). *An existentialist theology: a comparison of Heidegger and Bultmann.* New York: Harper & Row.

Marsden, G. M. (2006). *Fundamentalism and American culture* (2nd ed.). New York: Oxford University Press.

Meacham, J. (2006). *American gospel: God, the founding fathers, and the making of a nation* (1st ed.). New York: Random House.

Merton, R. K. (1970). *Science, technology & society in seventeenth century England* (1st American ed.). New York: H. Fertig.

Metzger, B. M., Coogan, M. D., & Oxford University Press. (1993). *The Oxford companion to the Bible.* New York: Oxford University Press.

Monk, R. (1990). *Ludwig Wittgenstein: the duty of genius* (1st American ed.). New York: Free Press: Maxwell Macmillan International.

Myers, C. (1988). *Binding the strong man: a political reading of Mark's story of Jesus.* Maryknoll, NY: Orbis Books.

Noll, M. A. (2002). *America's God: from Jonathan Edwards to Abraham Lincoln.* Oxford; New York: Oxford University Press.

Numbers, R. L. (2006). *The creationists: from scientific creationism to intelligent design* (Expanded ed.). Cambridge, MA: Harvard University Press.

Otto, R. (1958). *The idea of the holy: An inquiry into the non-rational factor in the idea of the divine and its relation to the rational.* New York: Oxford University Press.

Paley, W. (1831). *Natural theology: or evidences of the existence and attributes of the deity, collected from the appearances of nature.* Boston: Lincoln and Edmands (Original work published 1802).

Pannenberg, W., & Peters, T. (1993). *Toward a theology of nature: essays on science and faith* (1st ed.). Louisville, KY: Westminster/J. Knox Press.

Plato. (1961). *Plato: The collected dialogues, including the letters.* (E. Hamilton & H. Cairns, Eds.) New York: Pantheon Books.

Rad, G. V. (1962). *Old Testament theology.* New York: Harper.

Randall, L. (2005). *Warped passages: unraveling the mysteries of the universe's hidden dimensions* (1st ed.). New York: Ecco.

Reid, T., Beanblossom, R. E., & Lehrer, K. (1983). *Thomas Reid's inquiry and essays* (1st ed.). Indianapolis: Hackett Pub. Co.

Ryle, G. (1949). *The concept of mind.* London, New York: Hutchinson's University Library.

Shestov, L. (1966). *Athens and Jerusalem.* Athens, OH: Ohio University Press.

Sifton, E. (2003). *The serenity prayer: faith and politics in times of peace and war* (1st ed.). New York: Norton.

Skinner, B. F. (1953). *Science and human behavior.* New York: Macmillan.

Skinner, B. F., & Epstein, R. (1980). *Notebooks.* Englewood Cliffs, N.J.: Prentice-Hall.

Smith, L. D. (1986). *Behaviorism and logical positivism: a reassessment of the alliance.* Stanford, Calif.: Stanford University Press.

Snow, C. P. (1959). *The two cultures and the scientific revolution.* New York: Cambridge University Press.

Stahl, W. A. (2002). *Webs of reality: social perspectives on science and religion.* New Brunswick, NJ: Rutgers University Press.

Tillich, P. (1958). *Dynamics of faith.* New York: Harper.

Tillich, P. (1967). *Systematic theology.* Chicago: University of Chicago Press.

Vitz, P. C. (1977). *Psychology as religion: the cult of self-worship.* Grand Rapids, MI: Eerdmans.

Vriezen, T. C. (1967). *The religion of ancient Israel.* Philadelphia: Westminster Press.

Walker, W., & Handy, R. T. (1970). *A history of the Christian church* (3d ed.). New York: Scribner.

Weber, M. (1958). *The Protestant ethic and the spirit of capitalism* (Student's ed.). New York: Scribner.

Whitehead, A. N., & Russell, B. (1910). *Principia mathematica.* Cambridge University Press.

Wilson, E. O. (1978). *On human nature.* Cambridge: Harvard University Press.

Wilson, E. O. (2006). *The creation: an appeal to save life on earth* (1st ed.). New York: Norton.

Woolfolk, R. L. (1998). *The cure of souls: science, values, and psychotherapy.* San Francisco: Jossey-Bass.

Chapter 12

The Proliferation of Faith-Based Counseling: Booming While Psychotherapy Declines

Janet L. Cummings, Psy.D. and
Nicholas A. Cummings, Ph.D., Sc.D.

More people have been helped by reading the New Testament than by all of the psychotherapists combined.

—Albert Ellis

The statement by the late Albert Ellis, consistently voted along with Carl Rogers as the most famous American psychologist, is surprising since he openly declared his own lack of religious conviction. Ellis repeated this in several lectures during the era when psychology, and psychotherapy in general, were increasingly skeptical of religion and at times were even hostile toward it (Ellis, 1980). Paradoxically, during this same era (1990 to 2005) two phenomena emerged: (a) there was an increase of over one thousand percent in the study of religion by both research and practicing psychologists, accompanied by an explosion of publications addressing the importance in society of religious belief even as church attendance declined (Bartoli, 2007), and (b) there was a rapid proliferation of faith-based counseling, even as the number of Americans seeking psychotherapy from mainstream professionals declined and continues to decline (Young et al, 2002 and Sperry & Shafranke, 2005). Faith-based psychotherapy centers are booming and pastoral counseling is growing while most Americans are turning away from psychotherapy in favor of medication.

What is fueling the growing skepticism toward mainstream psychotherapy? Have publicized irreligious stances by psychiatry and psychology contributed to this rejection? Why are so many Americans willing to pay out-of-pocket for faith-based counseling when they could be taking advantage of their health insurance benefit? The polls consistently reveal that up to 90% of Americans believe in the existence of God, while 65 to 75% (depending on which poll you read) consider themselves religious as defined by an identification with one faith or another (e.g., Christian, Jewish, Muslim, Buddhist, Hindu). African-Americans traditionally have been more religious than the white majority even though this may be changing in the younger generation of blacks, while Latinos are predicted to change the future of America with their intensely devout beliefs and church attendance. Concurrently, according to a 2007 survey (Curlin), psychiatrists have been found to be the least religious of all medical specialties, and religious physicians are least likely to refer their patients to a psychiatrist (This was also reported in the *New York Times,* September 18, 2007). No such comprehensive survey of psychologists has been conducted, but there is no reason to believe other than that they would closely resemble psychiatrists on this dimension.

This chapter discusses the conflict between American psychology/psychiatry and religion, while visiting some more surprising statements from leaders in the field. Additionally, it assesses the concurrent boom in faith-based counseling centers, with suggestions for sound practice improvements, all stemming from first-hand experience. Intertwined is a consideration of the psychological importance of religious belief, and what the genetic and biomedical revolutions have to say about this seeming life-style imperative that would contradict decades of thought on this subject. Finally, suggestions are proffered for the rapprochement of mainstream psychology and religion.

The Schism between Religion and Psychotherapy

Historically there have been waves of militant atheism that have swept the United States (Curlin, 2007), and predictably American psychology's view of religion has seemingly coincided with these. There have been instances where psychological writings, especially that of Sigmund Freud, have actually fueled at least one of these waves. In the mid-eighteenth century, a devastating earthquake in Lisbon killed 60,000 people and fueled an outcry that a benevolent God would never allow this to happen. In the mid-nineteenth century advances in geology proved that the earth was much older than the 6,000 years decreed by the Bible. A third such wave of religious skepticism followed World War I, when a combination of Freud's psychoanalytic writings and Einstein's theories of relativity upset established views of the human psyche and the universe. A fourth such wave is underway, and one historian sees it as the result of the academic deification of Darwin's theory of evolution with its emphasis on scientific determinism, as well as a revulsion against Islamic extremism and its attendant violence (Johnson, 2007). For the psychological fields in particular the desire to emulate the precision of the hard sciences has contributed to a compulsion to negatively address religion, often fortuitously and without regard for, or an understanding of, the obvious importance and utility of a behavior so ubiquitous.

Revisiting some of the least quoted conclusions of religion's greatest detractors can be enlightening.

- ***Sigmund Freud,*** the founder of psychoanalysis, is largely responsible for the contentious relationship between religion and psychoanalysis, and perhaps psychology itself. Yet in later life he stated, "Once again, only religion can answer the question of the purpose of life. One can hardly be wrong in concluding that the idea of life having a purpose stands and falls with the religious system (Freud, 1930-1961, p. 76).

- ***Albert Einstein,*** whose theories of relativism would deny the existence of a deity as well as free-will, nonetheless concluded that acting as if people were responsible for their actions would psychologically prompt them to act in a more responsible manner. He stated, "I am compelled to act as if free will existed because if I wish to live in a civilized society I must act responsibly" (Isaacson, 2007, p. 392).
- ***Carl Jung,*** a student of Freud's who was banished from psychoanalysis by his mentor, never questioned the importance of religion. He advocated, "We must read the Bible or we shall not understand psychology. Our psychology, whole lives, our language and imagery are built upon the Bible" (Jung, 1976, p. 156).

Recently there have been a number of attempts to address the utility of faith, thus accounting for its ubiquitous presence throughout the centuries. Psychoanalyst Robert Langs (2007), for example, sees death anxiety, a condition peculiar to humans, as providing wisdom to faith and spirituality. When religious faith succeeds it quiets death anxiety and there is peace and tranquility; but when it fails there is violence and upheaval. Similar explanations are proffered by Hutchinson (2007) and Johnson (2007). The key interest in these more recent considerations is not so much whether religion fits scientific findings in evolution, relativity, or quantum mechanics, but its importance in the *adaptability* of human beings individually and collectively. This is within the province of psychology, and one which the discipline has only begun to explore.

Psychology's First Salvo

Although society's, as well as psychology's conflict between religion and science is long-standing, it did not explode in the United States into a contentious political battle until relatively recently. Traditionally religions were content to uphold their beliefs without involvement in the political process. Actually, the involvement of the clergy directly into politics was frowned upon and the ministers and priests who strayed were threatened with sanctions by their own sects. Early in American history churches in the North took the lead in opposing slavery. They also became politically active after World War I in pushing for the federal legislation which subsequently prohibited the distribution and sale of all alcoholic beverages. But thereafter, there seemed to be a generally accepted dictum that religion did not meddle in politics. Two events changed all of this. The first was the strong religious base of the Civil Rights Movement, and the second was the conceptual expansion of the Constitutional provision that forbade Congress from passing laws that infringe on freedom of religion into its present iteration of "separation of church and state."

The original conceptualization by the Founding Fathers allowed God in all facets of government as long as government did not restrict the citizens' freedom of religious expression and worship. Indeed, the history of American government is replete with allusions to God, and our public buildings and monuments are architectural and artistic expressions of faith (Gingrich, 2006). Suddenly, with the newly conceptualized separation of church and state, these traditions were attacked. Efforts to remove traces of God in government mounted, and eventually these spread from removing from public property such obvious religious symbols as crosses and the Ten Commandments to include such cultural objects as Christmas trees and menorahs.

It was then that the heretofore passive religious sectors sprang into political attack mode with such figures as Jerry Falwell and later Pat Robertson awakening the *silent majority*. Soon Roe v. Wade became the center of the firestorm, which to this day, still festers to the top of every political campaign.

Instead of staying above the contentious political fray, psychology fired its first salvo in 1979 during the APA presidency of Nicholas Cummings. A strong, concerted effort to make faith-based doctoral programs in clinical psychology ineligible for APA approval was mounted and would have passed the Council of Representatives had not the APA president ruled it out of order at three meetings of the Council, citing the then effective Leona Tyler Principle which required psychological research/practice evidence, as well as the Constitutional right of freedom of religion (Cummings & O'Donohue, 2008). The proponents were unable to show that faith-based doctoral clinical programs (e.g., Fordham, Fuller, Rosemead) were deficient in their education and training, and on that basis President Cummings repeatedly ruled it out of order. Had such a measure been approved by the APA Council and subsequently enforced, psychology would have been permanently branded anti-religious as constitutional challenges for years wound through the courts. Fortunately this did not happen, but soon the APA was deeply involved with its subsequent series of gratuitous proclamations that are still viewed by many as antireligious.

The Response from Religion

Although many devout Americans have become increasingly skeptical of psychology, only one denomination has taken the route of the Baptist Theological Seminary in Louisville, Kentucky which dropped psychology from its curriculum, substituting Biblical Counseling. This is the flagship seminary of the Southern Baptist Convention in Nashville, Tennessee and it had hoped other institutions that train psychologists and counselors would follow. Edward Shafranske, director of the Psy.D. program at Pepperdine University and a psychologist who has written extensively on the relationship between psychology and religion (Sperry & Shafranske, 2005), sees no intrinsic conflict between the two. Conflict occurs in reductionism in which psychology would view faith as a purely psychological phenomenon, or the opposite in which religion would view mental illness as the result of sin or demon possession (Gill, 2005).

To date no other training institutions have followed the Baptist Theological Seminary in banning psychology. To the contrary, faith-based training programs and internships continue to grow, providing the counselors for the nation's proliferating faith-based centers. In the only discernible negative reaction toward mainstream psychology, more and more Americans are entrusting their psychological problems to treatment in faith-based counseling centers where they can rest assured their spirituality will not be regarded as pathological.

The Religious Roots of Positive Psychology

After several unfortunate decades in which victimology dominated clinical practice, psychology finally began to gravitate toward positive psychology as had long been championed by Martin E.P. Seligman (2000). During this earlier period in clinical practice many conditions were seen as the inevitable result of societal or circumstantial oppression. Practitioners, rather than encouraging resiliency from their clients, remanded these "victims" to hopelessness, or at best limited hope (Zur, 2005).

Positive psychology is beginning to change the way we practice, while resiliency has become a prime subject of psychological research. Few, if any psychologists remember that what is now termed positive psychology made its first appearance as what has retrospectively been termed the *gospel of hope*. In 1952 Norman Vincent Peale, the pastor of the Marble Collegiate Church, published *The Power of Positive Thinking* which made the *New York Times* bestseller list for 182 weeks. Karlgaard (2007) sees the positive gospel as one brought to the New World in the 1600s "by the reformed Calvinists, made secular and practical by Benjamin Franklin, expressed as the Pursuit of Happiness by Thomas Jefferson in the Declaration of Independence, noticed by Alexis de Tocqueville, defined by Max Weber, and written into popular culture by Horatio Alger and others" (Karlgaard, 2007, p. 27).

Where Psychology Needs to Go

Until recently it was generally accepted in psychology and sociology that morality, and thus religious beliefs and spirituality, were molded and conditioned by society. Naïve Darwinian biology would suggest that the most selfishly aggressive animals would be the one's to survive; but the opposite seems to be true. The animals that were more likely to survive are those that evolved the ability to live in groups. And in the evolutionary process, humans who were able to do likewise by forming effective societies where individuals worked together, were also the winners. With the advances in genomics and molecular biology there has emerged this different view, as discussed by N. Cummings in a previous chapter of this volume.

Using ingenious psychological methods, Haidt (2007) probed the emotion of disgust and discovered *moral dumbfounding*, an instantaneous response in which people felt very strongly, but could not explain why. His explorations led him to view morality as two separate systems: (a) an ancient system that he called moral intuition that is based on emotion-laden moral behaviors that evolved before language was developed, and (b) a modern system that he calls moral judgment that came after language development, when people were able to articulate why something was right or wrong. Psychology, it seems, has for decades been limited to exploration of the latter. It was unable to explain why, or even to be aware, that morality was a survival-based evolutionary process that preceded language development. But this cast some light on why religious belief, no matter how primitive, has existed universally as adaptation. Exploring further the adaptive paradigm, it behooves psychology to begin to explore openly, and free from political correctness, a host of psychologically-related behaviors and conditions—instead of squandering its credibility on proclamations negatively addressing intelligent design, a subject best left to biologists who must wrestle with the origins of the species, and physicists who must speculate on the origins of the universe.

In contrast, the following suggested topics for investigation are all within the province of psychology, which has already disappointed the public in its failure to help solve issues resulting in social disorganization. Because religion and morality are off limits in the politically correct world of psychological research, a straightforward look as to how these ubiquitous issues impact on social disorganization have been long neglected. Some of these topics are:

- Religious conversion (Christian or Muslim) in prison has been the most effective rehabilitation for felons (Center for Substance Abuse Treatment, 1997). Psychotherapy is sadly ineffective with sociopaths; yet religious conversion succeeds where psychology fails. What can psychology learn here?

- Similarly, religious conversion has been very effective in ending a life of alcoholism and drug addiction, more so than psychotherapy (Quimette, 1997). Alcoholics Anonymous (AA) and its offshoots such as Narcotics Anonymous (NA), as well as all 12-step programs have a strong spiritual component, the so-called higher power to which the addict turns over his or her life. Again, how does religion succeed more often than psychotherapy?

- Religion has most often been a force for charitable works and for good, such as the experience of Wilberforce in ending the slave trade in England. But when religion changes from being a force for peace to that of violence (e.g., the Spanish Inquisition, Salem witch hunts, current extreme Islamic genocide), what are the reasons religion has failed to fulfill its adaptive role?

- Do rigid religious fundamentalists and militant atheists share common behavioral characteristics, with one being the mirror image of the other? Are there behavioral similarities among radical political ideologies that serve to screen-out facts that might be contrary to either the radical ideology or the fundamentalist beliefs?

- The Qu'ran and the Bible are replete with both peaceful and violent passages. What prompts a peaceful evangelical Christian who wants to preserve life by outlawing abortions resort to killing via the bombing of abortion clinics? What turns followers of an otherwise peaceful religion such as Islam into advocates for killing all infidels, and genocide for all Jews?

- African Americans have been among the most ardent church goers (Cosby & Poussaint, 2007 and Williams, 2007). As the younger generation continues to lose its faith, is that contributing to the social disorganization among blacks such as teenage pregnancy, school drop-out, crime, crack addiction and failure of fatherhood?

- Girls brought up in religious homes are less likely to become sexually active at a young age, and girls who do become sexually active early manifest more depression and a higher suicide rate. Yet psychotherapists have in the past promoted freedom of sexual expression and side-stepped morality. Is there a disconnect here? Is the APA's belated warning that in our society girls are being sexualized too early (D'Angelis, 2007) a step in the right direction and one that needs to be investigated further and possibly expanded so as to assess the role of morality?

- A surprising number of physicians not only encourage prayer, but they pray with their patients. Recently a meta-analysis of intercessory prayer showing positive results was published (Hodge,

2007). Because of small samples and design flaws the promising results have limited generalization. But these limited results support intriguing questions: Does prayer have a positive effect on the body's healing and immune systems? Are people who pray more optimistic and therefore happier and healthier? Or does prayer simply have a placebo effect?

- The monastic system within the Roman Catholic and Orthodox Christian Churches, which began in the early centuries following the birth of Christianity, has proven itself useful in the containment of mental illness. Within any society, there exists a percentage of the population who needs to *drop out* of society. In the current nomenclature, these individuals are generally referred to as *schizoid* or *schizotypal*, or as *schizophrenic* in more severe cases. For many centuries prior to the advent of psychotherapy and psychotropic medications, these individuals would often seek solace in the confinement of a monastery or in the isolation of monastic hermitude. These monastics would be charged with the writing of prayers, hymns, and essays on theological issues. Because their church as a whole would not permit deviation from the teachings of the Church fathers, these monastics seldom invented new religious beliefs or systems, as is often the case in modern times when thought-disordered people become strongly focused on theological issues. In fact, the traits in these individuals, which might be viewed as pathological today, were an asset within the monastic system, as they were able to endure (and even welcome) lengthy periods of isolation while focusing nearly all their energies on their spiritual work. Thus, these individuals were indeed more than merely contained; they were given important tasks and the respect of their churches as a whole. While pockets of monastics still exist in many parts of the world, and to a lesser extent in the United States, this method of containing mental illness has largely been replaced by more costly (and in many cases less effective) means.

Where Faith-Based Counseling Needs to Go

In a relatively short period of time, mainly since the mid-1990s, faith-based counseling has done remarkably well in filling the religious diversity void that exists in psychology and mental health training programs and clinics (Schulte, Skinner & Caliborn, 2002; Corenett, 1998; and Evans, 2003). However, evidence-based research comparing these programs with mainstream psychotherapy has lagged behind and is essentially absent. There are currently two studies in the very early phase of comparing the effectiveness of faith-based centers with community mental health centers, but most of the research to date has investigated these training programs to the degree to which they have accomplished their dual mission to provide effective psychotherapy while respecting religious diversity (Richards & Bergin, 2000). To be fair, the thrust toward evidence-based psychotherapy in psychology is relatively recent in its current magnitude, and the emphasis has been toward investigating existing or emerging interventions, mostly cognitive (Chambliss et al, 1996). Faith-based counseling has, to the extent it is true in treatment centers in general, employed these evidence-based interventions. But eventually the question of whether the inclusion of faith has adulterated effectiveness must be addressed. Until this question is investigated, the authors have suggestions as to where faith-based programs must go.

The first author of this chapter supervises over fifty counselors and counseling trainees in a faith-based center serving a congregation and evangelical population of more than twenty thousand evangelical Christians. When she first assumed this role over a decade ago, it was apparent to her that improvement in clinical effectiveness was needed. The line between treatment and worship was blurred, and a misplaced over-compassion rendered the counseling center vulnerable to manipulation and exploitation by Axis II patients, especially those with borderline personality disorder, antisocial personality disorder, and certain types of hysteria. The intensive retraining and subsequent ongoing supervision of the large staff have made this the most sought-after counseling internship in the state, now attracting top applicants nationally, and more importantly, have resulted in a remarkably effective outpatient treatment center for an extensive repertoire of psychological conditions.

During this time she has witnessed the demand for faith-based counseling grow exponentially, both locally and nationally, while referrals to mainstream psychotherapy practice are declining. A number of her trainees, upon receiving their state licenses, launched immediately successful private practices. One such graduate told her he was opening his private office in a remote and sparsely populated locale only because he lived there. She cautioned that this was an unlikely place to do so, but he went ahead and did so, anyway. To his supervisor's surprise, the demand for his services was so great that within two months his time was filled and he had a waiting list. Furthermore, his prospective patients were eager to pay out of pocket, rather than seek covered services through their health plan's network. This is not uncommon for religiously inclined prospective patients whose skepticism has heretofore resulted in their having forgone psychotherapy.

As several recent studies have shown (Cummings, 1996-2007), in our university training programs openly religious faculty and students are a small minority, while the faculty disinterest in, and even bias against religion is reflected in our curricula. Even worse, openly religious faculty may not be hired or may be denied tenure or promotion, while students might be punished with lower performance ratings, even when their coursework grades are high (Richards & Bergin, 2000). Consequently, our profession is trained and subsequently lives in a culture that leaves it unprepared to address in an effective, unbiased manner the important spiritual crises of religious patients.

The second author of this chapter has collected scores of complaints of religious discrimination from both faculty and students, some egregious enough to be referred to an attorney for legal redress. Although these are anecdotal, their numbers are staggering in an era when even one such instance of prejudice is unacceptable. However, it coincides with Redding's (2005) assertion that psychology is woefully lacking in socio-political diversity.

With patients who had attempted previous psychotherapy before coming to a faith-based counseling center, the most frequently voiced complaint is that they remained silent on a number of issues they discerned were of disinterest to the therapist, and consequently were not able to fully relate to the therapy and to benefit from it. Perhaps the greatest counter-transference (i.e., inability of the therapist to relate to the patient's therapeutic goals) stems from this lack of socio-religious diversity in our profession. Thus, in retraining psychologists and counselors to function in faith-based centers (but ideally in *any* psychotherapeutic environment), the greatest need is that of counteracting our profession's irreligious attitudes. However, this lack of religious understanding and tolerance may be so entrenched in our profession that to belabor it may be futile. Of importance to faith-based centers designed to offset this bias is the avoidance of a different kind of pitfall.

The authors would proffer the following characteristics of professionals functioning in an effective faith-based counseling center:

- The professional is empathic and understanding of the importance of faith in the patient, and its importance in the patient's life.
- While recognizing the importance of faith and encouraging it as indicated, there is a difference between worship and psychotherapy. For example, prayer is important, and may be encouraged. But prayer is not psychotherapy.
- The clinician is highly trained in effective, evidence-based psychotherapy and does not rely on religious conviction to fill gaps in his or her training.
- Spirituality may mean Catholic, Protestant, Jewish, Muslim, Hindu, Buddhist or any other religious conviction, and the clinician must be empathic to the patient's faith even when it markedly differs from her or his own.
- A skilled clinician recognizes that militant atheism, rigid scientism, and even intense political ideology may be secular substitutes that mimic religious fundamentalism and might well be approached accordingly.
- How faith and clinical acumen are combined has led to the promulgation of a number of models for this integration, none of which is satisfactory as one-size does not fit all. Flexibility designed to meet each individual patient's need is not only desirable, but therapeutically required in a skilled practitioner.
- In summary, the effective counselor in this setting has a faith-based side and a clinical side, with each complimenting the other and without substituting one for the other.

Case Illustrations

The following vignettes of actual cases are illustrative of the kinds of patients seen in faith-based counseling centers and in faith-based independent practice.

Prayer is not psychotherapy. After an exchange of greetings with the therapist at the beginning of the first session, the patient asked the therapist to kneel with him in prayer. In this prayer he asked for God's wisdom to guide the therapist in counseling him. It was obvious throughout the first session that the patient was using religious dialogue as a way of avoiding discussion of his problems. When he began the second session by asking the psychologist to again kneel in prayer, the therapist interrupted, stating that prayer was an important way to receive help, but it was God-given and he ought not to have to pay for someone to join him in prayer. The patient, he pointed out, was paying a rather stiff fee for psychotherapy, not prayer. This had a salient effect on the patient, who became responsive to interpretations of avoidance, and soon opened up with his problem.

My past lives. A man who was obviously suffering from sexual addiction revealed that his spiritual advisor had discovered that, in a past incarnation, the patient was a close friend and admirer of Casanova. He accompanied him on many sexual exploits, and the advisor attributed his sexual compulsivity to the conditioning of his behavior in this past life. The psychologist did not question the veracity of what was obviously serving as an excuse for his out of control sexual behavior, but seemingly agreed with the spiritual advisor that if he learned this behavior from Casanova, what was once learned can through therapy be unlearned. This satisfied the patient who settled into therapy, but it was apparent to the psychologist that had he questioned the concept of a previous life, the patient would have lost confidence and quit. This was confirmed in the therapy as it became apparent that the patient had been using the alleged Casanova tie as an excuse for flagrantly abusive sexual behavior.

Only fools rush in. A depressed Roman Catholic woman with not only severe suicidal preoccupation, but also a strong likelihood she would kill herself, confided that the only thing preventing her from doing so was that suicide is a mortal sin that remands one to hell. The counselor's own belief was that God would not so punish someone who was mentally ill, but he refrained from challenging her belief. Rather, his obligation was to strengthen anything that might prevent her almost inevitable suicide. He interpreted, "You are saying it would be foolish to end your short-term misery on this earth by exchanging it for an eternity of misery." This reframing augmented the patient's faith and kept her alive until the combination of psychotherapy and medication reduced the severity of her depression and constant threat of suicide.

Avoiding "hard time." The counselor was an African American two-time ex-felon who, during his second imprisonment, experienced a religious conversion which turned his life around. After his release he prepared himself to be a lay counselor and subsequently joined the staff of a faith-based counseling center. He was remarkably effective with black teenagers who already had embarked on a life of drugs and crime and were soon to ascend to felon status. He had a style of blunt confrontation combined with paradoxical intention. Thus, he avoided all religious talk, and using prison-yard lingo and the worst of street slang, he conceded that the young patient was headed for the slammer so he wanted to be helpful by instructing him on the best way to con the system, get a light sentence, and thus avoid hard time. His directness, history as an ex-convict, and his intense interest in each boy soon bonded him as the black father figure these youth never had.

It would not be long before each patient began to ask how he avoided his third and final incarceration (the state had a three-strikes-and-you're-in-for-life law), and it was then (and only then) he talked of his religious faith that had turned his life around. He was consistently effective with seemingly incorrigible black teenage boys, running circles around his fully educated and trained colleagues.

Gay is sinful. A man who had experienced same-sex attraction since his youth presented for counseling. He had a history of two extremes. At times he had led an openly gay, very promiscuous lifestyle, while at other times he had sought psychotherapy aimed at altering his sexual orientation. The patient viewed his promiscuous behavior, as well as his sexual orientation, as sinful because of his fundamentalist Christian background. His astute therapist helped him distinguish between orientation and behavior, and to adopt a lifestyle that the patient believed to be consistent with his Christian beliefs. At the same time, the patient was helped to accept his sexual orientation, and to stop viewing himself sinful because of it.

Hiding behind Scripture. A patient made a point of letting his counselor know in the first few minutes of the first session that he was an avid churchgoer who takes the Bible literally. As the session progressed, the patient disclosed a history of relationships in which he had been abusive and unfaithful, as well as a history of flirting with alcohol and drug abuse which had led to a recent job loss. In a way that was both confrontational and compassionate, the therapist began pointing out the discrepancy between the patient's reported beliefs and his behavior. Each time the therapist confronted the patient in this way, he would dodge the issue by quoting the Bible. The therapist persisted in this approach, and the patient eventually admitted that his reported beliefs and lifestyle did not line up and he became willing to work in psychotherapy to alter the behaviors that had caused his relationship and occupational difficulties.

The man is the heads of the house. A couple presented for intake with the triage counselor at a faith-based counseling center. The husband complained that the wife was not submissive, and that she did not respect his God-given headship in the family. The wife complained that the husband was very controlling, and that he often used the Bible to berate and control his family. The triage counselor decided to assign this couple to individual counselors instead of to a marriage counselor. The husband's therapist assigned him to do an in-depth study of the Apostle Paul's advice for family relationships (Ephesians 5 and 6; Colossians 3), and used the homework assignment to redefine the husband-wife relationship as mutually submissive. In particular, he used Paul's analogy that the husband, as the head, should love his wife as Christ loved the church. At the same time, the wife's therapist helped her to respond in positive ways to her husband's changes, thus giving him the respect he desired from her.

Let me hide myself in Thee. A woman brought her middle-age single brother in for evaluation. The previous Christmas she brought him home from the Greek Orthodox monastery where he had been living for the past eight years as a "lay monk" who performed maintenance and odd jobs for the monastery. She, her husband and the three children had such a good time reconnecting with him that his sister prevailed upon him to stay with them long enough to readjust back into society. Within less than a month the patient became withdrawn, and by the second month he was hearing voices. Psychotropic medication eliminated the auditory hallucinations, but the patient's withdrawal steadily increased and soon it was difficult to get him to come out of his bedroom. It was learned in the evaluation session that the patient had two psychiatric hospitalizations in the past, but after entering the monastery he was tranquil and contented while he basked in the appreciation for his excellent maintenance work. All the while he was protected from the mainstream society that was so frightening to him. The counselor persuaded the family that without this protection the patient would soon be re-hospitalized, or at best he would live marginally under heavy medication. His sister agreed and the patient happily returned to the monastery.

Summary and Conclusions

Psychology's relationship with religion has been paradoxical at best, and contentious at its worst. In its efforts to be scientific, perhaps over-compensating for its status as a so-called soft science, it has neglected investigation of the positive aspects of religion, particularly the adaptive nature of faith that has made it both ubiquitous and ever-present throughout recorded history. Even militant atheism in its zeal to counteract religion has its fervency, often surpassing the zealotry of religious fundamentalism. That there may be "secular religiosity" is underscored by the recent assertion of scientist and author Paul Davies (2007) that science has its own faith-based belief system. All science proceeds on the assumption that nature is ordered in a rational and intelligent manner. One could not function as a scientist if the universe was thought of as a meaningless jumble of odds and ends haphazardly juxtaposed. As we have seen in a previous chapter of this volume, such a belief system led even Albert Einstein, an avowed non-deist, to accept what today is called "intelligent design."

Psychology's contentiousness with religion, even to the point of often regarding it as a manifestation of pathology, has not only resulted in the neglect of appropriate research into its adaptation quality, it has resulted in a growing skepticism toward psychology by a large segment of the American population. Most Americans believe in God, and the unfortunate disdain of religion in some segments of psychology, has led to a rapid proliferation and subsequent growth of faith-based counseling centers and independent counseling practices. In this view, psychology has seemingly disqualified itself from relating to a large segment of the population it has pledged to serve. In the meantime, persons of faith have espoused the importance of counseling and psychotherapy by responding with therapeutic address minus the godlessness. As faith-based counseling grows, in its counter-reaction it often fails to clearly demark what is regarded as religion and what is considered psychotherapy. Recommendations are proffered to make faith-based counseling more effective and less parochial. A well-trained faith-based counselor must be able to respect and treat persons of all faiths, even those other than his or her own, as well as treat persons who profess no religion whatsoever. Unfortunately, traveling such a faith-based, but unbiased therapeutic course may draw criticism from some individuals on both sides of the religious-irreligious spectrum. But sound counseling from a well-trained psychotherapist is compatible with faith, and such excellence must be the goal of the proliferating faith-based counseling centers and independent practices.

References

Bartoli, Eleanora (2007). Religious and spiritual issues in psychotherapy practice: Training the trainer. *Psychotherapy: Theory, Research, Practice, Training, 44(1),* 34-65.

Center for Substance Abuse Treatment (1997). *Recovery from substance abuse and addiction: Real people tell their stories.* Rockville, MD: Substance Abuse and Mental Health Services Administration (SAMHSA).

Chambliss, D.L., Sanderson, W.C., Shoham, V., Bennett Johnson, S., Pope, K.S., Crits-Christoph, P., Baker, M., Johnson, B., Woody, S.R., Sue, S., Beutler, L., Williams, D.A., & McCurry, S. (1996). An update on empirically validated therapies. *The Clinical Psychologist, 49,* 5-18.

Cornett, C. (1998). *The soul of psychotherapy: Recapturing the spiritual dimension in the psychotherapeutic encounter.* New York: Free Press.

Cosby, B., & Poussaint, A.F. (2007). *Come on, people.* Cambridge, MA: Cambridge Press.

Cummings, N.A. (1996-2007), Personal communications from psychology faculty and students, most of it unsolicited.

Cummings, N.A., & O'Donohue, W.T. (2008). *Eleven blunders that cripple psychotherapy in America: A remedial unblundering.* New York: Routledge.

Curlin, F.A. (2007, September 7-9). A survey of attitudes toward religion in clinical practice. *Psychiatric Services.*

D'Angelis, T. (2007, April). APA task force report decries culture's sexualization of girls. *Monitor on Psychology,* 51.

Davies, P. (2007, November 24). *New York Times,* Op-Ed.

Ellis, A. (1980). Psychotherapy and atheistic values: A response to A.E. Bergin's "Psychotherapy and religious values," *Journal of Counseling and Clinical Psychology, 48,* 635-639.

Evans, K.M. (2003). Including spirituality in multicultural colunseling: Overcoming counselor resistance. In G. Roysircar, D.S. Sandhu, & V.E. Bibbins, Sr. (Eds.), *Multicultural competencies: A guidebook of practices,* pp. 161-171. United States: Association for Multicultural Counseling and Development.

Freud, S. (1930). *Civilization and its discontents.* New York: Norton. (Reprinted in 1961).

Gill, R.E. (2005, September-October). Baptists replace psychology with "Biblical counseling." *National Psychologist,* 12.

Gingrich, N. (2006). *Rediscovering God in America: Reflections in the role of faith in our nation's history and future.* Nashville, TN: Integrity House.

Haidt, J. (2007). *The happiness hypothesis.* Richmond, VA: University of Virginia Press.

Hodge, D. (2007). A systematic review of the empirical literature on intercessory prayer. *Research on social work practice, 17,* 174-187.

Hutchinson, R.J. (2007). *The politically incorrect guide to the Bible.* Washington, DC: Regnery Publishing.

Isaacson, W. (2007). *Einstein: His life and universe.* New York: Simon and Schuster.

Johnson, J. (2007, October 8). Militant atheism. *Forbes.*

Jung, C. (1976). *The visions seminars: From the complete notes of Mary Foote* (Vol. 1). Zurich: Spring Publications.

Karlgaard, R. (2007, November 12), The gospel of hope. *Forbes,* 27.

Langs, R. (2007). *Beyond Jahweh and Jesus.* Lanham, MD: Jason Aronson.

Quimette, P.C., Finney, J.W., & Moos, R.H. (1997). Twelve-step and cognitive-behavioral treatment of substance abuse: A comparison of treatment effectiveness. *Journal of Counseling and Clinical Psychology, 65,* 230-240.

Redding, R.E. (2005). Sociopolitical diversity in psychology: The case for pluralism. In R.H. Wright & N.A. Cummings (Eds.), *Destructive trends in mental health: The well-intentioned path to harm,* (pp. 303-324). New York: Routledge (Taylor and Francis).

Richards, J.S., & Bergin, A.E. (Eds.) (2000). *Handbook of psychotherapy and religious diversity.* Washington, DC: American Psychological Association.

Schulte, D.L., Skinner, T.A., & Claiborn, C.D. (2002). Religious and spiritual issues in counseling psychology training. *Counseling Psychologist 30(1),* 118-134

Seligman, M.E.P., & Csikszentmihalyi, M. (2000). Positive psychology: An introduction. *American Psychologist, 55,* 5t-14.

Shafranske, E.P. (Ed.) (1996). *Religion and the clinical practice of psychology*. Washington, DC: American Psychological Association.

Sperry, L. & Shafranske, E.P. (Eds.) (2005). *Spiritually oriented psychotherapy*. Washington, DC: American Psychological Association.

Williams, J. (2007). *Enough: The phony leaders, dead-end movements, and culture of failure that are undermining black America*. New York: Three Rivers Press (Random House).

Young, J.S., Cashwell, C., Wiggins-Frame, M., & Belaire, C. (2002). Spiritual and religious competencies: A national survey of CACREP-accredited programs. *Counseling and Values, 47,* 22-33.

Zur, O. (2005). The psychology of victimhood. In R.H. Wright & N.A. Cummings (Eds.), *Destructive trends in mental health: The well-intentioned path to harm,* (pp. 45-64). New York: Routledge (Taylor and Francis Group).

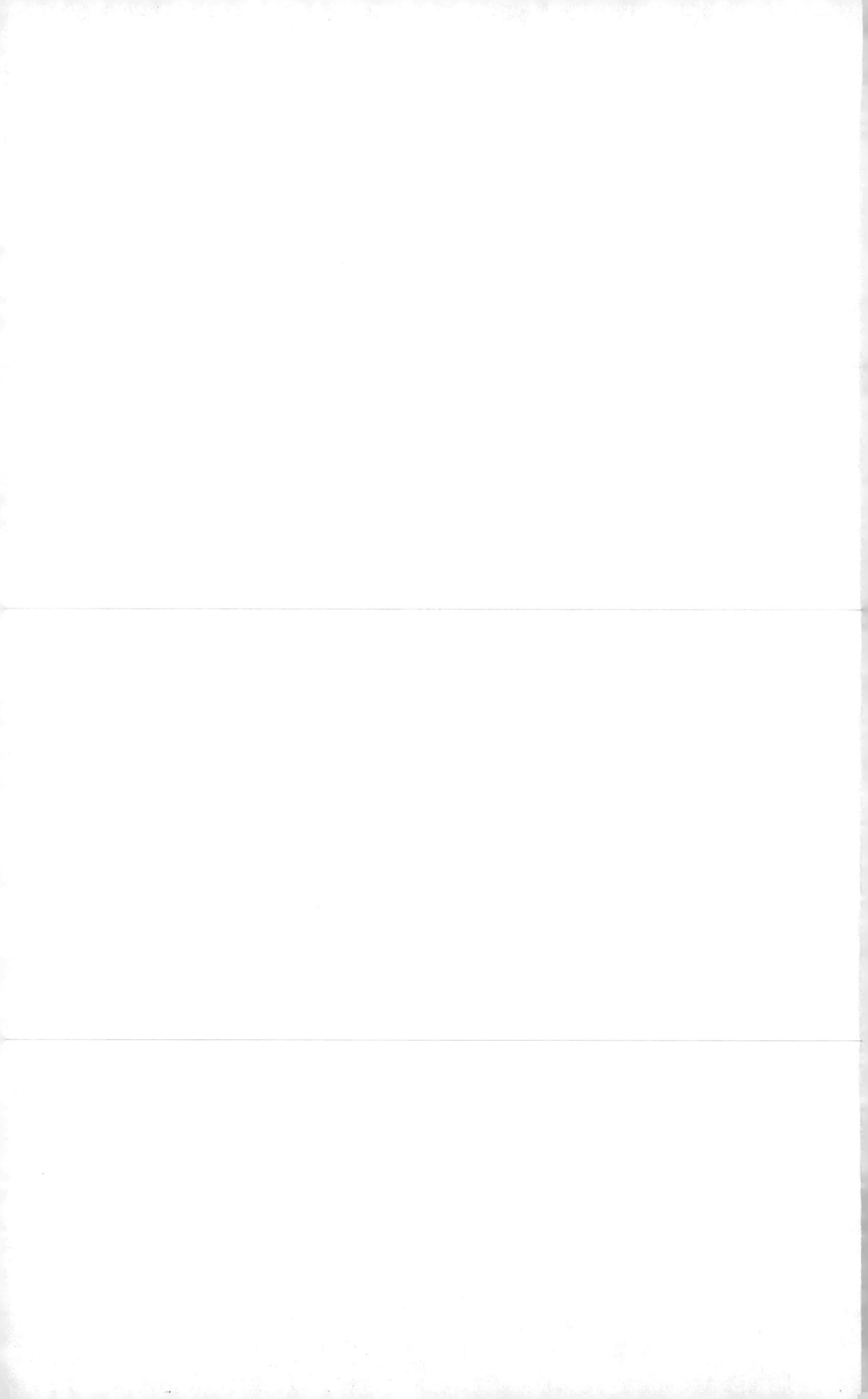

Index